Community Movements in Southeast Asia

I0105410

COMMUNITY MOVEMENTS IN SOUTHEAST ASIA

An Anthropological Perspective of Assemblages

Edited by

Ryoko Nishii and **Shigeharu Tanabe**

Silkworm Books

ISBN: 978-616-215-186-6
© 2022 Silkworm Books
All rights reserved

First published in 2022 by
Silkworm Books
430/58 M. 7, T. Mae Hia, Chiang Mai 50100, Thailand
info@silkwormbooks.com
www.silkwormbooks.com

Typeset in Minion Pro 11 pt. by Silk Type
Printed and bound in the United States by Lightning Source

CONTENTS

Part 3: Networks and Globalization: Land, Life, and Movements

ACKNOWLEDGEMENTS

This publication is a part of Grants-in-Aid for Scientific Research (KAKENHI), Scientific Research (A) (Overseas Scientific Investigation), 2017–2020: "Community Movements in Mainland Southeast Asia under the Transforming Power Formation in Globalized World" (Project No.17 H01648).

During the implementation of this study, an international symposium entitled "Rethinking 'Community': from Case Studies in Mainland South East Asia" was held at the Myanmar-Korea Local Knowledge Center, the University of Yangon, Myanmar, on 24 August 2018 to present an interim report on results. This symposium was co-organized by the Department of Anthropology, University of Yangon. We would like to give our heartfelt thanks to Prof. Mya Mya Khin of the University of Yangon for her help in organizing the symposium. In addition, an international seminar on "New Aspects of Community Movements in Southeast Asia" was held online on 10 September 2020 to summarize results. Although this seminar was originally planned to be held in Chiang Mai, Thailand, it was rescheduled online due to the spread of COVID-19. We wish to thank Malee Sitthikriengkrai for presenting a paper from Chaing Mai. We also would like to express our sincere gratitude to Apinya Feungfusakul and Kwanchewan Buadaeng for their highly informative comments.

Finally, I would like to acknowledge that the authors of this book are supported by Grants-in-Aid for Scientific Research from the Ministry of Education, Culture, Sports, Science and Technology and the Japan Society for the Promotion of Science (Project Nos. 15K16904, 23510306, 21520825, 24520918, 18K01172, 25770303, 17H00948).

On behalf of all authors, we would like to express our gratitude to everyone who made this project possible.

Ryoko Nishii
May 2021

INTRODUCTION
Community Movements in Southeast Asia

RYOKO NISHII

From the state to "community movement"
—an anthropological perspective

In recent years, the world has been filled with cases in which the state apparatus of violence is on full display. The collapse of the Arab Spring which is popular uprising against the current government between 2010 and 2012 in Arab countries, the armed suppression of democracy protests in Hong Kong, Thailand, and Myanmar highlight the state not as protector of its citizens, but as violent device for oppression.

"The democratic state," says David Graeber, "has always been a contradiction in terms" (Graeber 2020: 122, 117). The state, by its very nature, can never be truly democratic; it is fundamentally nothing more than a means of organizing violence.[1] Tosihito Kayano shares Graeber's view that the origin of the state is the acquisition of control through violence and that the state is not established by the people for their own security, but by violently superior agents who control the people and take their wealth. Therefore, for the state, the protection of the population is just an incidental and derivative activity (Kayano 2005: 104–105).

The modern nation-state was established by transforming the inhabitants of territories divided by national borders into citizens, transforming them into state subjects of a collective entity called the nation. Kayano says that the formation of nation-states is nothing but the process of "democratization" of state violence toward the people. "Democratization" in this context derives from its meaning as the formation of a nation as a cultural community through the establishment of a national language and the implementation of public education. The most important effect of the democratization of state violence is the disappearance of military confrontations between the state and its population (Kayano 2005: 199). By becoming, albeit potentially, the bearers of state violence, the population escapes the dichotomy between total submission to state violence and deadly resistance (ibid. 202).

However, in the current pro-democracy demonstrations in Southeast Asia, such as in Hong Kong, Thailand, and Myanmar, where people are confronted with regimes dominated by the military (a powerful and violent state apparatus), the people are sometimes forced to make such a choice. These situations cannot be viewed from the perspective of progressive history, where democratization is part of the progression from the state as a primordial violent apparatus to a full-fledged nation-state. It may be that to explain what is happening assumptions of the inevitable existence of the state as an institutional device need to be discarded in favor of a return to the fundamental nature of state as a vehicle for power.[2]

One perspective of relativizing the state was recently presented by David Graeber and James Scott. It can also be seen in anarchism, in which the political ideal is equal collectivity without the state. By the fact that we live in an environment that includes the physical and institutional aspects of our daily lives as a starting point, instead of the assumed organic totality of an existent "nation," we can free

ourselves from conventional thinking and approach reality with
flexibility.

In anthropology, Graeber cites Marcel Mauss as the founder of the
anarchist theory of the state because he disclosed that ". . . societies
without states and markets became so because they wanted to live
that way." Next, Pierre Clastres, author of *Society Against the State*
(*1974*), asserted that the stateless people of the Amazon did not
fail to match the Aztecs or Incas in forming civilized societies, but
rather refused to command others through violence. Graeber sees a
parallel between Mauss' gift economy and Clastres' argument that
stateless societies were in fact trying not to provide fertile soil for
inequality (Graeber 2006: 61–63). In Southeast Asia, this discussion
of stateless societies was continued in James Scott's Zomia (Scott
2009). Zomia, a vast mountainous region between mainland
Southeast Asia and China [a huge massif of mainland Southeast
Asia, running from the Central Highlands of Vietnam westward
all the way to northeastern India and including the southwest
Chinese provinces of Yunnan, Guizhou, and western Guangxi.].
Beyond merely taking advantage of its geographical isolation from
centers of state power, much of Zomia has "resisted the projects of
nation-building and state-making of the states to which it belonged"
(ibid. 19).

"The community movement," which is the subject of this book, is
an attempt to see the workings of power in people's collectivity from
the perspective of people's lives, while relativizing the perspective
that assumes an indispensable state uniting territory and people.
"Community movement" is a concept combining "community"
and "social movement," conceived to encapsulate social processes
emerging from collectivities of people that cannot be captured by
conventional views.[3] The community movement concept relativizes,
or rather resists, using the existence of social institutions like the state

in capturing the reality of power relations arising from and involving people in the places where they live.

In terms of collectivity, hierarchies can be created depending on the orientation of how relations between people are maintained. Alternatively, anarchistic orientations try to maintain equality. The power to control relationships between people arises from collectivity. The community movement framework uses the fundamental relationships between people in the places where they live as a starting point. The community may be described in terms of the holistic interactions between individuals, in the manner of Martin Buber's "I and Thou" micro-level face-to-face situations. In anthropological terms, it refers to relationships with unstructured potential that Victor Turner calls "communitas".[4] Power becomes effective when people subject themselves to such primordial relations as part of collectivity.

Shigeharu Tanabe shows persuasively how fundamental relationships reveal and affect those involved in community movements (Chapter 1). In describing "an assemblage of resistance," he shows that resistance signifies constructing a "subject," referring not only to the refusal of negative or oppressive power, but to creating or reproducing other kinds of hegemony, related practices and knowledge. "Assemblage of resistance" is a term that enables us to elucidate not only the practices of "resistance" against dominating or hegemonic forces and discourses, but more generally whole spheres of domination over everyday practices and lifestyles among individuals. Tanabe analyzes the case of hermits and yogis in northern Thailand which have developed into a "counter-hegemony" against modern political and administrative systems and the centralized Buddhist *sangha*. For these hermits and yogis, the ultimate freedom is to find the meaning of life, that is, to resist the "present" by determining their own styles of thinking and living, and transforming themselves to construct their own form of "subject."

Community movements as perspectives with which to relativize the state

How these subjects construct nations is the focus of Benedict Anderson's theory of nationalism as "imagined community." Anderson used the potential of "communitas" to explain the function of nationalism. He discussed the nation-state under nationalism as an imagined community reaching a size that required the limitations of face-to-face knowledge to be transcended. Here, the violent state evokes a community of people with personal ties to the nation, whose natural collective actions turn them as subjects into a nation.

The question this book poses is how communities are influenced by and respond to power in actual small-scale face-to-face situations. The nation-state cannot survive on violence alone. It needs to lead people to act on their own accord. As mentioned earlier, people must be made to act freely as part of the exercise of power through the establishment of a national language and the implementation of education.

The example of Myanmar in Part II deals with exactly how the state creates the citizenry it wants through education and how the people subject themselves to it. These chapters show the dynamics of an assemblage, where power does not act in one direction, such as from the top down, but through a complex intertwining of various elements, with unexpected results. This mirrors Hannah Arendt's analysis of totalitarianism: that there are no "causes" but only "origins" in history (see Chapter 3).

Myanmar's first general election in 2011 transferred power to a civilian government, ending almost 50 years of military rule. In the following 2016 general election, the National League for Democracy (NLD) led by Aung San Suu Kyi won an overwhelming victory. Alongside the progress of democratization beginning in 2010, controls over political speech have loosened, allowing previously suppressed anti-Muslim sentiment to revive, mainly among Buddhist monks.

In the meantime, clashes between predominantly Muslim Rohingya and Rakhine Buddhists in 2012 led to widespread religious conflict between Buddhists and Muslims across the country. The religious conflict also revitalized the 969 movement, with its anti-Islamic tendencies, among some Buddhists and led to the formation of the Association for the Protection of Race and Religion, or "Ma Ba Tha." Around the same time, Buddhist "Sunday schools" were formed, a phenomenon that has been overlooked or simply considered part of the anti-Islamic movement.

Keiko Tosa in Chapter 4 analyzes the complex relationships between Ma Ba Tha and the various streams of Sunday schools. Tosa's field research reveals Sunday school education fostering independent thought and critical thinking, in contrast to the rote learning of mainstream Myanmar schools, describing the effects as follows: "The development of human resources capable of appropriately expressing criticism and opinions is recognized as an issue for Myanmar society as democratization progresses. Under the military regime, politics usually proceeded in the form of "rule" imposed from above, and there were few opportunities to express opinions from below." The implications of this new form of education for the future of Myanmar are great.

Ayako Saito in Chapter 5 sheds light on Muslim-Buddhist relations from the rarely covered Muslim perspective. According to the 2014 census, Buddhists and Muslims compose 87.9% and 4.3% of Myanmar's population, respectively. Of the Muslim population, 20% refer to themselves as "Bamar Muslims," distinguishing themselves by their efforts to understand and interact peacefully with non-Muslims. Though increasingly anxious in the face of a buoyant anti-Muslim movement, they have managed to create and maintain cordial relationships with their neighbors. In a recent example, a volunteer group operating out of a Yangon mosque provides food to people hospitalized or quarantined due to COVID-19 has received several rounds of domestic media coverage. Saito also reports on how Muslims are providing formal training to help their children integrate into Burmese society, drawing on their experience running Islamic training courses for elementary school through to university students, especially during summer holidays. This education aims to instill a consciousness of being "indigenous Muslims." Saito portrays Bamar Muslims as trying to live as model Burmese citizens in Burmese society, conscious that although anti-Muslim sentiment is currently waning, it may flare up at any time.

Tadayuki Kubo in Chapter 6 focuses on the Kayah ethnic minority. Kayah State uses three Kayah language writing systems, including the Romanized alphabet and Burmese script adapted for transliteration. The third, a system developed by Karenni national leader Khu Hteh Bu Peh, was approved in 2013 as the official Kayah script and named "Kyebogyi" (instead of 'Karenni', which has anti-government connotations). This move appeared to coincide with the ending of conflict and the beginning of reconciliation. Kubo insists that Kyebogyi is neither Karenni nor Kayah, but a depoliticized ethnic language; it cannot be clearly positioned as counter-hegemonic by analyzing its naming process. Kubo sheds light on the Kayah use of language to avoid confrontation and become good subjects of Myanmar, noting that minority languages have not only been oppressed, but used as a tool for anti-government movements. He explores the process of language and literary education at the heart of political movements and their consequences beyond politics.

All chapters on Myanmar discuss aspects of nation-building that were taking place before the February 2021 coup d'état , as well as community movements that emerged after democratic reform in 2011.

The authors unanimously stress that it is impossible to predict how the situation will change in the future. However, Kubo noted that how people confront state power will remain central to discussions.

These cases in Myanmar illustrate the complexities of how individual community members interact with power. Using Bourdieu's concept of "habitus," Tanabe explains that "governmentality is an attempt to intervene and change people's customary acts, or modes of practice. In this context, individuals are given a certain amount of authority to assume self-responsibility in social life. While self-regulating, this makes 'the individual' in the community no longer a mere subject of power, but a part of it, subjected to it" (Tanabe 2008: 152–157).

The word "community" in "community movement" relates to how relationships seen as imaginary have at their core micro-level face-to-face and physical interactions. At this fundamental level, people are embedded in the power structure of the state and even connected to organizations and networks beyond the state. Community movements are involved in and subordinate to the power structures that act on the community and motivate individuals. However, it is a micro-movement process that resists and adapts for its own survival. Derived from "community" and "social movement," "community movement" is the process by which people create alternative communities and worlds that can persist under inescapable hegemony. This book illustrates the process with cases from the field.

Community movements as assemblages

Community movements emphasize coincident formation, characterized by diversity and heterogeneity, in contrast to the conventional social movements formed prior to the 1960s, which were based on political integration and cultural and class homogeneity. This idea is based on the discussion of collective action by Melucci, one of the leading exponents of the "new" social movements. "New social movements" refers to collective action found in today's complex societies, as opposed to the playing out of historical trends by dogmatic uniform actors. "Such a misunderstanding can be corrected only by rejecting the assumption that collective action is a consistent reality. Only by this rejection can we discover the plurality of perspectives and relations of meaning crystallized in any collective act (Melucci 1997: 15)."

Melucci says that "newness" depends on the production of new cultural codes in networks that lie beneath the surface, undetectable in the visible acts of social movements. While traditional social movements were openly visible and active in politics, collective action in new social movements is produced outside the political sphere, with actors functioning as provisional non-institutionalized ad hoc representatives. This new type of movement pinpoints and manifests the power relations of the political system to address and confront the larger issues affecting human life in complex societies (Melucci 1997: 41–2, 90).

This view leads us to see community movements as assemblages, without assumptions of a pre-existing organic wholeness. The word "assemblage" is reminiscent of Deleuze's "diversity, which includes many heterogeneous terms, and in which relations are established by joint action." For example, Deleuze sees the "man-horse-stirrup" assemblage as a new symbiotic force in which man and animal enter into a relationship and transform each other into a whole new body with unique capabilities (Deleuze, Parnet 1980: 107–8). Bennett is inspired by Deleuze's assemblage in her thoughts on political philosophy. Expanding on Deleuze, she incorporates not only human but also non-human elements in this assemblage, which she describes as an "ad hoc grouping of diverse elements, of vibrant materials" (Bennett 2010: 23).

Ryo Takagi in Chapter 2 looks at voice and community radio assemblages against the backdrop of Thailand's political situation, which has been volatile following Prime Minister Thaksin Shinawatra's removal in a military coup in 2006. The nation remains divided, with fortunes seesawing in conflicts focused on Thaksin. This fragmentation and confusion has led to massive anti-government protests, leaving many casualties. After the 2014 coup, a military-led government took control of the political process and imposed extensive free-speech restrictions. It remained in power after the death of King Bhumibol Adulyadej in 2016 and the 2019 general elections. Student protests continued throughout 2020, aggravating division and confusion in Thailand and further complicating control of the nation.

In this state of flux, Takagi follows the community movements associated with three radio stations through diverse combinations of events. For example, a listener tunes in to a community radio station by chance and so learns about a medical subsidy program that saves his life and leads him to become a DJ. Another DJ attends a Bangkok political demonstration and later spreads empathy to his listeners by sharing the horror he experienced there through breathing, silence and voice. Takagi vividly describes how each listener and community is transformed through the voice of the radio.

Ryoko Nishii also casts community movement as an assemblage of human and non-human elements countering hegemony in the political milieu of Thailand. After the massacre at Thammasat University on 6 October 1976, many students escaped the government crackdown by fleeing to the forest to join the Communist Party. The forest strongholds were already populated with peasants and ethnic minorities before the students arrived. A large number of Hmong people associated themselves with the Communist movement in

1960s Thailand. Nishii looks at three Hmong communities and relates their respective memories to current movements and circumstances. One group of Hmong is involved in an ongoing land restitution movement, as the site of their original village has been incorporated into a national park. Their memories of the rice mill, burned village, rice fields and orchards, and the impressions left upon them by repeated visits to, and ancestral rituals conducted at these sites have sustained the land restoration movement for 30 years.

Manuel DeLanda, who envisions a new society based on Deleuze's theory of the assemblage, contrasts the assemblage with the concept of organic society. An organismic society is made up of intrinsic relations, where the constituent parts are constituted by their very relations to other parts within the whole (DeLanda 2006: 9). In contrast, the assemblage is a totality made up of various relations of extrinsic nature. The constituent parts of the assemblage first break away from the assemblage and connect to different assemblages, where they interact differently (ibid., 10–11). As Melucci puts it in "New Social Movements," relationships between parts are only incidentally determined. The key question is not "what is society?" but rather the process of "how does society come to exist as what it is?" That is to say, it does not posit society as a given whole.

In viewing community movements as assemblages, we can see the process of "society coming to exist," by which Melucci's invisible relationships change power systems. In other words, the concept of "community movements" as an assemblage sheds light on real-life power dynamics that have hitherto not been adequately captured by social science.

Community movements in a globalized world

Southeast Asian nations are run by various types of regimes, ranging from democratic to authoritarian. Although relationships between residents and authoritarian governments differ, every country is influenced by international organizations. None are wholly independent.

ToshihiroAbe in Chapter 9 shows that even citizens of countries on the global periphery cannot avoid involvement in globalization or its primary impact on them of farmland deprivation. The three chapters in Part III deal with the day-to-day realities of such scenarios in the globalizing economies of Thailand, Laos and Cambodia.

Nobuko Koya in Chapter 7 points out two aspects of Thai agricultural policies: modernization/industrialization since the 1960s under the influence of foreign multinational entities and sporadic/spontaneous diversification of rural agricultural methods since the 1980s, away from "agriculture for sale" toward "agriculture for living." Koya analyzes the Inpaeng Network, which started integrated farming in the mid-1980s and expanded to 900 villages with more than 100,000 members by the 2000s. "Integrated" or "mixed" farming creates a unique assemblage of products, spanning grains, vegetables, fruits, herbs, trees and fowl. The assembling pattern is not set by the network and there is no clear distinction between members and non-members. The network was anti-authority in essence, but later supported officially. Its success lay in its practices aligning with the King's support for a "sufficiency economy" in response to the 1997 Asian currency crisis. Koya emphasizes that as well as containing new farming methods, integrated farming also marks changes in personal outlook in life away from concerns about being rich or poor; participants contend that they are not rich but not poor either. This highlights cases of successful accommodation with global economic influences.

Some Laotians and Cambodians have, in contrast, managed to resist outside influence. In Chapter 8, Tomoko Nakata discusses a community movement of villagers opposed to land-grabs. Although Laos' "*Chintanakan Mai* (New Thinking)" economic reforms shifted its economy from centrally planned socialism toward market-oriented capitalism, the country has maintained a single-party regime since its founding in 1975. The present regime is often characterized as authoritarian, with virtually no freedom for people to object to the government's policies. As the government created domestic laws to promote the economy, the state and foreign actors, including the World Bank and Asian Development Bank (ADB), have increasingly intervened in people's lives. However, independent civil society organizations are nonexistent, and international NGOs are restricted to extending and supplementing official government policies, programs and objectives, with few active linkages to local groups.

Against this background, Nakata examines how some locals struggled to sustain themselves after losing a large part of their farmland to the development of large-scale rubber plantations. She describes vividly how villagers shifted cultivation into a conservation park across a river, all the while refusing to pay tolls and fees. To facilitate frequent crossings, they built a rope bridge spontaneously and voluntarily, without official leadership, planning or administration. All stakeholders, recognizing the utility a rope bridge would bring, autonomously decided to be involved in its construction and to contribute equally with their labor and money to accomplish the project together. We might say that this was a uniquely Laotian form of resistance for survival.

Whereas the aforementioned case studies from Laos and Thailand can be characterized as cooperative interactions between potential allies through spontaneous engagement in autonomous actions/ movements, Toshihiro Abe's Cambodian study in Chapter 9 shows how collaborators change with movements. Specifically, in this case villagers adapted to changing political circumstances by turning their local anti-land-grab appeal into a global issue.

During the Khmer Rouge regime (1975–1979), private land holding was forbidden and official land ownership documents were lost. The period between the end of the civil war and the early 1990s was marked by unregulated movements of people. Under the 1992 Land Law, the concession system was reintroduced with strong support from international organizations, particularly the World Bank. Actors in the movement shifted their strategy from mobilizing local support for governmental policy change to negotiating with foreign stakeholders on economic land concession issues, incorporating the global justice movement framework.

Unique to the Cambodian case is the way the movement engages with the outside world. For example, in *Avatar*-themed performances, residents from mountain forest areas in northwest Cambodia donned green clothing, leaf hats and primitive face-paint, intentionally mimicking characters from the Hollywood movie. They repeatedly appeared in Phnom Penh and their hometown to protest "illegal logging and mineral mining and taking a toll on the ancient forest." Using images from and harnessing the global popularity of Hollywood movie, the performance appealed not only to locals, but also to foreign media. Incomplete understanding of symbolic imagery from the global Avatar phenomenon was smoothly bridged with such traditional icons as scarecrows. While the community movement in Laos took advantage of governance gaps to bridge literally a river to maintain livelihoods, the community movement in Cambodia bridged locals and the global community.

In summary, the community movement as an assemblage is distinct from conventional social movements that assume certain forms of homogeneity, such as solidarity and unity. Furthermore, it is characterized by the process of creating dynamism through the contingent organization of "communitas" as unstructured interrelationships among heterogeneous and diverse people. The movement does not originate from a fixed, pre-determined institutional entity, such as the state. Instead, the state and various institutional constructs change while constituting the assemblage. The concept of "community movement" is an attempt to capture the process of how people move and act in search of a better life, even as the process entangles and affects them. In other words, the concept of community movement as an assemblage captures the micro-movements in which people are engaged throughout their daily lives, while maintaining a perspective that relativizes the state. This gives a new perspective on the changing reality of Southeast Asia in the current milieu of globalization.

Endotes: Introduction

1. Democracy is defined by Graeber as follows: "Democracy, then, is not necessarily defined by majority voting: it is, rather, the process of collective deliberation on the principle of full and equal participation. Democratic creativity, in turn, is most likely to occur when one has a diverse collection of participants . . . free of a preexisting overarching authority" (Graeber 2013: 186).

2. The current anti-government protests have been influenced by changes in communication tools and the digital revolution in ways that cannot be captured in the context of face-to-face state violence. What started as an online clash between Thai and Chinese youths in the spring of 2020, with Taiwanese and Hong Kong youths supporting their Thai counterparts, has become a new form of protest, using social media to demonstrate without central leadership, developing a sense of sympathy and solidarity in opposing undemocratic institutions. Their informal title, "Milk Tea Alliance," comes from local forms of milk tea popular across these nations (Yoshioka 2020a, 2020bc). Demonstrators against the coup d'état in Myanmar in February 2021 were also reported to have "joined" this online alliance. (This title was suggested by Kota Oguri: "Teacups in the Storm: Thinking about Hong Kong and Southeast Asian Coffee Culture from the Perspective of the 'Milk Tea Alliance.'" Society for the Cultural Anthropology of Taste, 11 March 2021). Such cross-regional and cross-national connections force us to reconsider contests between states as power apparatuses, with their nationally bounded structures and their respective inter-connected peoples. Note, however, that these new communications tools can also be used for suppression and control by those in power. Forms of communication are also changing, with such analog means as letters and leaflets regaining prominence.

3. The concept of "community movement" was proposed by Tanabe, the co-editor of this book, and the collected results of the joint research group that was the predecessor to this research group. The results were published in *Communities of Potential: Social Assemblages in Thailand and beyond* (2016). For more details, see Tanabe 2016, "Introduction."

4. Turner describes the non-structural potential of "communitas" as something that is still attached to the structure without becoming active, relying in part on Henri Bergson's concept of "élan vital, life-force" (Tanabe 2016: 9).

References

Bennett, Jane. 2010. *Vibrant Matter: a Political Ecology of Things.* Duke University Press.

DeLanda, Manuel 2006. *A New Philosophy of Society: Assemblage Theory and Social Complexity.* Bloomsbury.

Deleuze, Gilles, and Claire Parnet. 1980. *Duruzu no shisou* (Deleuze's Thought). Translated by Tamura Takeshi. Tokyo: Thaishukanshoten (in Japanese).

Graeber, David. 2006. *Anakisuto jinruigaku no tameno dansho* (Fragments of an Anarchist Anthropology).Translated by Kohso Iwasaburo. Tokyo: Ibunsha (in Japanese).

————. 2013. *The Democracy Project: A History, A Crisis, A Movement.* Penquin Books.

————. 2020. *Minshushugi no hisiyoukigen nituite: "aida" no kuukan no minshushugi* (There Never Was a West: Or, Democracy Emerges From the Space in Between). Translated by Kataoka Daisuke. Tokyo: Ibunsha (in Japanese).

Kayano, Toshihito. 2005. *Kokka towa nanika* (What is the State?). Tokyo: Ibunsha (in Japanese).

Melucci, Alverto. 1997. *Genzai ni ikiru yuboumin atarasii koukyoukuukan no soushutsu ni mukete* (Nomads of the Present: Social Movements and Individual Needs in Contemporary Society). Tokyo: Iwanami Shoten (in Japanese).

Scott, James C. 2009. *The Art of not Being Governed: An Anarchist History of Upland Southeast Asia.* New Haven & London: Yale University Press.

Tanabe, Shigeharu. 2008. *Kea no komyuniti kitatai no eizu jijoguru-pu ga hirakumono* (Community of Care: What AIDS Self-Help Groups in Northern Thailand Open Up). Tokyo: Iwanami Shoten (in Japanese).

————. 2016. "Introduction: Communities of Potential." In *Communities of Potential: Social Assemblages in Thailand and Beyond*, edited by Shigeharu Tanabe, 1–18. Chiang Mai: Silkworm Books.

Yoshioka, Keiko. 2020a. "Mirukuti doumei, kanryoku tono amakunai kankei, innbouronn mo isshuu (Milk Tea Alliance's not-so-sweet battle with power kicks off conspiracy theories)." *Asahi Shimbun*, 4 September 2020 (in Japanese).

————. 2020b. "Wakamono no ikari ga hajiketa! kenishugi to tatakau tai, hongkong, Taiwan no mirukuti doumei, tai no wakamono ni naniga okite irunoka (Young people's anger has burst! The Milk Tea Alliance of Thailand, Hong Kong, and Taiwan to Fight Authoritarianism: What's Happening to Thai Youth) (1)." *Ronza*, 6 September 2020 (in Japanese).

————. 2020c. "Wakamono no ikari ga hajiketa! kenishugi to tatakau tai, hongkong, Taiwan no mirukuti doumei, tai no wakamono ni naniga okite irunoka (Young people's anger has burst! The Milk Tea Alliance of Thailand, Hong Kong, and Taiwan to Fight Authoritarianism: What's Happening to Thai Youth) (2)." *Ronza*, 7 September 2020 (in Japanese).

Part 1

Community Movements as Assemblages: Resistance, Voice, and Memory

Chapter 1

THE ASSEMBLAGE OF RESISTANCE IN CRISIS
Buddhist Hermits of King's Mountain in Northern Thailand

SHIGEHARU TANABE

Introduction

This chapter deals with the Buddhist *thamma* (Pali: *dhamma*) practices among the hermits and the associated organizations featured in King's Mountain (*khao phra racha*) in Northern Thailand. It focuses on multiple kinds of Buddhist practitioners, such as hermits (*roesi*) and yogis (*pha khao* or female hermits), who practice *thamma* together in their own ways. Their peculiar body of practices is quite different from that in ordinary monasteries or nunneries under the overwhelming Establishment of the Community of Buddhist Monks, or *sangha* (*khana song*). As I have touched on elsewhere (Tanabe 2016a, 3–8), such an organizational feature could be properly analyzed in terms of the concept of "assemblage," a dynamic configuration consisting of diverse people, originally put forward by Gilles Deleuze and others. As well as those who are outside the state *sangha,* such as hermits and yogis, even some insider monks within the *sangha* and laypeople gathered in King's Mountain try to liberate their imaginations toward their own future. Amid the overwhelming hopes and enthusiasm among those people, we can detect a resistance to the massive and solid *sangha* and the administrative institutions.

What I call an "assemblage of resistance" here could function as "counter-hegemony" through constructing multiple "subjects"[1] and their relationships therein.[2] For instance, Juliane Schober's study (2014, 32–53) also develops in parallel on a religious virtuoso *weikza* in Burma who inspires a counter-hegemonic imagination as opposed to the modernizing reformist Buddhist center. The case of the hermits and yogis in King's Mountain has been developed as a "counter-hegemony" against the modern political and administrative systems and the centralized Buddhist *sangha*. "Deterritorializing," or getting themselves out from the established Buddhist institutions, they have trodden their autonomous paths, while keeping in contact with other outside groups and institutions. This chapter, thus, intends to identify the ways of constructing such "subjects" of resistance; and the processes whereby the community as an "assemblage of resistance" was split up in the fluid situation that emerged after the death of their leader, Phra Pho Pan (1932–2016).

The assemblage of resistance

I have discussed elsewhere the organizational concept of "assemblage" (Tanabe 2016a: 3–9). It elucidates not only the stabilized and consistent state of internal affairs, but also refers to the dynamic processes in which constituent parts are always moving and entering into alliances with others or, to the contrary, antagonizing or resisting others in and around the assemblage.[3] An assemblage is not a structure or system, nor an essential entity (DeLanda 2006: 9–10). What constitutes the King's Mountain hermitage is a sort of interpersonal network of individual activities under the tutelage of Hermit Phra Pho Pan (hereafter "Pan," see Fig. 1) with certain independence, in which hermits and yogis are connected with outside organizations or assemblages, such as Buddhist monasteries and their alliances. It would also be pertinent to look at another feature in which an assemblage could relate to a mixture of hierarchies of pre-existing institutions and newly emerging organizations (DeLanda 2006: 5–6), as illustrated by the HIV/AIDS self-help groups of Northern Thailand in the late 20th and early 21st centuries (Tanabe 2008: 189). "Assemblage of resistance" is a term that enables us to elucidate not only the practices of "resistance" against the dominating or hegemonic forces and discourses, including Buddhism, but more generally the whole spheres of domination over everyday practices and lifestyles among individuals, or what Foucault calls "a lifestyle, a way of thinking and living" (Foucault 1984, iii).

Figure 1. Hermit Phra Pho Pan at King's Mountain, 2012

Bearing this in mind, to understand how people achieve their purposes in and out of the assemblage in King's Mountain, we need to pay due attention to the concept of "the virtual" (*le virtuel*) of Henri Bergson. The virtual contains potential or capacity that could be "actualized" (not realized) in a visible form by a process of "actualization" or "differenciation." However, the virtual or potential is actualized in terms of various different lines along which "actualization" or "differenciation" takes place: for instance, life may be actualized as plant, animal, human, Buddhist or whatever (Deleuze 1988, 97; Patton 2000, 36–7). The hermits, yogis and others in King's Mountain thus actualize their own potential or capacity, which would have remained untapped or underdeveloped before they came up to King's Mountain. Pan himself had already actualized his own meditation technology of *samatha* (serenity) and *vipassanā* (insight) while he was at Doi Saphanyu Samnak, Mae Wan district (1981–1993) before coming to King's Mountain in 1997 (Tanabe 2004a, 102–4). After resuming activities there, the interactions with the many hermits and yogis who settled in or stayed temporarily have enormously contributed to further refining his meditation technology, actualizing the potential to generate abundant *nimit* (Pali: *nimitta*) or visions.[4]

In King's Mountain, one such feature of *nimit* is associated with the configuration of Foucauldian "heterotopic" space, or "an alternative real space" as I have described elsewhere (Tanabe 2016b: 27; 2016c: 122). Pan and other hermits and yogis have visualized their own "heterotopic" styles and images (see Foucault 1986, 27), which include a variety of buildings, such as a monastery (*vihara*), pagodas (*phrathat* or *cedi*), or Buddhist sculptures, paintings and other objects quite different from those normally seen in other Buddhist monasteries or hermitages. Such features of the site seem to reflect one of the heterotopic aspects of resistance to the dominating and hegemonic contemporary Buddhism. It could be said that the people in King's Mountain have transformed their subjugated "subject" into one bearing a new "mode of thought and life" detached from hegemonic Buddhism, in terms of what Sato Yoshiyuki (2008, 313–14) calls a strategy of "construction of interiority." Such heterotopic features of resistance in King's Mountain have emerged from its organizational quality of "assemblage." The aggregate of hermitages and nunneries could thus be seen as an assemblage that is the fertile soil for actualization of one's potential or capacity. As Arturo Escobar and Michal Osterweil (2010, 191) plausibly point out, the significance of interacting individuals and parts within such an assemblage is firmly embedded in the negation of the modernist conceptions of totality and essence.

Furthermore, the assemblage of resistance in the case of King's Mountain could be comprehended in terms of the organizational features derived from the concept of "deterritorialization" put forward by Gilles Deleuze and Félix Guattari (1987, 291–2). The Buddhist modernization in Northern Thailand has proceeded as a "territorialization" that produces endless currents of Buddhist centralization provided with a close connection with the nation-state centered in Bangkok. Against such Buddhist "territorialization," we have come across many instances where local monks have rather developed their own ways of conduct in accepting indigenous discourses and practices. Such currents have spread out especially since the late 19th century, when the centralized *sangha* became dominant in many parts of Northern Thailand. This trend can be detected and could be called "deterritorialization"—the streams getting rid of the territorializing forces of modernized Buddhism. In Northern Thailand, the *khruba* (venerable teacher) tradition exemplified by Khruba Sri Wichai and Khruba Khao Pi in the early and mid-20th century represent the most eminent ways of "deterritoialization," resisting the centralized Buddhist *sangha,* remaining within it on the one hand, while on the other becoming a hermit (*roesi*) who is, in most cases, completely outside the *sangha,* pursuing his own way of practicing *thamma.* The hermit way of *thamma* practices, not being placed under the hegemonic Buddhist *sangha,* has spread not only among male hermits but also female yogis (female hermits),[5] and those close to them as disciples or followers in Northern Thailand. In addition, we have to note that such male and female Buddhist practitioners should not be seen simply as a "minority" divided or expelled from a "majority," but as "minoritarian." This is not a state forced by the majority, but refers to hermits or yogis who are in the process of escaping the state of minority, as defined by the dominating majority. To consider this in the framework of Deleuze and Guattari (1987, 291), what we will see is "hermits" and "yogis" in the orbits in which they have taken flight (*la fuite*)[6] to transform themselves into something else, escaping the hegemonic Buddhist regime. They intend and are eager to "become (*devenir*)" a Buddhist rather than a Buddhist monk, or even a Buddha. "Becoming" is a kind of politics of the virtual; the process of "becoming a Buddha"[7] is one of the crucial points of departure toward resistance against the "present" within the assemblage of King's Mountain (Tanabe 2016c, 129–30).

Tracks of the hermits and yogis

King's Mountain has long been a site of "becoming a hermit" or "becoming something else" for most of the hermits, including Hot and Pan, as well as others. For those who have joined the hermitage or nunnery, a certain sort of "becoming" is a necessary point of departure to transform their life-circumstances. At the same time, they, consciously or unconsciously, have to keep constantly to their passion to transform themselves as a "minoritarian," a life of seeking their own Buddhist way detached from the hegemonic Buddhism. As I mentioned elsewhere, some of Pan's cases of "becoming" relate to his long-sustained symbiosis with animals, as represented in "becoming" himself a buffalo to pull the plough over his rice-fields (Tanabe 2016b, 39n5); and by the planned symbiotic project of the "Walled Palace for Cows and Buffaloes (*wang wiang ua khwai*)" (Fig. 2) in Ban Mai Sawan, which is an extension of a utopian village community originally constructed by him in the 1970s (Tanabe 2004a, 27, 89–94; 2016b, 23).

Figure 2. Hermit Pan and colleagues talking about the planned symbiotic project in Ban Mai Sawan, 26/11/2013

The King's Mountain hermitage is one of the Buddhist assemblages that emerged from participation by a number of "deterritorialized" people who settled, or stayed temporarily, as hermits, yogis, or other kinds of "minoritarian," since the late 1990s. The hermitage has basically been equipped with self-organizational features as an assemblage characterized by its multiplicity, heterogeneous components, liaisons, alliances, or networks, as indicated by Deleuze. As he said, such features include symbiosis and sympathy derived from alliances, alloys or even "contagions, epidemics, the wind like magicians" (Deleuze and Parne 1987, 69). Furthermore, he indicates the relationship maintained between the constituent parts: "it is the set of the affects which are transformed and circulate in an assemblage of symbiosis, defined by the co-functioning of its heterogeneous parts" (*ibid.*, 70). Such significant features of relationship can be detected in many ways among the hermits and yogis and are linked to the processes of actualization of their potentials in their "deterritorializing" tracks.[8] Thus, in the following paragraphs, I pick up the three cases of Yogi Regina (nun), Tu Chan (monk) and Ruesi Hot (hermit) to trace their tracks of symbiosis and affect, and their attained goal at Pan's passing in 2016.

Yogi Regina

Yogi Regina met Pan for the first time in 1991 at Doi Saphanyu Samnak[9] located about 5.8 km to the southwest of King's Mountain. She, still in her early 30s, was a spirit-medium and ordained as a yogi or "female hermit" at Doi Saphanyu. As I described elsewhere (Tanabe 2016b, 31–2), since her early career she had long experienced "becoming something else" or being possessed by spirits.[10] The prevalence of professional spirit-mediumship in Northern Thailand is a relatively recent phenomenon, with strong influences, largely from central Thailand, since the 1960s, becoming extremely popular in Chiang Mai urban areas in the 1980s–90s. It could be said therefore that Regina's spirit-possession started along with the rapid social changes in rural areas around San Pa Tong district, basically caused by the capitalist development diffused from central Thailand. Another noteworthy feature is, as I touched on elsewhere, that the spirits that possessed her sometimes reflect a nationalist hero, such as King Naresuan (reigned 1590–1605) (Tanabe 2016b, 31). In addition, her practices include making *baisri* ornaments (cooked rice offerings with folded leaves and flowers) on occasions for propitiating Hindu deities, spirits, and the Buddha, and reading *ongkan* (divine prescriptions) on the occasion of inviting Hindu deities (*thewada*). All these features observable among Regina and her followers are quite different from legitimate modernized Buddhism and also from the traditional practices long maintained by the villagers in the area.

From "becoming" spirits as a spirit-medium and practicing Hindu conventions as a yogi, we can detect that Regina's thoughts and practices during the past several decades reflect her perpetual deviation from the authentic, legitimate and long-accepted traditions. This seems to be her own "deterritorializing" path from legitimate hegemonic Buddhism, which reflects, moreover, an unshakable path of actualizing the self. It is her "minoritarian" actualization of her own potential that would not, otherwise, be attained. Such actualization processes could not be fully realized without Pan's support and alliance since the period at Doi Saphanyu Samnak in the early 1990s until his death in 2016. The contingent encounter with Pan seems to have provided her with an opportunity to develop her own feminist thought in order to oppose the everlasting male domination in the Buddhist *sangha*. She has gained steady support and resources for the life of yogis in King's Mountain. Soon after her arrival at King's Mountain, Regina established a nunnery with several nuns for daily *thamma* practices.

In 2009, Regina had begun to dedicate her efforts in cooperation with Pan to construct Chedi Chet Thawip (Seven Continents Pagoda), a pagoda exclusively for the heroines in the myths and history of Northern Thailand and beyond at the site of Ho Thao Thammikarat (The Hall of Righteous King), at the northern end of the compound.[11] Before that, Pan had already begun to construct a huge pagoda called Chedi Sri Lanna (Pagoda of Glorious Lanna) at the center of King's Mountain, dedicated to the male heroes with the principal image of Phra In (Indra).[12] While this male pagoda had been under construction until just before the death of Pan in 2016, construction of the female pagoda was delayed and finally stopped in the early 2010s due to financial or other reasons. Surprisingly, a significant change was made around the time of Pan's death to the principal figure at the center of the male pagoda. The Hindu god Phra In was replaced by Phra Maha Chakraphat (転輪聖王), an ideal Buddhist king in ancient India who is also one of the main Buddhist symbols of the royalist Thammayut sect. Accordingly, the name Chedi Sri Lanna was replaced by Chedi Maha Chakraphat (Maha Chakraphat Pagoda) in 2015 (Cohen 2019, 163n39). It is not clear whether this significant change was initiated by Pan himself toward the end of his life. However, the change from Phra In to Phra Maha Chakraphat seems to be highly indicative of an intervention from the royalist Thammayut sect.[13]

Before Regina came to King's Mountain, she had already kept close contact with Luang Ta Ma at Wat Tham Muang Na in Chiang Dao district, Chiang Mai province, who was one of the high-ranking monks in the royalist Thammayut sect in Northern Thailand.[14] However, he didn't appear when making merit for the funeral (*kan bamphenkuson*) of the late Pan held at Ban Mai Sawan, the village he constructed in the 1970s, for six days from 23 to 28 April 2016. The funeral was basically organized by his sons, a brother, and followers

Figure 3. Installation of *chat* (multi-tiered spire for celebration), 25/04/2017 (Photo: Witoon Buadaeng)

Figure 4. Maha Chakraphat Pagoda with *chat* on the top, 16/01/2019

in and outside the village, while Yogi Regina remained only as a host of merit-making rites for several days. The final day of cremation (*chapanakit*) on 28 April was held with more than 1,000 people paying their condolences, including hermits, monks, Karen novices, and villagers not only from Chiang Mai but also from many parts of Northern Thailand.

Thereafter, Luang Ta Ma's influence over the hermitage and nunnery became increasingly evident and he began to introduce to King's Mountain important ritual practices, including chanting the Chakraphat mantra (*suat mon phra maha chakraphat*) on many occasions under the Thammayut denomination (Cohen 2019, 176). One of the most symbolically significant events was held on 25 April 2017, which is widely regarded as the first anniversary of Pan's death (20 April 2016), but more likely to correspond with the date of King Naresuan's death on 25 April 1605. Luang Ta Ma presided over the installation of the Chakraphat spire on the top of the pagoda while chanting the Chakraphat mantra over the King's Mountain hermitage (Cohen 2019: 176; see Figs. 3, 4). This event seems to be a symbolically and substantially significant moment in establishing the domination by the Thammayut sect over the King's Mountain hermitage and nunnery, while Pan's lifelong accomplishment since the mid-20th century was almost fading away. Not so long after that ceremony, in August 2017, the images of Luang Pu Du and Luang Pho To were cast and placed to the north of the Chakraphat pagoda, followed in 2018 by the Chakraphat image to the south (Cohen 2019, 173). These figures, Chakraphat, Luang Pu Du and Luang Pho To, closely associated with Luang Ta Ma, became the main symbols of King's Mountain (Fig. 5). Accordingly, the prominent images formerly representing the hermitage of Northern Thai or Lanna tradition, such as the statues of many hermits, Khruba Sri Wichai, and Khruba Khao Pi were withdrawn from its central part.

Figure 5. Poster Thot Pha Pa (off-season offering of robes) at King's Mountain on 25 April 2017. Luang Ta Ma at the center with his teachers, while Phra Pho Pan is put aside on the both sides. Phra Chakraphat image and Maha Chakraphat Pagoda on the top.

Yogi Regina had, since the 1990s, been a close comrade of Pan, and her firm feminist thoughts and practices toward the "deterritorializing" path were developed maintaining the symbiosis with other yogis and hermits in the assemblage. After Pan's death, however, her direction was radically transformed to "reterritorialize" the whole assemblage of King's Mountain into a more integrated and modernized Buddhist institution like other contemporary monasteries. Radical and reversal changes she currently advocates are to restore the northern part of King's Mountain as a meditation park open to people from outside and to transform the remaining southern part into an officially registered monastery, not a hermitage, under the state *sangha*. With this plan she clearly intends to develop the whole area of King's Mountain as a registered monastery within the Thammayut sect under the leadership of Luang Ta Ma. At this point, Regina seems to have stopped from her long "flight," beginning to "reterritorialize" herself into the main stream of Thai Buddhism. Such conversion from flight toward "minoritarian" actualization hasn't been confined to Regina, but also extends to other hermits and yogis, and to Tu Chan who has been very close to her (Fig. 6).

Figure 6. Regina and Chan at the ceremony of installing *chat*, 25/04/2017 (Photo: Witoon Buadaeng)

Tu Chan

Tu Chan, a monk in his mid-30s born in Chiang Mai city, had been a foreman at the construction site of Chiang Mai Night Safari Park in his 20s. During that period, by chance he briefly met Pan in King's Mountain. After he resigned from his job at the construction site, Chan became particularly close to a ceramist friend near his house who produced Buddhist images and pottery. On the friend's advice, he read a book on the history of Luang Thep Lok Udon, a legendary Sri Lankan monk, which deeply inspired him on Buddhist beliefs and practices. Then Chan made an image of Luang Thep Lok Udon and thereafter continually produced Buddhist images, amulets (*phra phim*) and other products. Before that, he had been ordained briefly as a monk for 15 days at Wat Umong, a famous monastery to the west of Chiang Mai city. Thereafter, he frequently visited Pan at King's Mountain and also became acquainted with Yogi Regina, who invited him to stay there as a white-robed hermit (*nung khao hom khao*) in 2010. In those days, he was close to Roesi Suthon, another resident hermit in the hermitage, who was a specialist in writing *yan* magical scripts[15] and who tattooed (*sak yan*) Chan's whole body.

Thus, Chan took a step forward on the track of "deterritorialization" in King's Mountain and pursued *thamma* as a hermit together with producing Buddhist images and amulets. Fortunately, Chan has been able to pursue his own Buddhist path evading any strict monastic rule but under Pan's merciful protection. He is close to Yogi Regina and often worked as her driver when she visited monasteries and pagodas to make offerings of *baisri* ornaments to propitiate deities, spirits and the Buddha, and to read divine prescriptions (*ongkan*) inviting deities. Although since his youth he had been interested in pursuing Buddhist ascetic practices, he could not follow the Buddhist ordained life in terms of the strict code of

monastic disciplines (*winai song*). After his fateful encounter with
Pan in King's Mountain, however, Chan strongly sympathized with
his idea of flexible Buddhist practices for everybody to find their
own way. Under this elastic way of Buddhist life, Chan has been able
to actualize his own way of Buddhist practices combined with the
artisanship that has enabled him to produce molded Buddhist images
and amulets. Although having been something of a dropout from
the institutional framework of Thai Buddhism, he has successfully
constructed his own "subject" of resistance against the Buddhist
regime by pursuing his craftsmanship within the broad-minded space
of the King's Mountain hermitage.

Working together with Regina, Chan often visited Tu Lung Sawat
at Wat Phra That Upkaeo Chamthewi in Hot district of Chiang Mai
to help make rice and flower offerings of *baisri* on many occasions of
making merit (*tham bun*) to the pagoda. Tu Lung Sawat is an elder
brother of Khruba Anan at Wat Don Chan in Chiang Mai city who
has been keen to participate in many rural development projects
and is also famous for his exorcist rituals (*phithi lai phi*) for those
who are possessed by evil spirits. Together with Khruba Thong Suk
at Wat Buwak Khrok Noi, a grandson of Khruba Sri Wichai, these
monks have maintained a close relationship with Pan, Regina, Chan
and other hermits and yogis in King's Mountain for quite a long
time. They are classified, in a sense, as monks in the traditional Maha
Nikai sect and, at the same time, some of them are popularly entitled
"*khruba*," or "venerable teacher." It could be said that the assemblage
of King's Mountain has been surrounded by or become a part of
another assemblage, or a network, of "*khruba*" monks in Northern
Thailand, being distinct from those in the modernist and reformist
Thammayut sect, at least up until around the early 2010s.

Chan, who had grown up under such masters of Northern Thai
traditional Buddhism, however, began to follow a different path. As

I mentioned earlier, Pan's health began to seriously deteriorate in the early 2010s[16] and the hermits and yogis set about searching ways of maintaining the hermitage and their own life after his predicted death. Under such critical circumstances, Regina and Chan began to contact Luang Ta Ma and other monks at Wat Tham Muang Na and other monasteries of the same lineage in Chiang Dao district, about 180 km to the north of King's Mountain. Luang Ta Ma, one of the most prominent Thammayut monks in Northern Thailand, constructed a new cave monastery—Wat Tham Muang Na—in the territory of the Shan ethnic group's Muang Na village, Chiang Dao district. The construction was suggested by his teacher Luang Pu Du Phromapanyo (1904–1990) at Wat Sa Kae in Ayutthaya province, a Thammayut respected meditation master in Central Thailand. In response to Regina's courteous and devout invitation, Luang Ta Ma visited the ailing Pan at King's Mountain on several occasions since around 2015 and suggested to change the name of the pagoda at the center to Chedi Maha Chakraphat (Maha Chakraphat Pagoda), as I touched on before. Since around that time Chan seems to have begun to sympathize with Luang Ta Ma's straightforward attitude toward contemporary Buddhism and up-to-date ideas. Finally, Chan ordained as a monk for the second time immediately after Pan's death in 2016 at Wat Pa Thara Phirom, Chiang Dao district, a monastery under the supervision of Luang Ta Ma.

Tu Chan thus finally stepped forward into the territory of hegemonic Buddhism by withdrawing from his "subject" of resistance. Or alternatively, it might be said that after a long period of ambiguous and ambivalent resistance while on "flight," he was finally able to join the Thammayut sect in order to find a possible way for King's Mountain to survive as a place for pursuing *thamma* for the younger generations, including himself, Regina and others. In short, even though King's Mountain came under the supervision of the Thammayut sect, Chan and other members still envisaged that it could take on Pan's legacy of "minoritarian" symbiosis and affects within the assemblage. Paul Cohen records, however, one of Chan's saddest episodes of casting a Chakraphat image similar to Pan's face that tells much about the sense of loss:

> [Chan] organized the casting of a bronze chakkavatti [Chakraphat] image to be placed in the temple-hall of the King's Mountain pagoda . . . In his devotion and love for Pan, Chan playfully fashioned the face of the image to resemble that of his teacher! He received a stern rebuke from Phra Chao Khun Rithirong [the high-ranking Thammayut abbot at Wat Pa Dara Phirom, Mae Rim district, Chiang Mai], who declared that such a composite image was not permissible and that the face would require changing! In short, a Thammayut temple King's Mountain is unlikely to have the religious freedom it once experienced as an autonomous hermitage under Phra Pan's tutelage (Cohen 2019, 174).

Tu Chan's episode is concerned not only with the problem of religious freedom, but more significantly with the sense of loss derived from the negation of his artistic sense and practice nurtured and embraced with affect and symbiosis within the assemblage.

It would be relevant to reckon how Regina and Chan take into consideration their own relationship with Luang Ta Ma and his royalist sect of Thammayut in terms of their future. From an organizational point of view, their relation to the Thammauyut sect while keeping a close linkage with the King's Mountain hermitage and nunnery can be regarded as a recently established "exteriority of relations," denoting that it can be a part of the Thammayut sect while protecting its independence as an assemblage. This kind of fusion can be detected in many cases among assemblages and similar organizational settings in modernity, as I mentioned at the beginning of this chapter and in some related works (DeLanda 2006, 11; Escobar and Osterwel 2010, 191). For Regina and Chan, the newly established relationship with the Thammayut sect as an "exteriority of relations" might be one of the possible ways by which King's Mountain could survive for generations of Pan's disciples as an established site of Buddhist practices in the form of a monastery, hermitage, meditation park or whatever. As Cohen (2019, 173) argued, they must have considered that the site of King's Mountain could otherwise be taken over by capitalists in collusion with the local administration. Nevertheless, it could be said that their path means the end of resistance for those who had tried to get clear of hegemonic Buddhism through the assemblage of "minoritarian" and "deterritorialization," as was quite evident since the late 1990s up until the early 2010s. In short, Pan's legacy might be carried on by new generations, but only in pieces; it might be tough to restore or restart in the future the ontological quality and organizational power accumulated at the King's Mountain hermitage and nunnery over these past several decades.

Hermit Hot

Since Hot settled for the second time at the King's Mountain hermitage in 2014, he has enthusiastically provided visitors with fortune-telling (*poet kam*), reversing fortune (*kae kam*), and ways to cure a variety of illnesses. A practitioner of such fortune-telling, curing, inscribing sacred formulae and letters or *yan* (Pali: *yantra*) and so forth is derived from what is commonly called in Northern Tai *yokawachon* (Pali: *yogāvacara*), a "practitioner of spiritual discipline" or "meditation practitioner" (Crosby 2000: 141; 2013: 155n26; Tanabe

2016c: 129). The *yokawachon* tradition has long been prevalent as a technique or *wicha* (magical lore) among the monks and ex-monks in and around the Buddhist monasteries, not only in the North but also Central and Northeast regions up until today. As I explained elsewhere (Tanabe 2016b, 29; 2016c,123), Hot first learned the technologies of fortune-telling, reversing fortune, cures, and inscribing *yan* through his father-in-law while living in Lampang in the late 1990s through the early 2000s. We should pay much attention to the fact that he was able to overcome his own long experiences of mental illnesses and sufferings by devoting himself to meditation practices, including serenity (*samatha*) and insight (*vipassanā*). We have to bear in mind that he has obtained and become proficient in these technologies in order to save his own life through relieving his ailing "subject." For Hot, King's Mountain has been a space to emancipate himself from his own illnesses through meditation and to apply it to cure and make good use of it for other people; in other words, it is for him a site of "becoming a subject" as a healer by utilizing the traditional technologies together with avoiding highly modernized and hegemonic Buddhism. In this way, as often feasibly pointed out for ex-sufferers who recovered and became healers in traditional lore and medicine, including *yokawachon*, Hot has emerged after a long and thorny pilgrimage "from sufferer to healer."

Although the case of Hot is similar to that of Pan, the former is more often embedded in the processes of serenity meditation (*samatha*), as often observable in his fortune-telling and curing for visitors (Fig. 7). In the hermitage, Hot normally sits in front of a visitor and concentrates his mind on one point, and for a while enters the state of absorption, or *khao chan* (Pali: *jhāna*). When he begins to give blessing to the visitor, his voice becomes high or deep depending on the embodying Buddha (Tanabe 2016c, 127). This means that Hot is able to become a Buddha within his body through meditation and it would be pertinent to say that his "becoming" is very similar to the cases of spirit-possession[17]. To use Michael Taussig's phrase, Hot "yields into and becomes Other" (Taussig 1993, xii). The "becoming a Buddha" among the hermits could share a quality of transformation through "affective contacts" similar to the cases of spirit-mediumship in Northern Thailand, as I argued before (Tanabe 2013a, 182–84). Hermit Hot steadily maintained a prominent quality of "liminality" and continuously remained as a crucial part of a collective "communitas" of the retreat. Finally, he succeeded to the position as the head of the King's Mountain hermitage, while Pan moved to his previous site at Ban Mai Sawan in 2014.

Figure 7. Hermit Hot wrist-tying (*mat moe*), 31/10/2014

Since he came up to King's Mountain in 2007 and later from 2014 onward, Hot has been quite close to Pan's relatives and the villagers in Ban Mai Sawan, Pan's former base in the 1970s. As Cohen puts it, Hot has also sympathized and supported Pan's legacies centered at maintaining "a community of hermits dedicated to the practice of meditation and the nurturing of loving-kindness (*mettā*) for others" (Cohen 2019, 175). In particular, the notion of "loving-kindness" has long been shared not only by the hermits and yogis in King's Mountain, but also the villagers of Ban Mai Sawan, probably since its beginning in the 1970s. Generally speaking, this Buddhist notion has long been associated with the millennial notion of Phra Sri Ariya Mettrai, a future Buddha (the advent every 500 years), shared by the people in Northern and even Northeast and Central regions. According to Pan, the era of Phra Sri Ariya had already begun in this world before he moved to King's Mountain in the late 1990s. For Pan and other hermits and yogis, it has been said that the descending of Phra Sri Ariya already happened in 1993, as indicated in an inscription discovered at a cave in the area of Taton in Bago division near Karen State in Burma (Tanabe 2016b, 32–4; 2016d, 1–3). Subsequently, Pan constructed a huge reclining image of Phra Sri Ariya Mettrai in 2012 (Fig. 8), which marked a significant "event" to participate in a new world or "new space-times" (Deleuze 1995, 176) for people inside and outside King's Mountain. For the hermits and yogis, the advent of Phra Sri Ariya will bring to humans the significance of "loving-kindness," which has long been undervalued within the contemporary capitalist system. Another point Pan emphasizes is Phra Sri Ariya's "loving-kindness," rather than Goutama Buddha's "intelligence" (*sati paññā*), which is an invaluable human potentiality that should constitute an important element among communities and political leadership in the contemporary world (Tanabe, 2021).

Pan's millennialism has been deeply embedded in his notion of Buddhist (utopian) values and even in everyday social practices, particularly focusing on saving poor villagers, orphaned children and sick persons in neighboring communities. Such millenarian values have been shared with Hot's project of saving poor children. For Pan and Hot, what is called "loving-kindness" is not only awarded to the believers by their deep devotion to Phra Sri Ariya, but more significantly moves them to give their sympathy and alliances to those who should be saved. In other words, Phra Sri Ariya, according to Pan, has already come into our hearts and we now need to set out to save those who need relief (Tanabe, 2021). In this way, the notion of Phra Sri Ariya and the associated "active utopianism"[18] have been widely shared by many villagers in Ban Mai Sawan and other communities with which Pan or Hot have established relations.

Figure 8. Reclining Phra Sri Ariya, full of *metta* (loving-kindness), 14/02/2013

With such a principle of "active utopianism," Hot could not tolerate Regina and Chan's plan of submitting the entire property of King's Mountain to the authoritarian and royalist Thammayut sect represented by Luang Ta Ma and others. His relationship with Regina and Chan, who were disciples of Pan and at the same time deeply influenced by Luang Ta Ma, worsened around 2014, and the conflict between the two became critical after Pan's death in April 2016. In the midst of such despair and hopelessness, Hot left the King's Mountain hermitage to found his new site of "becoming" in a village in San Pa Tong district about 15 km to the southeast in 2018.

Resistance and value

Amid Pan's worsening health, and the subsequent increasing influence on the King's Mountain hermitage and nunnery of Luang Ta Ma of the Thammayut sect since the mid-2010s, the hermits and yogis were urged to decide their own future directions. The ways of resistance against the domination of the Buddhist *sangha* and the related political powers have been varied in terms of individual direction, as described in the previous section. This is because the hermits and yogis have their own different problems and directions toward their solution, which could be allowed to exist flexibly together within the King's Mountain as an assemblage. In other words, the hermits and yogis as "minoritarian" can live together through "affective contacts" (Tanabe 2013a, 186–88) and actualize their own potentials through symbiosis and sympathy derived from alliances within the assemblage.

At this point, a question could be raised as to why and how they are able to actualize their own individual potentials within King's Mountain as an assemblage. To respond to this question, we have to reveal their value and the related meaning to life that promote and foster symbiosis among the multiplicity in the assemblage of the hermits and yogis in King's Mountain. David Graeber argues, based relevantly on Terence Turner (1979), working on the Kayapo of central Brazil, that it is the "politics of value" that trace the fundamental question of what value is:

> We are back, then, to a "politics of value," but one very different from [Arjun] Appadurai's neoliberal version. The ultimate stakes of politics, according to Turner, is not even the struggle to appropriate value; it is the struggle to establish what value *is*. (Graeber 2001: 88).

For the hermits and yogis, the ultimate freedom is to find out the meaning of life, or—as Graeber (2001: 88) stresses—the freedom to decide "what is the life worth living." To put it another way, for the hermits and yogis, the ultimate freedom is resistance to the "present" by detecting their own style of thought and life and transforming themselves to construct their own "subject." Such resistance is to realize their own value of life, which could be inspired and welled up through the interactions between those who gathered in the assemblage. At this point, it would be appropriate to contend that a "politics of value" can emerge, not in individuals as anarchist theorists such as Graeber presumably presuppose, rather in an assemblage or community, always keeping internal multiplicity such as in the King's Mountain hermitage and nunnery. In other words, it is an assemblage that "actualizes" and maintains what value *is*. The resistance is for the hermits and yogis to produce and act for something more than "opposition," as Sherry Ortner (1995: 191) plausibly argues, which must allow a multiplicity of ways to "actualize" value, which hitherto remains underdeveloped and hidden. In this sense, it could be said that resistance is directed toward the ultimate freedom through "actualization" of the potential or capacity contained or covert within the individual hermits and yogis.

Among the hermits in King's Mountain, one of the obvious differences from the main stream of modernist and "universalist" Buddhism relates to their strong attachment to *nimit,* "mental image" or "vision," derived from *samatha* serenity meditation. Their *nimit* images, often a sign for construction of a Buddhist site or structure, are also connected with the more routine creation and use of magical objects, such as *yan* (*yantra,* sacred scripts of heart syllables) (Tanabe 2017). This is one "minoritarian" way of actualizing their own value in their lives, largely detached from the main stream of contemporary Thai Buddhism. Then, it should be noted that their strong attachment to *samatha* serenity meditation is different from the practices of modernized Thai Buddhism, which normally lay a stronger focus on *vipassanā* reflexive meditation. The latter has recently become increasingly associated with modern self-reflexivity, being popular among the new generations of Buddhist monks and lay people in contemporary Thailand. On the contrary, the practices strongly engrossed in *nimit, samatha* and *yan* among the hermits are closely associated with what Crosby (2000, 141; 2013, 4, 154–5n26) calls the *yogāvacara* (*yokawachon*) tradition that has still survived in many parts of South and Southeast Asia up until present, despite the growing domination of hegemonic modernized Buddhism.

For Hot, "becoming" somebody or something else through *nimit* emerges from *samatha* or serenity, and constructs a new "subject" or *tua ton,* in other words, getting out of being subject to authorities or powers prevalent in modernity—that is resistance. Not only for Hot but also many hermits, yogis and visitors, King's Mountain has been a site for "becoming" through which they are able to find what is value for oneself, that is, "becoming" is creating an indispensable value peculiar to oneself that won't be pursued elsewhere. King's

Mountain has been a site for continuously creating and preserving such values as opposed to generalized, globalized or capitalist ones. "Loving-kindness" or *metta* (Pali: *mettā*), together with "compassion" or *karuna* (Pali: *karunā*), are such values attached to the people in King's Mountain. Certainly, Pan's notion of "loving-kindness" is originally derived from the traditional, though highly abstract, Buddhist notion of *metta*. For him and his fellows it is, however, more concretely concerned with fundamental human potential. So far as I have known from conversations with Pan over many decades, his notion of "loving-kindness" is a fundamental value overarching the thoughts and practices of the hermits and yogis in contacting others in blessing, divination, curing, praying for visitors or fellows in King's Mountain. If we interpret it in a Spinozian and Deleuzian context, Pan's notion of "loving-kindness" largely corresponds to "affect" or "affective contact" deeply embedded in the body itself (Tanabe 2013a, 184–86).

"Loving-kindness" or "affect," not simply psychological "emotion," can go far beyond the self, intruding into others, human and nonhuman, and entering into alliances with them (*ibid.*, 189–90). Such a notion of "loving-kindness" is deeply embedded in a human value or potential concerned with symbiosis among the multiplicity, i.e. different peoples, ethnic groups, or nonhumans, and with sympathy and alliances with the feeble, old, poor, sick, orphaned children, or nonhumans. Such a value looks like a fantasy in the midst of the modern capitalist and political regimes, but could lead to revitalize worthwhile paths among the "minoritarian" peoples.

Value based on "loving-kindness" or "affect" in this way can organize a certain fabric of assemblage that allows the residents to have frequent contact with a variety of outside peoples without withdrawal from the world, quite different from the traditional notion of "*roesi*" or "hermit," indicating a Buddhist who resides in the deep forest away from human settlements. The hermits inhabiting King's Mountain could thus survive and adhere to their ultimate freedom through a wide range of resistance against the whole spheres of domination over individual everyday practices and lifestyles. In this regard, the ultimate freedom for the people in King's Mountain is resistance against the "present" through "becoming" someone else or something else, detecting their own style of thought and life to construct their own "subject."

Conclusions: The assemblage in crisis

With the death of Phra Pho Pan in 2016, the conflicts over the territory and leadership over the King's Mountain hermitage and nunnery rose to the surface. Since around the period of construction in the late 1990s, King's Mountain retreat has established firm relationships with the monasteries of the traditional Maha Nikai sect, such as Wat Phra That Doi Suthep, Wat Buwak Khrok Noi, and Wat Don Chan around Chiang Mai, and Wat Upkaeo Chamthewi in the Hot district of Chiang Mai. Since around 2015, King's Mountain, however, began to establish an increasingly close relationship with Luang Ta Ma at Wat Tham Muang Na in Chiang Dao district, which is one of the bases of the hegemonic and modernist sect of Thammayut. In so doing, the King's Mountain retreat came under the strong influence of Abbot Chao Khun Rithirong, the high ranked Thammayut monk at Wat Pa Dara Phirom, Mae Rim district (Cohen 2019, 173).

Since the late 20th century, many social scientists, including anthropologists, have argued against the rise of neoliberalism and its harsh effects and related powers, including suppression, depression, or hopelessness among the peoples concerned. Many social scientists have, subsequently, begun to turn their attention toward the ways

48

of resistance among the oppressed and those suffering under such overwhelmingly harsh conditions.[19] Political scientist James Scott has already argued "everyday forms of resistance" (1985) and "hidden transcripts" (1990) as modes of resistance, including those non-obvious acts of resistance among the peasantry. Importantly, Sherry Ortner asserts that most recent ethnographic studies lack focus on the subjective experience of the actors in resistance including their intentions, desires, fears, depression and hopelessness, and need to "reveal the ambivalences and ambiguities of resistance itself" (Ortner 1995, 190; 2016, 65–66).

In addition to such earlier arguments by Scott and Ortner, we could develop a further direction by introducing the Foucauldian context of "subject." As this chapter has advocated in the preceding sections, resistance should be understood in terms of the way of constructing "subject" rather than "opposition" to the powers embodied in the nation-state, institution, organization, or more comprehensively, "governmentality" in general. In other words, resistance signifies constructing a "subject" that refers not only to refusal of any negative or oppressive power, but, more hopefully, to creating or reproducing other kinds of hegemony and related practices and knowledge, rather than aiming narrowly at constituting a new establishment or institution.

As I have discussed elsewhere, the hermits' resistance in King's Mountain is, in general, against the "present," or against the present state of modernized Buddhist practices and the related discourses (Tanabe 2016b, 38–9). More precisely, however, its core process rests on constructing a "subject" resisting the newly encountered reality through Buddhist practices, especially meditation. In other words, it is aimed at overcoming the present state of oneself by transforming it into a certain potential state or "becoming" (*devenir*) something else or somebody else (Foucault 1982, 216; Sato 2008, 313–20). As I have discussed earlier, Regina, Chan and Hot got into the world of Buddhism and, when faced with the reality of rigid and inflexible Buddhist institutions incorporated in the state, wished to be able to resist such a harsh situation. They have steadily tried to construct their own "subject" by becoming something else while in meditation or other practices. For those in King's Mountain, resistance is to deny obedience to the dominating regime of Buddhist *sangha* or its cultural discourses through the newly created "subject" (Tanabe 2016b, 13–5). The assemblage that had played an enhancing role in such an aspect of resistance has, however, been split up with the death of Pan and faced with a crisis under the offensive launched by the hegemonic royalist Thammayut sect in recent years.

As Ortner plausibly puts forward:

> Resistance can be more than opposition, can be truly creative and transformative, if one appreciates the multiplicity of projects in which social beings are always engaged, and the multiplicity of ways in which those projects feed on as well as collide with one another. (Ortner 1995: 191)

In this sense, the resistance among the hermits and yogis in King's Mountain can be seen as pointed in many directions in terms of their own Buddhist thoughts and practices, but finally split into two parts and a multiplicity of ways of practicing *thamma* within the assemblage bringing it into a crisis.

The King's Mountain hermitage has been an assemblage of endless resistance to the Buddhist *sangha* and its discourses that have been constructed through modernization since the late-19th century. Such an assemblage is, as Graeber puts forward, a site for preserving and operating the "destituent power"[20] derived from the multiple imaginative powers among those assembled. It should be said that such powers are never for institutionalization, but for promoting anti-institutionalization itself (Graeber 2009, 60–1). Certainly, hermits and yogis in King's Mountain have continuously accumulated "destituent power" transcending the state *sangha* and administrative institutions. Since the death of Pan in 2016, however, such power of the assemblage has been split up under the rising establishment power of the Thammayut sect headed by Luang Ta Ma. The "assemblage of resistance" embodied by Phra Pho Pan has been in crisis, on the one hand, and on the other the "reterritorialization" toward the established Buddhist order has begun to spread into the remaining hermits and yogis.

In considering such a critical situation in King's Mountain, it is pertinent to recall the fundamental principle contained in a multiplicity of the assemblage, which is based on "connection and heterogeneity," or Deleuze and Guattari's "rhizome," i.e. subterranean stems, not roots and radicles. When an assemblage expands its connections with outer elements, individuals or institutions, it necessarily changes in nature. Deleuze and Guattari (1987, 9) stress that under such a crisis "a rhizome may be broken, shattered at a given spot, but it will start up again on one of its old lines, or on new lines." King's Mountain has also been what Deleuze (1986, 122–23) calls a "fold (*pli*)" as a zone of "subjectivation" or the "center of cyclone," a particular site for resistance that is apt to modify or overturn the surrounding power relations. Actually, the King's Mountain hermitage and nunnery have long been such a "fold" and will continue to be so, even though some prominent stems are withdrawing from the front line of the immortal rhizome.

Endnotes: An Assemblage of Resistance in Crisis

The fieldwork on which this chapter is based was carried out in Chiang Mai province in Thailand between 2014 and 2020. I am grateful to Kwanchewan Buadaeng and Apinya Feungfusakul for their deliberate and constructive comments in the online seminar "New Aspects of Community Movements in Southeast Asia" held on 10 September 2020. My gratitude also goes to Ryoko Nishii for her helpful comments on the draft at the final stage and to Witoon Buadaeng for his ceaseless and thorough support in my research in King's Mountain and for providing me with his photos taken during the fieldwork.

1. "Subject" here denotes what Foucault writes as follows: "There are two meanings of the word *subject*: subject to someone else by control and dependence, and tied to his own identity by a conscience or self-knowledge. Both meanings suggest a form of power which subjugates and makes subject to" (Foucault 1982, 212).

2. In order to grasp the configuration of an assemblage, it would be useful to compare the development of people's imagination emerged in movements against the globalizing power in recent years. We should then pay attention to imagination boiled up among the newly emerging assemblages or communities, which is plausibly called "constituent imagination" by Shukaitis and Graeber (2007, 11). The power that emerges is not one which is rooted in the institutionalized order, but arises in the process which people are about to recreate by mobilizing their imagination. It is, however, never a power directed toward institutionalization, but a "destituent power" to the contrary (Graeber 2009, 60–1).

3. In addition to *A Thousand Plateaus,* Deleuze's concept of assemblage is concisely elaborated in his dialogues with Claire Parnet. He develops a variety of aspects of assemblage, ranging from "assemblage of man-animal-manufactured object," "regimes of utterances," "territory" to "deterritorialization" (Deleuze and Parnet 1987, 69–76).

4. His experiences of flashes leading to *nimit* of constructing a monastery at an ancient site of the monastery later called Wat Doi Saphanyu are described in Tanabe (2004, 102–4). Concerning the concept of *nimit* (Pali: *nimitta*), see Crosby (2013, 15).

5. Concerning yogi or *mae chi* in Northern Thailand, see Muecke (2004).

6. Deleuze and Guattarri's concept of "flight (*la fuite*)" signifies a process of "becoming" or transforming oneself into something else. In referring to the arahant ideal among forest monks in Northeast Thailand, James Taylor (2008, 161) aptly points out that the process "implies a reconfiguration of the mind-body complex to a new subject-placement."

7. The process of embodying the full constituents of Buddhahood, or a Buddha within, is described in detail in Buddhaghosa's *Vissuddhimagga*. See Crosby (2013, 15–6).

8. For the processes of actualization of potentials among "deterritorialized" people such as HIV/AIDS self-help groups in Northern Thailand, see Tanabe (2008, 161–88).

9. It was not yet registered as a monastery within the state *sangha*. Later, it was registered and Pan donated it to Wat Phra That Doi Suthep to the west of Chiang Mai city, one of the monasteries Khruba Sri Wichai had restored in the 1930s.

10. Concerning the processes of spirit-medium's "becoming" in Northern Thailand, see Tanabe (2002, 43–67; 2013a,176–92).

11. The construction of Chedi Chet Thawip (or Chedi Wirasattri) was planned to propitiate Hindu derived goddesses, including Mae Thorani (Goddess of the Earth), Mae Pho Sop (Rice Goddess), Mae Khongkha (Goddess of the Ganges) and the more recently introduced Bodhisattwa Mae Kwan-im (観世音菩薩), and so forth. The planned construction site is at the northern end of the compound where Ho Thao Thammikarat was initially constructed for Pan's residence in the late 1990s, but he later moved to the southern part of the compound.

12. Chedi Sri Lanna was originally planned to propitiate the four Hindu Gods (Phra In as the head, Phra Siwa, Phra Narai, and Phra Phrom) and the historical and mythical figures including Lua King Wilanka, Chao Kho Mue Lek, Phaya Mangrai (Chiang Rai), Chao Thip Chang (Lampang), and, according to Pan, even Chao Mae Chamthewi, the Mon queen of Haripunchai kingdom (Lamphun) in the 12th century.

13. According to Hermit Hot, the name of Chedi Sri Lanna was changed to Chedi Maha Chakraphat at the suggestion of Luang Ta Ma in 2015 (interviewed at his residence in San Pa Tong district on 20 November 2019).

14. Phra Chao Khun Rithirong at Wat Pa Dara Phirom in Mae Rim district, Chiang Mai is a more senior figure of Thammayut sect in Northern Thailand (Cohen 2019, 173). For the advancement of the Thammayut sect in Northern Thailand since the latter half of 19th century, see Ferguson and Shalardchai Ramitanondh (1976) and Taylor (1993, 82–8).

15. Concerning writing *yan* scripts by Pan and other hermits in King's Mountain, see Tanabe (2017, 5–9).

16. The ritual of extending life (*suep chata khon*) was held at the Chedi Sri Lanna (later changed to Chedi Phra Chakraphat) for a weakened Pan in October 2015 (Cohen 2019, 171).

17. For the practitioner's experiences of a dream and its interpretation in the cases of spirit-possession, see Tanabe (2013b, 166–74).

18. This kind of Buddhist movement or revolt, in a variety of scales in Thailand and Burma, has been called an "active utopianism" (Sakisyanz 1965; Cohen 2001, 234).

19. For a detailed and useful review on the recent anthropological works on resistance, see Fiona Wright in the entry "resistance," *The Cambridge Encyclopaedia of Anthropology* (2016, 1–13).

20. Concerning a "destituent power," see Note 2. Patrice Ladwig (2014, 325–26) detects what he calls "millennialism with revolutionary potentialities" among the cases of peasant revolts associated with pre-modern Lao and Thai Buddhism. It is also possible to identify revolutionary potentialities founded on the "destituent power" in the form of Buddhist "active utopianism," having arisen among the hermits and yogis in King's Mountain. Tanabe (1984, 90–102) also analyzes the revolutionary potentialities based on "ideological practices," including supernaturalism, military lore and the sacred-water bathing during Phya Phap rebellion in late 19th century Chiang Mai.

References

Cohen, Paul. 2001. "Buddhism Unshackled: The Yuan 'Holy Man' Tradition and the Nation-State in the Tai World." *Journal of Southeast Asian Studies* 32(2): 227–47.

———. 2019. "The Death of a Thai Hermit: A Case Study of Religious Transition and Schism in a Buddhist Community." *Journal of Southeast Asian Studies* 50(2): 154–78.

Crosby, Kate. 2000. "Tantric Theravāda: A Bibliographic Essay on the Writings of François Bizot and Others on the *Yogāvacara* Tradition." *Contemporary Buddhism: An Interdisciplinary Journal* 1(2): 141–98.

———. 2013. *Traditional Theravāda Meditation and Its Modern-Era Suppression.* Hong Kong: Buddha Dharma Centre of Hong Kong.

DeLanda, Manuel. 2006. *A New Philosophy of Society: Assemblage Theory and Social Complexity.* London: Continuum.

Deleuze, Gilles. 1986. *Foucault.* Translated by Seán Hand. Minneapolis: University of Minnesota Press.

———. 1988. *Bergsonism.* Translated by Hugh Tomlinson and Barbara Habberjam. New York: Zone Books.

———. 1995. "Control and Becoming." In Gilles Deleuze, *Negotiations 1972–1990.* Translated by Martin Joughin. New York: Columbia University Press.

Deleuze, Gilles and Félix Guattari. (1980) 1987. *A Thousand Plateaus: Capitalism and Schizophrenia.* Translated by Brian Massumi. London: Athlone Press.

Deleuze, Gilles, and Claire Parnet. (1977) 1987. *Dialogues.* Translated by Hugh Tomlinson and Barbara Habberjam. London: Athlone Press.

Escobar, Arturo and Michal Osterweil. 2010. "Social Movements and the Politics of the Virtual: Deleuzian Strategies." In *Deleuzian Intersections: Science, Technology, Anthropology,* edited by Casper Bruun Jensen and Kjetil Rodje. New York: Berghahm Books.

Ferguson, John P. and Shalardchai Ramitanondh. 1976. "Monks and Hierarchy in Northern Thailand." *Journal of the Siam Society* 64(1): 104–50.

Foucault, Michel. 1982. "The Subject and Power." In *Michel Foucault: Beyond Structuralism and Hermeneutics,* edited by Hubert L. Dreyfus and Paul Rabinow. Brighton, Sussex: Harvester Press.

———. (1972) 1984. "Preface." In *Anti-Oedipus: Capitalism and Schizophrenia,* edited by Gilles Deleuze and Félix Guattari, London: Athlone Press.

———. (1967) 1986. "Of Other Spaces." *Diacritics* 16(1): 22–7.

Graeber, David. 2001. *Toward an Anthropological Theory of Value: The False Coin of Our Own Dreams.* New York: Palgrave.

———. 2009. *Shihonshugi-go no sekai no tameni: atarashii anarchism no shiza* (For the world of post-capitalism: A new anarchist perspective). Translated by Kohso Iwasaburo. Tokyo: Ibunsha. (in Japanese).

Ladwig, Patrice. 2014. "Millennialism, Charisma and Utopia: Revolutionary Potentialities in Pre-Modern Lao and Thai Theravāda Buddhism." *Politics, Religion and Ideology* 13(2): 308–29.

Muecke, Marjorie. 2004. "Female Sexuality in Thai Discourses about *Maechii* ('Lay Nuns')." *Culture, Health and Sexuality* 6(3): 221–38.

Ortner, Sherry. 1995. "Resistance and the Problem of Ethnographic Refusal." *Comparative Studies in Society and History* 37(1): 173–93.

———. 2016. "Dark Anthropology and its Others: Theory Since the Eighties." *HAU: Journal of Ethnographic Theory* 6(1): 47–73.

Patton, Paul. 2000. *Deleuze and the Political*. London: Routledge.

Sakisyanz, Emanuel. 1965. *Buddhist Background of the Burmese Revolution*. The Hague: Martinus Nijhoff.

Sato, Yoshiyuki. 2008. *Kenryoku to teikou: Foucault, Deleuze, Derrida, Althusser* (Power and resistance: Foucault, Deleuze, Derrida, and Althusser). Kyoto: Jinbun Shoin. (in Japanese).

Schober, Juliane. 2014. "The Longevity of *Weikza*." In *Champions of Buddhism, Weikza Cults in Contemporary Burma*, edited by Bénédicte Brac de la Perriere, Guillaume Rozenberg, and Alicia Turner. Singapore: National University of Singapore Press.

Scott, James. 1985. *Weapons of the Weak: Everyday Forms of Peasant Resistance*. New York: Yale University Press.

———. 1990. *Domination and the Arts of Resistance: Hidden Transcripts*. New Heaven: Yale University Press.

Shukaitis, Stephen and David Graeber. 2007. "Introduction." In *Constituent Imagination: Militant Investigations, Collective Theorization*, edited by Stephen Shukaitis and David Graeber. Oakland (Cal.): AK Press.

Tanabe, Shigeharu. 1984. "Ideological Practice in Peasant Rebellions: Siam at the Turn of the Twentieth Century." In *History and Peasant Consciousness in South East Asia*, Senri Ethnological Studies, No.13, edited by Andrew Turton and Shigeharu Tanabe. Osaka: National Museum of Ethnology.

———. 2002. "The Person in Transformation: Body, Mind and Cultural Appropriation." In *Cultural Crisis and Social Memory: Modernity and Identity in Thailand and Laos*, edited by Shigeharu Tanabe and Charles F. Keyes. London: RoutledgeCurzon.

———. (1986) 2004. *Nung lueang nung dam: Tamnan khong phu nam chao na heang Lannathai* (Wearing yellow robes, wearing black garb: The story of a peasant leader in Northern Thailand). Bangkok: Chulalongkorn University Press.

———. 2008. "Suffering, Community, and Self-Government: HIV/AIDS Self-Help Groups in Northern Thailand." In *Imagining Communities in Thailand: Ethnographic Approaches*, edited by Shigeharu Tanabe. Chiang Mai: Mekong Press.

Tanabe, Shigeharu. 2013a. "Spirit Mediumship and Affective Contact in Northern Thailand." In *Duai Rak: Essays on Thailand's Economy and Society for Professor Chatthip Nartsupha at 72*, edited by Pasuk Phongpaichit and Chris Baker. Bangkok: Sangsan.

————. 2013b. "Reibai no yume to hyoui (Dream and spirit-possession by spirit-mediums)." In *Seirei no jinruigaku kita tai ni okeru kyodousei no politikusu* (Anthropology of spirits: Politics of communality in Northern Thailand). Tokyo: Iwanami Shoten. (In Japanese).

————. 2016a. "Introduction." In *Communities of Potential: Social Assemblages in Thailand and Beyond*, edited by Shigeharu Tanabe. Chiang Mai: Silkworm Books.

————. 2016b. "Hermits of King's Mountain: A Buddhist Utopian Movement in Northern Thailand." In *Communities of Potential: Social Assemblages in Thailand and Beyond*, edited by Shigeharu Tanabe. Chiang Mai: Silkworm Books.

————. 2016c. "Resistance through Meditation: Hermits of the King's Mountain in Northern Thailand." In *Scholarship and Engagement in Mainland Southeast Asia: A Festschrift in Honor of Achan Chayan Vaddhanaphuti*, edited by Oscar Salemink. Chiang Mai: Silkworm Books.

————. 2016d. "The Advent of Phra Sri Ariya: Hermits of King's Mountain in Northern Thailand." Paper presented at the seminar "Past and Present of the Future: Ancient and Contemporary Predictions about Thai Buddhism," organized by École Française d'Extrême-Orient (EFEO), Bangkok on 28–29 January 2016 (unpublished).

————. 2017. "A Network of Magical Objects (*yan*) among the Hermits of King's Mountain in Northern Thailand." Paper presented at the 13th International Conference on Thai Studies, Chiang Mai, 16 July 2017 (unpublished).

————. 2021. "*Phra Sri Ariya long ma prot sat korani yipun kap lanna* (Phra Sri Ariya descends to save all living things: Cases from Japan and Northern Thailand)." Paper presented in the online seminar on "Phra Sri Ariya Descends to Save All Living Things: Cases from Japan and Northern Thailand," at the Japanese Studies Center, Faculty of Humanities, Chiang Mai University, Chiang Mai on 14 January 2021 (unpublished).

Taussig, Michael. 1993. *Mimesis and Alterity: A Particular History of the Senses*. New York: Routledge.

Taylor, James. 1993. *Forest Monks and the Nation-State: An Anthropological and Historical Study in North-Eastern Thailand*. Singapore: Institute of Southeast Asian Studies.

————. 2008. *Buddhism and Postmodern Imaginings in Thailand: The Religiosity of Urban Space*. Farnham (Surrey): Ashgate Publishing.

Turner, Terence. 1979. "Anthropology and the Politics of Indigenous Peoples' Struggles." In *Cambridge Anthropology* 5: 1–43.

Wright, Fiona. 2016. "Resistance." Entry in *The Cambridge Encyclopaedia of Anthropology*, edited by F. Stein, S. Lazar, M. Candea, H. Diemberger, J. Robbins, A. Sanchez and R. Stasch, 13pp. http://doi.org/10.29164/16resistance.

Chapter 2

REASSEMBLING THE COMMUNITY OF VOICE
Community Radio in Northern Thailand

RYO TAKAGI

Introduction

Thailand has been in turmoil ever since Prime Minister Thaksin
Shinawatra was forcibly removed in a military coup in 2006. The
nation remains divided, with seesawing fortunes in conflicts focused
on Thaksin.[1] This fragmentation and confusion has led to massive
anti-government protests against the regimes in power, with many
casualties.[2] After the 2014 coup, a military-led government took
control of the political process and imposed extensive free-speech
restrictions. It remained in power after the death of King Bhumibol
Adulyadej in 2016 and the 2019 general elections. Student protests
continued throughout 2020, aggravating division and confusion in
Thailand and further complicating control of the nation.

This chapter focuses on the community of local political radio
stations and their survival in the face of significant fluctuations in
contemporary Thailand's power structure and how the community
continues to transform by reorganizing its assemblage. The study
addresses the community radio stations in Chiang Mai, Northern
Thailand, initially established to support the pro-Thaksin Red Shirts
and subsequently closed and reopened since the coup in 2014 due to
free-speech controls (Takagi 2018, 139–145).

The theoretical underpinnings of this study include the argument by Tanabe ed. (2016), which explores, from the perspective of movements, the reality of a new type of community emerging in Southeast Asia. It focuses on constructing a new community type in diverse formats incorporating diverse people as parts of a movement, rather than a conventional community based on homogeneous identities (Tanabe 2016, 3–4). The concepts that have attracted attention are assemblage (a combination of multiple diversities) and potentials.[3] The assemblage concept, raised in *A Thousand Plateaus* (Deleuze and Guattari 1987), is a dynamic arrangement composed of combined diversities, such as heterogeneous forces, systems, individuals, objects and natural elements.[4] Its constituent parts have a degree of autonomy. Individuals and parts possess great power, rather than the uniform whole.[5] Assemblage is useful to understand the dynamics of a new community apart from conventional perspectives, focused on a combination of diverse parts and the actualization of their potential (Tanabe 2016, 1–4). Tanabe ed. (2016) explains how the assemblage of a community builds from the relationships among individuals and parts, how the potential of its components are actualized and exerted, and how individual potential, through the experience of negotiating and collaborating with external people and systems, transforms the community itself (Tanabe 2016, 3–6).

This chapter examines how political community radio stations in Chiang Mai, Northern Thailand, were affected amid notable fluctuations in the power structure of contemporary Thailand. It also explores how they have been trying to reassemble the community by actualizing diverse individual parts.[6] In so doing, it considers the following two points.

The first is a departure from the emphasis on interpersonal relationships alone as constituent parts of a community to focus on diverse non-human elements,[7] such as voices or opinions expressed on the radio and social media. These non-human factors can be as potent components or mediators as human factors.[8] The concept of assemblage includes diverse human combinations with a wide variety of non-human elements.[9] This chapter focuses on non-human factors as constituent parts of the aggregate and discusses how they enabled the community to reassemble its assemblage.

The second point is the power of radio as an individual component or a mediator in the community. Here, we explore how casual, personal voices heard once live on the radio, can affect community reassembly.[10]

Three featured community radio stations in Chiang Mai are Radio Station A in the city center, Radio Station B in the suburbs, and Radio Station C in a remote, provincial rural area. Here, we provide an overview of each community radio station and how it has endured the fluctuating power structure in Thailand since 2006. We explain how the radio stations reassembled their communities during this time and the impact of radio voices, social media, and face-to-face meetings as mediating forces.

From political conflict and a divided nation to control in Thailand

First, I would like to present a basic overview of the fluctuations in the power structure that have occurred since 2006, leading Thailand from political conflict to control by a military government, and ultimately to nationwide turmoil.

One of the triggers for conflict, division and turmoil in contemporary Thailand was the removal of then-Prime Minister Thaksin from power by a military coup in September 2006. Thereafter, conflict developed between a pro-Thaksin faction on one side and an anti-Thaksin faction on the other. This event caused a grave rift in the nation. Despite two elections, in 2007 and 2011, such division and turmoil led to large-scale anti-government demonstrations. Many casualties resulted until the 2014 coup, with the two sides repeatedly switching places as offense and defense.

Fundamentally, the conflict focused on two organizations, the Red Shirts of the United Front of Democracy Against Dictatorship (UDD) on the pro-Thaksin side and the Yellow Shirts of the People's Alliance for Democracy (PAD) on the anti-Thaksin side.[11] Recent political conflicts in Thailand divided the nation into different parts, with many pro-Thaksin residents in the north and northeast and anti-Thaksin groups in the capital area around Bangkok and the south.

Thereafter, in May 2014, Army Chief Prayut staged a coup to stop the conflict and turmoil between the pro-Thaksin UDD and the anti-Thaksin People's Democratic Reform Committee (PDRC), which had taken over from the PAD. Proclaiming that the coup intended to control the ongoing political turmoil and restore order in the nation, Prayut founded the National Council for Peace and Order (NCPO). This military coup marked the beginning of extensive control of free speech, even resorting to the crime of lese-majesty.

Control by the military government was primarily targeted at pro-Thaksin forces and employed strict surveillance. In March 2019, elections took place for the House of Representatives.[12] Prayut was re-elected prime minister through a joint vote, along with appointed members of the Senate, and his regime continued. The repression of opposition forces also continued, forcing the dissolution of the breakthrough Future Forward Party, among others. Large-scale student demonstrations opposing the current government continued into 2020. As of today (October 2021), the political stalemate is causing the country to descend further into turmoil.

As the present agitation sends shockwaves throughout the nation, community radio stations in Chiang Mai primarily support the pro-Thaksin faction. Since Thaksin was born in Chiang Mai, the city is a stronghold for his forces, with substantial support in rural areas. After the military coup in 2014, the province came under intense scrutiny and became the principal target of free-speech controls. Community radio stations supporting pro-Thaksin movements were initially highly active, but later suffered heavy control and situational fluctuations (Takagi 2018; 2019).

This chapter clarifies how local community radio stations reassembled their communities and survived destabilization and fluctuations in the power structure.

Community Radio Station A in Central Chiang Mai

Community Radio Station A is a well-known radio station based in the center of Chiang Mai, with a service area reaching many communities in the province.[13] It was the first radio station established during the political confrontation after 2006. Because of its early active stance, it became subject to strict control by the military-led government. The power structure changes affected this radio station the most, resulting in repeated closures and reopenings.

The radio station first broadcast in 2008. Its mission was to serve local content to Northern Thailand residents and to provide an alternative to Bangkok media. It received financing from local politicians and other entities; residents also donated funds and other goods. In 2013, it broadcast for 18 hours from 6 a.m. to midnight, Saturdays, and Sundays, without a break. Content varied during the week, with popular music being played between national news and regional Chiang Mai news. It featured a political talk show called

Sapha Café, with commentary on regional culture by intellectuals, experts on law and the environment, Buddhist lectures by monks.

The daily broadcast continues with alternating DJs in two-hour block sessions.[14] Each DJ routinely holds his/her daily program at a scheduled time and broadcasts his/her thoughts and opinions. A lawyer or intellectual familiar with regional culture may become a DJ, just as area residents or merchandizers may voice their views on daily life and politics. Many listeners look forward to such programs featuring opinionated residents.

Diversity strengthens community

The diversity of people actively involved in the operation of Radio Station A is notable: politicians at the national, provincial, and city level; provincial business managers who provide facilities and funds; corporate workers; lawyers; self-employed doctors; teachers; students; Buddhist monks; shared-ride *Songthaew* taxi drivers; merchants; homemakers; and even city garbage collectors. Diverse people from every level were actively involved in the operation of this radio station. Furthermore, both Buddhists and Christians were involved in station management.

Two local residents were actively involved with station operations. Mr. Alom (pseudonym), the former owner of a trading stall, is currently a DJ at the station. He was born in 1954 of a father from Pakistan and a mother from Chiang Mai. After graduating from elementary school, he started selling small goods around the Chiang Mai city market. He later made a living selling a crêpe pastry called *roti* in a street stall. He came to work for Radio Station A as a result of an illness. According to Mr. Alom, he had not been able to afford the hundreds of thousands of baht for the cost of medical treatment to cure his life-threatening disease, but owing to the 30-Baht Health

Care policy, he could now afford treatment. An acquaintance from Radio Station A gave Mr. Alom information about this policy, which helped him secure treatment and saved his life. Now, Mr. Alom is a DJ at the station, and his story reveals an intriguing coincidence where illness led to work at the radio station.

Due to the unaffordable cost of medical treatment, Mr. Alom was, to some extent, resigned to die. However, the radio program he was listening to while setting up his street stall ended up saving his life. He was listening to political commentary on community radio when he learned about the possibility of using the 30-Baht Health Care Policy, introduced during the Thaksin administration. While listening to the radio commentary, an acquaintance involved in the radio station happened to be a guest listening to the same commentary. Fortunately for Mr. Alom, such a coincidence allowed him to visit the radio station through his acquaintance.[15] Mr. Alom was thus able to familiarize himself with the procedures for subsidizing his medical expenses and began to build a relationship with the radio station.

In those days, Mr. Alom did not have time to read newspapers. His primary source of information was the radio he listened to at work. In a strange twist of fate, Mr. Alom happened to be listening to that evanescent radio program while in the presence of his acquaintance at the radio station, a coincidence that saved his life. Furthermore, this experience allowed him to become involved in the radio station as a DJ, which later helped the radio station gain more community strength.

Mr. Alom is not only a DJ but also receives phone calls and messages from listeners. Occasionally, he speaks to callers on live radio. He says encounters with unknown listeners (strangers) provide a source of encouragement as he battles his illness.

Another person is Mr. Ban (pseudonym), who made his living on a bicycle, collecting garbage and converting it to money. Mr. Ban said he got acquainted with people from the radio station on garbage-collecting trips to the facility. He gradually began cleaning work there and received meals and wages in return. People started to recognize him as a responsible member of the station. Mr. Ban frequented the stations enough so that his familiarity increased to the extent of daily involvement with visiting politicians and lawyers at the station. The transistor radio that previously hung on Mr. Ban's red bicycle for garbage collection plays Radio Station A continually. When he is out on garbage runs, he often initiates conversations with strangers to talk about what he hears on the radio.

In this way, Radio Station A performed an impactful public service by connecting respected politicians, business people, and legal professionals to ordinary residents who initially had no connection to the station. This synergy enhanced the diversity of station operations. It went beyond a one-way exchange from the radio station to listeners through radio broadcasts to enable a reciprocal dynamic from station audiences. Furthermore, through daily face-to-face contact surrounding the radio station, fellow strangers who typically had little contact met and cooperated.

Control of free speech and the use of religious rituals

However, this situation has been greatly affected by socio-political turmoil since 2014. Following an approximately one-year long broadcast suspension period, the station was operational once again on the condition that nothing political would be aired. The new content primarily comprised songs and local commercial advertisements, with news broadcasts from central Bangkok. According to one of the DJs, it was critical to continue broadcasting to deliver the voice of radio to residents and not disrupt the connection to loyal listeners.

Nonetheless, Radio Station A was in a difficult situation. Broadcasting and related activities were severely limited. Meanwhile, countermeasures were taken in an aggressive attempt to suppress the relationships of people formerly involved in radio broadcasting. In these circumstances, gatherings were restricted, so people formerly involved in radio sought connection in religious rituals. Specifically, on 10 July 2014, to celebrate the Buddhist ritual, *Wan Khao Phansa*,[16] about 60 members of former radio stations crowded into pickup trucks to visit the nine city temples and donated to the monks at each temple. Because the primary purpose of *Wan Khao Phansa* donations was religious, the gathering was not restricted. According to a former radio station adviser who participated, the religious ritual was an opportunity to keep members connected. In this way, radio community members maintained their connection while avoiding strict government control.

These actions represent a reassembly of station activities, previously dominated by broadcasting and politics, amid the shifts in the power structure resulting in free-speech control. In other words, in addition to voices, face-to-face gatherings, such as religious rituals, which previously were less important, became emphasized as an essential component of the community and a mediator for reassembling and reconnecting the community itself.

Community Radio Station B in Suburban Chiang Mai

Real audience voices

Community Radio Station B broadcasts from the suburbs of Chiang Mai city.[17] Ms. Charm (pseudonym), born in 1962, is at the center of Radio Station B. She was born and raised locally and worked in a tourist souvenir shop in the city. In 2008, when Radio Station A was established, she decided to participate as a DJ.

In 2012, she left Radio Station A and opened Radio Station B in a city suburb with financial assistance from local politicians and others. Ms. Charm, a distant relative of former Prime Minister Thaksin, said her original purpose was to support the pro-Thaksin movement.

Ms. Charm took to the airwaves as a central DJ, and as of March 2014, six DJs were broadcasting about 14 hours a day. Central to Radio Station B were people with diverse backgrounds. These included local village assembly members, teachers, people involved in the city tourism industry, and farmers. At that time, the broadcast content was almost the same as Radio Station A. During Ms. Charm's DJ block, there were listener calls and messages, and listeners' voices aired over the radio via phone. In this regard, Ms. Charm explained, it was important to "deliver and spread the public's voice rather than unilaterally deliver news and information from Bangkok to listeners." Moreover, the conversations between the listener and DJ were sometimes in the language of Northern Thailand, and from the listener's side, a voice in one's own language was appealing.

The unique factor about Radio Station B was that it broadcast real listener voices in their own dialects in public spaces via the radio. Many of the audience's comments included their opinions on politics, but also included discussions about their circumstances. For example, a listener told Ms. Charm that her son had passed his university entrance exam, and the DJ congratulated her on the radio. The congratulatory laughter of Ms. Charm was shared, not only with the listener but also with the entire audience, as a real voice in public space via the radio, encouraging them to celebrate together. A real voice resonates directly as physical sound and creates emotions on the spot.[18] The evanescence of the voices on the radio produced real and uplifting sensations within the listening community, ultimately reinforcing it.

Use of social media and commerce in community expansion

Spoken words at Radio Station B were relayed on net radio via the Internet. Because it was Internet radio, audiences throughout Thailand and around the world could listen without geographical limits. Collaboration between these contemporary media and radio is also seen in the use of social media.[19] Radio content and conversations with listeners are repurposed online and on Facebook, becoming ever more popular as a source of news, entertainment and business.

DJ's words on the radio are heard only once by the audience. Conversely, words exchanged on social media remain on record in the form of texts, photos and videos. Radio Station B posts some parts of its program content on social media. Facebook, in particular, is used as a platform to share public content through texts and pictures. In the case of LINE, although communication was more private and limited to selected groups, there were times when radio content went viral. Content sent by listeners via LINE or Facebook was discussed by the radio DJ. In other words, social media, in addition to the DJ's voice, is positioned as an important component to stimulate the audience community.

Another characteristic feature of Radio Station B is that it tried to create a daily connection with residents and the community. Ms. Charm installed a small workshop at home to produce folk craft merchandise for tourists. There, she gathered local young people who didn't have permanent jobs and gave them work using folk crafts. At the time, more than 10 young people were based at the workshop. By selling folk crafts produce at souvenir shops in the city, the young people could earn some money. Ms. Charm explained that one purpose was "to help local villagers." In a similar vein, Ms. Charm's Radio Station B provided local poor children with donations for learning support and distributed blankets for the elderly in the winter.

In this way, Radio Station B was a forum for residents to exchange opinions and interact. In other words, besides radio broadcasting, such activities as handicrafts provided opportunities for face-to-face connection between the people involved in radio stations and local residents. Various people gathered at the station, including DJs, station workers, local politicians and campaigners, neighboring residents, souvenir producers, and merchants dropping in to sell souvenirs at city stores.

With radio at its core, diverse components of the assemblage, such as live interactions with listeners on social media and face-to-face gatherings organized through folk crafts, exerted their power or potential to reassemble and restructure the community of Radio Station B.

Unfortunately, Radio Station B's activities became subject to major constraints in the political turmoil after 2014. About a year later, the radio station was permitted to reopen on the condition that it would not broadcast any political material. Again, the content was limited to popular songs and advertisements. Eventually, Ms. Charm stepped down from her post as an operator and DJ of the radio station.

Radio Station B is an example of a community entity that retained a wide variety of people and internal components, while unable to rearrange or reassemble them to respond adequately to the coup and the subsequent shifts in the power structure and the constraints on free speech. Regretfully, the radio station could not make use of its components, which led to its debilitation.

Community Radio Station C in Rural Chiang Mai

Community Radio Station C serves a remote rural area of Chiang Mai province.[20] It was established as a community radio station in 2009 and was initially based in district a neighboring its current location. In 2010, the radio station expanded and transferred to its current location.

In April 2009 and again from March to May 2010, pro-Thaksin forces staged massive anti-government demonstrations in Bangkok against the anti-Thaksin forces in power at the time. As a result, the anti-Thaksin regime ordered the military to use force to unilaterally suppress the demonstrations, resulting in a large number of casualties. In response to the armed suppression of the pro-Thaksin demonstrations in Bangkok, the pro-Thaksin forces tried to regroup with bases in the rural areas in the north and northeast. Radio station C was established at this time and expanded its activities. It was precisely the political support for the pro-Thaksin forces that prompted the founding of Radio Station C.

Like Radio Stations A and B, the primary activity of Radio Station C was to broadcast voices. Its DJs were actively in favor of political support for the pro-Thaksin forces. This chapter focuses on the weekday programs that were broadcast in 2013 for 17 hours from 5 a.m. to 10 p.m. From the early morning, DJs specializing in different fields, such as forestry conservation, news from central Bangkok, health-related topics (including medicinal plants), welfare and education policies, local news and traditional literature of Chiang Mai, local history and agriculture, and popular music, ran their programs in two-hour blocks. Different programs aired on weekends, and local monks often gave long lectures on Buddhism. Popular songs and traditional local music were played between these programs, and as with Radio Stations A and B, the DJs interacted with the audience by transmitting live calls.

Two people: Transforming lives through radio

This section focuses on the diversity of DJs involved in Radio Station C and other people who supported the radio station, including two of its principal members.

Born in 1948 in Lamphun, a province neighboring Chiang Mai, to a farming family, Mr. Daeng (pseudonym) became a tenant farmer after completing four years of compulsory elementary education. He married at 21 and experienced major political change in 1973 (at 25) when the military government at the time was overthrown by student movements. Later, as urban students moved into the rural areas to live with farmers, Mr. Daeng became involved in the burgeoning farmers' movement, eventually serving as a district vice-chairman for the Farmers' Federation of Thailand.[21] The district chairman, five years older than Mr. Daeng, was a well-known farmers' movement leader, and they became deeply engaged in the movement for farmers' rights.

Gradually, right-wing forces in Thailand recovered their lost ground and resorted to assassinating leaders of the students' and farmers' movements (Haberkorn 2011; Surichai 1983). One night, Mr. Daeng was assaulted by a group of strangers. The scar of the assault remains on his right cheek. Shortly after the military and the right-wing coup that toppled the civilian government and imposed martial law in 1976, Mr. Daeng, fearing for his safety, decided to take his wife and children with friends to hide in the jungle near the provincial border. At that time, many students' and farmers' movement leaders convened in the jungle to live and continue their activities, sharing communist ideologies.[22] After two years of jungle life, Mr. Daeng and started a new life in a completely new region in 1978.

He still lives in a rural district of Chiang Mai. He dedicated himself to selling pork at the market, bought his land and house, and opened a local restaurant. For three decades, he was not actively involved in politics until the military coup ousted Thaksin from power in 2006. When Thaksin became prime minister, Mr. Daeng was exposed to policies catering to rural areas and the poor. He was emotionally supportive of such policies from the beginning, although it was not until 2006 that he actively engaged with the pro-Thaksin movement. According to Mr. Daeng, the overthrow of the Thaksin regime, which had been generous to rural areas, in a military coup resonated with the hardships he had experienced in the 1970s, enticing him back to the movement. This was how Mr. Daeng, who had been involved in the farmers' movement in the 1970s and had lived in the jungle, became a force within the modern pro-Thaksin movement as well as a key player in the pro-Thaksin community radio station established in 2008.

Mr. Daeng is a radio DJ who broadcasts every weekday afternoon for two hours. According to Mr. Daeng, he never expected to become a DJ, but in retrospect, radio was one of the few media he was familiar with as a child and one he listened to daily during his life in the jungle. His jungle radio played a shortwave broadcast of the Communist Party of Thailand from Chinese territory. The radio, with its characteristic "communist style," was a source of entertainment during his life in the jungle. The importance of radio broadcasting and the characteristic DJ style that he learned at that time would prove useful in his later experience as a DJ.

Mr. Eak (pseudonym), a man from a neighboring district, was born in 1961 into a garlic farming family, but in his 30s, after marriage, he spent several years as a migrant worker at a factory in Singapore. Later, he returned to his hometown and started a business manufacturing and selling ant poison, his profession ever since. He learned how to make ant poison from a Chinese man he met in Singapore. According to Mr. Eak, while in Singapore, he became aware of the economic disparity within Thailand and the class divide between individuals, which made him realize the importance of having money and the need to develop poverty-stricken rural areas of Thailand. He says that his involvement with Radio Station C was shaped by his experience as a migrant in Singapore and meeting Mr. Daeng and others involved with the radio station.

Mr. Eak also described his participation in a 2010 demonstration in Bangkok as the catalyst for his devotion to his role at the radio station. He recounted his experience of sleeping and eating on the streets of Bangkok for two weeks with pro-Thaksin supporters from other provinces, and the exhilaration of standing on a huge stage in downtown Bangkok to express his opinions. He still remembers the three-minute speech he gave on stage.

The rhetoric of some of the metaphors used in that speech was elaborate. For example, he argued that society is like a stupa (*chedi*). In other words, the higher you go, the fewer people you see, and only a few can secure a place at the top, but neither a *chedi* nor society can stand without its foundation at the bottom. He made this metaphor his own after hearing it in various speeches during his involvement with social movements. He often brings it up in conversation.

Mr. Eak's participation in the Bangkok demonstrations is critically important from another perspective, one of suppression by the government's military in May 2010. He says he will never forget how he and his colleagues from the radio station and others ran from the soldiers armed with teargas and guns. Some people from the same radio station who participated in the demonstration were wounded and had to be taken to the hospital; he described in detail the chaotic situation at the time. Immediately after telling the story, there was a moment of silence as he reminisced about those days and choked up.

According to Mr. Eak, after returning to Chiang Mai he shared this experience on the radio as a DJ. He recalls that he was sometimes at a loss for words during live broadcasts and fell silent. However, he often received words of encouragement from the audience for those moments of silence. Once, when he was forced to switch to music after a prolonged pause, he received a large number of encouraging messages on LINE immediately afterward. He stopped the music and began to receive calls from listeners who were also in tears. Although he was the voice of a live broadcast, it seems to have been a moment when the audience shared his sorrow.

Mr. Eak also recounted that his experience in Bangkok had given him a new sensibility after returning to his hometown. His ordeal of heading to the Bangkok demonstration with some of his colleagues at the radio station and being subjected to governmental armed suppression inspired him to share the decisive moment of fleeing from the forces. He believes this shared experience of the fear of oppression laid the foundation for the shared radio station activities in which they continue to engage to this day. The sharing of a decisive experience among people from diverse backgrounds is integral to sustaining the bonds of the radio station community (assemblage).

These individuals are just two of the many diverse people involved with Radio Station C. Before the coup, seven main DJs worked at the radio station. Besides the two described above, a variety of people gathered at this community radio station to engage in its activities. Among them were teachers from local primary schools, part-time university lecturers, local government officials, owners of small restaurants and grocery stores, farmers, homemakers and monks. Sometimes a Buddhist monk would lecture on the radio, and at other times a Christian DJ would talk about the Bible. Although the audience was mainly Thai Yuan people, it also included ethnic minorities living in the mountains and emigres from China who had escaped the hardships of the post-World War II era. Listeners sometimes called in during broadcasts via mobile phones. The members of Radio Station C were diverse, and its listeners were not only diverse but also strangers to each other. Through interaction with the DJs on the radio and social media, each formed part of the assemblage.

While people from diverse backgrounds were involved in the activities of Radio Station C, there was a distinctive lineage of connections in this station related to Mr. Daeng's background. It was a network of people who had been engaged in political movements in the 1970s and had hidden together in the jungle.[23] A few of them lived in Radio Station C's local district, but others lived in the neighboring province and came to visit from far away to serve as substitute DJs on holidays. They had not necessarily been actively engaged in politics since the 1970s, but many of them supported Radio Station C's activities after Mr. Daeng became involved.

The background to these circumstances is also related to the nationwide pro-Thaksin trend. Specifically, the UDD, a national pro-Thaksin organization called the Red Shirts, became active around 2008. Some of its members were leading figures of the movement in the 1970s, who had continued their activities in the jungle and later became leaders of the UDD (Kanokrat 2016, 250–262). Their ideology was reflected in contemporary policy proposals to support rural areas and the poor. UDD schools were promoted in rural areas, wherein central UDD leaders spoke directly to the residents to gain leverage for pro-Thaksin groups. Under these circumstances, the network of people involved in the movement in the 1970s mediated and contributed to the formation of new activities at Radio Station C. In other words, this is an example of the reassembly or the reaggregation of onetime bonds after more than three decades.

Characteristics of radio broadcasting and vocal techniques

This section discusses the characteristics of radio broadcasting at Radio Station C, especially Mr. Daeng's voice. As noted, Mr. Daeng is not a trained DJ or announcer. He is an amateur DJ who never thought he would become one until he turned 60. On air, Mr. Daeng has a unique broadcasting style.

First, he divides the two-hour program slot into several parts. He starts with an introduction, followed by news stories gleaned from the Internet and social media, newspapers, and television and a discussion of events related to the radio station, personal events, or experiences, insterpersed by music. Paid advertisements promoting local shops and products play out between each segment. News stories, in particular, are updated daily. He purchases three daily newspapers and clips articles for his broadcasts. Despite dividing the program into parts, the demands of a constant flow of orally communicated information, two hours a day, every day, requires a good deal of preparation.

Another of his tweaks is the rhythm and inflection of his voice. He interjects formulaic words with characteristic intonation and rhythm, especially in the introduction and at the end of his slot. The basic wording is borrowed from traditional poetry. These verses, read on air with a musical intonation—some fast, others slow—provide variation. Although the literary expressions in verse are difficult to understand in parts, the unique rhythmic intonation of his voice sounds pleasant to the ear. Mr. Daeng's live voice is evanescent and resonates with listeners. Sometimes he interrupts these phrases to improvise and introduces the day's events with the same musical intonation used to read the verses. According to Mr. Daeng, this inflection and rhythmic ingenuity were inspired by the unique speaking style of the Thai

Communist Party, which he heard in the jungle in the 1970s. He explained that it focuses audience attention on the content, enabling listeners to figure out immediately which DJ was speaking.

Another characteristic of Mr. Daeng's voice is that unlike the announcers and presenters we encounter daily in mass media, his speech is not always fluent. During his interjections after reading a news story based on a newspaper, he occasionally stammers, stutters, misspeaks and pauses. This non-fluent speech represents the natural speaking style of a real person.[24] Further, listeners say they often pay more attention to stories punctuated with stammering, corrections and silence. The comments and opinions of the DJ expressed with these stutters and pauses attract the audience's attention and allow them to connect emotionally with the story.

The last feature of DJ Daeng's radio broadcasts is the use of social media. In addition to newspapers and the Internet, previously mentioned as sources of information for his programs, an important source of information is social media, including Facebook, LINE, Twitter, and YouTube. With social media, the content remains on record through texts, photographs and videos, spread through personal accounts and other means, allowing repeated viewing at any time. In this sense, social media content contrasts to the single experience of his voice on the radio. Of course, the possibility of "fake news" exists, but there is also a great deal of valuable information not covered by mass media. Furthermore, while community-based information used to be passed on only by word of mouth, today social media plays an important part in this process.

For example, Mr. Daeng once used information received from neighbors on LINE to inform the public of a regular market held at a temple in the area. On another occasion, he used information received via LINE from residents of a remote mountain area to report on road conditions during the rains. Furthermore, when political demonstrations took place in Bangkok and Chiang Mai, he presented up-to-the-minute information sent by acquaintances via social media on the radio. On these occasions, he often described the photos and videos taken at the scene and sent via social media. Sometimes, immediately after featuring the information sent via LINE on the radio, he broadcast phone calls directly from the sender on air to open a public discussion in greater depth. The presentation of information sent via social media on the radio increased the number of people contributing in this way.

Social media has become an indispensable component for both DJ Daeng and the radio station's information network. The radio voices and social media have become essential parts of the radio station's community (assemblage), creating synergy between the two.

Response to control, religious rituals and health product sales

Radio Station C, which expanded its broadcasting activities to support pro-Thaksin forces, was, like other radio stations, heavily affected by the coup in 2014 and subsequent control of free speech. On the night of the coup, armed troops sent from Chiang Mai stormed Mr. Daeng's home to take him into custody. Mr. Daeng was not present at the time, but his eldest son was taken into custody instead. Later, Mr. Daeng returned home and took his son's place and was held for a week at a military facility in another district. His mobile phone was taken away, and all the information recorded on it was copied and stored by the military. Radio Station C shut down and remained closed for over a year. When Mr. Daeng was released from custody, he was forced to sign a Memorandum of Understanding (MOU) stating that he would not engage in political activities. About a year later, as the military-led regime continued, a new permit was issued to reopen the radio station, but it was banned from broadcasting any political content. For about five years from the coup until just before the new general election in 2019, military officials continued to monitor the whereabouts of Mr. Daeng and the content of his weekly radio programs.

Under these circumstances, Radio Station C was forced to engage in different activities, taking some of the same measures as Radio Stations A and B under the same circumstance. Since the station was allowed to resume broadcasting only as long as political content was avoided, the content was limited to popular songs, local traditional music, daily community events and advertising for pesticides, fertilizers, farm machinery, local shops and restaurants. All current news was censored in advance in Bangkok and Chiang Mai.

Radio Station C's response to the absolute control of free speech was to have its core members actively participate in religious rituals in the same way as Radio Station A and sometimes to host religious events. One of the core members attended community rituals for new monks, weddings and funerals whenever it was possible to represent the radio station, which also organized seasonal religious rituals celebrated with community members. As governmental control reduced the opportunity to create ties through radio broadcasting, these religious events directly addressed the radio community's ties with participants through face-to-face gatherings. These measures reassembled the community and ensured its survival.

In addition to the use of religious rituals, Radio Station C made a new and unique attempts to reassemble and maintain community ties. It began to advertise health products, such as revitalizers and herbal supplements, taking orders over the phone and via social media. Station staff delivered the products. Although Mr. Daeng did not like this approach, he believed it was the only way the radio station could survive the constraints specified in the MOU, which severely restricted the content of radio programs by eliminating political material. This new approach was a mixed bag; it had both negative and positive aspects. It prevented long-standing ties with listeners from being disrupted. In particular, it ensured the continuation of an interactive system that allowed listeners to get in touch with the radio station in one way or another, rather than simply listening to the programs. Previously, people used to voice their opinions about political news on radio broadcasts over the phone or on social media, but this was impossible under the restrictions on free speech. To compensate, health-related products in which the audience was interested were advertised and sold on the radio.

The health products sold included liquid revitalizers and herbal supplement pills, which were generally expensive, ranging from 500 to 1,000 baht per box. When the benefits of these products were advertised on the radio, the radio station received orders by phone or via LINE, and the staff personally delivered the products to customers by car. While health products may seem irrelevant to the radio station activities, the interactive nature of commerce played an important role in the community. In many cases, customers who placed orders were new listeners, people that Mr. Daeng had not previously met. Some lived in the mountains, over 30 minutes away by car. Visiting the homes of listeners he had never met, even in small numbers, provided him with an opportunity to talk and build relationships. In a way, the health products were an excuse to visit people's homes. Furthermore, he called the listeners who had purchased products during his program to share their opinions and review products on air. This further advertised the products and sustained the connection between audience and radio station, even under speech restrictions.

Without the sales of health products, there would have been no means of connecting the anonymous audience to Mr. Daeng. The products, as objects, were important components of the assemblage in the sense that they actualized the buried connection between them.

Conclusion

This chapter has examined how community radio stations in Chiang Mai adapted to governmental restrictions on freedom of speech amid power structure changes in contemporary Thailand. Communities were reassembled while actualizing the potential of diverse individuals, components and mediators. The final section summarizes the salient points of three cases in three radio communities discussed in this chapter.

The first point is the diversity of the people involved in all three radio stations. Tanabe ed. (2016) indicates that the current reality of a community as a movement cannot be grasped by focusing only on the uniform and general aspects of a community based on conventional homogeneous identities. On the contrary, focusing on how new communities are created with an assortment of individuals and parts in diverse forms sheds light on novel aspects. The three cases discussed in this chapter precisely fit the characteristics of assemblage, defined as the consolidation of diverse elements.

People from all walks of life were involved in radio station activities. At Radio Station A, Mr. Alom sold *roti* at a street stall, and Mr. Ban made his living collecting garbage; at Radio Station B, young people gathered to produce folk crafts items. Radio Station C featured Mr. Daeng, who had previous involvement in the 1970s political movements and had lived in the jungle. Thrown into the turmoil caused by the shifts in the power structure of Thailand as a whole and the surrounding environment, people from diverse backgrounds who never would have met under ordinary circumstances were brought together through the voices on the radio. New relationships and communities were built and reassembled through mediators, such as radio station activities and movements.

The second point is to understand the radio community in the three radio stations as an assemblage, a dynamic arrangement of diverse elements combining heterogeneous forces, systems, individuals, objects and natural factors, both human and non-human, such as the voices on the radio and social media, as relevant to the assemblage as humans. Without the radio voices or social media, it would have been impossible for these radio stations to form the assemblages discussed in this chapter.

Mr. Alom of Radio Station A was able to receive treatment for his illness because he happened to be listening to a radio program. By becoming involved in the radio station as a DJ, he gained a large audience, and the radio station gained additional community power. When Ms. Charm of Radio Station B broadcast her audience's live voices in dialect, she provided a meaningful community service. When she reacted with joy to her caller's celebration of his son's admission to a university, she connected with her listeners on an emotional level.

In addition to the live voices, such social media as LINE were critical components in activating the community involved in the radio station activities and their listeners. For Mr. Daeng of Radio Station C, in particular, the number of listeners sending information increased by transmitting social media news on the radio. In this case, the non-human elements of the voices of the radio and social media became indispensable components of the radio station's assemblage.

The third point concerns the physical properties of voice as a significant component of the assemblage. The live voice on the radio is a single, evanescent experience that permeates and resonates with the listener and is another component in the construction of the assemblage. The uplifting live voice of Ms. Charm expressing her congratulations at Radio Station B is one example. Another example is Mr. Eak's unintentional tearful silence at Radio Station C, which captivated the attention of his diverse and unspecified audience, prompting them to send many empathetic messages of encouragement via LINE. Yet another example is the rhythm and inflection of the uniquely expressed voice of Mr. Daeng at Radio Station C. The percussive characteristics of his speech, embellished with stammering, stuttering and mistakes, represent the very characteristics of a live, natural voice. These characteristics of live radio attracted listeners and provided an opportunity for them to become emotionally involved with and sympathetic toward the speakers.

The fourth point concerns the role of face-to-face communication, in addition to non-human elements, such as voices and social media, in the formation of an assemblage. In each of the three radio stations described, with the potency of radio at its core, various face-to-face communications contributed to the assemblage. For example, Mr. Ban, who earned his living collecting garbage, routinely frequented and interacted with people at Radio Station A. Radio Station B provided an opportunity for local youth and souvenir vendors to interact through folk crafts. Another example is the strategic use of face-to-face religious rituals organized at Radio Stations A and C to maintain community ties, regardless of restrictive free-speech controls. In addition to people, their voices, and social media, face-to-face communication was an essential component of the assemblage. The mutual activation and manifestation of each component's potential continuously created and reassembled radio communities.

The fifth and final point is how the shift in the power structure, particularly since the imposed free-speech controls in 2014, affected the community of voice created by the radio stations and how these communities adapted and sustained themselves by reassembling their assemblages. Radio Stations A and C tried to reassemble by bringing face-to-face religious rituals to the fore. Radio Station B excluded politics from its programming content, failing to make sufficient changes in the reassembly of its components, resulting in a loss of vitality for the radio community. Radio Station C developed a unique approach, advertising and selling health products to reassemble the community using the power of each component, including radio, social media, and face-to-face communication.

In short, as radio communities suffered from power structure fluctuations in contemporary Thailand, but responded resourcefully. They reassembled and modified their activities to the extent allowed under the circumstances, manifesting the potential of various individuals and constituent parts. In the process, diverse individuals, as components of the community, maximized and actualized their own potential. For example, Mr. Alom of Radio Station A survived a life-threatening illness and gained a large audience as a DJ. Mr. Ban transformed from being garbage collector to a supporter of the pro-Thaksin movement. Local young people gathered at Radio Station B to engage in folk crafts, fulfilling their potential through their involvement in radio station activities while earning cash income with support from Ms. Charm. Mr. Eak of Radio Station C went from being involved in local business to being the voice of protesters in Bangkok. Mr. Daeng became a DJ and re-engaged in contemporary politics based on his long-dormant experiences during the 1970s.

Finally, not only human beings, but also radio voices, social media, and face-to-face communication exerted power as important parts of the assemblage. They made the most of their respective characteristics, becoming mediators through which the assemblage recalibrated in response to the power structure changes. It will be interesting to see how important these attempts at self-transformation will become when free-speech control is finally lifted.

Endnotes: Reassembling the Community of Voice

1. After the 2006 military coup, conflict mainly developed between a pro-Thaksin faction on one side and an anti-Thaksin faction on the other.

2. See Hewison (2012); Nelson (2010); Nostitz (2014); Pavin ed. (2014).

3. See Tanabe (2016, 3–6). "these individuals and constituent parts, instead of being a unified totality, contain the "virtual" (*le virtuel*) potential or capacity therein" (Tanabe 2016, 3).

4. See Tanabe (2016, 3–4); Deleuze and Guattari (1987, 71; 88–91; 323–337; 503–505). See also Deleuze and Parnet (2012). "The assemblage is co-functioning, it is 'sympathy, symbiosis'" (Deleuze and Parnet 2012, 39); "It (an assemblage) is a multiplicity that is made up of many heterogeneous terms and that establishes liaisons, relations between them, across ages, sexes and reigns—different natures. Thus, the assemblage's only unity is that of co-functioning: it is a symbiosis, a 'sympathy'" (Deleuze and Parnet 2012, 39). Bruno Latour also focused on the assemblage. "After having done extensive work on the 'assemblages' of nature, I believe it's necessary to scrutinize more thoroughly the exact contact of what is 'assembled' under the umbrella of a society" (Latour 2005, 1). And Latour also focused on heterogeneous elements of "social." "Even though most social scientists would prefer to call "social" a homogeneous thing, it's perfectly acceptable to designate by the same word a trail of associations between heterogeneous elements"(Latour 2005, 4).

5. See Tanabe (2016, 5); DeLanda (2006). "In fact, the reason why the properties of a whole cannot be reduced to those of its parts is that they are the result not of an aggregation of components' own properties but of the actual exercise of their capacities" (DeLanda 2006, 11).

6. The concept of "reassemble" is related *Reassembling the Social: An Introduction to Actor-Network-Theory* (ANT) by Bruno Latour (Latour 2005). "This book on how to use ANT for reassembling social connections is organized," "through which procedures is it possible to reassembling the social not in a society but in a collective?"(Latour 2005, 16). "If the social is a trace, then it can be retraced; if it's an assembly then it can be reassembled" (Latour 2005, 127). See also "we always have to start again, start again from the middle, to give the elements new relations of speed and slowness which make them change assemble, jump from one assemble to another" (Deleuze and Parnet 2012, 69–70).

7. Deleuze and Parnet took an example of an assemblage of the type man-animal-manufactured object: Man-Horse-Stirrup. "The stirrup replaced the energy of man by power of the animal. This is a new man-animal symbiosis, a new assemblage of war" (Deleuze and Parnet 2012, 52). "Social aggregates might not be made of human ties" (Latour 2005, 41), "no science of the social can even begin if the question of who and what participates in the action is not

first of all thoroughly explored, even though it might mean letting elements in which, for lack of a better term, we would call non-humans" (Latour 2005, 72).

8. Focusing on "mediator," Latour maintains that while in most modern theories of action the relations between the cause and the effect are fixed, his ANT "pictures of *concatenations of mediators* where each point can be said to fully act" (Latour 2005, 58–59). Such mediators "transform, translate, distort, and modify the meaning or the elements they are supposed to carry" (Latour 2005, 39). As Michel Callon's study (1986) of the scallop-fishermen of St Brieuc Bay shows, "fishermen, oceanographers, satellites, and scallops might have some relations with one another, relations of such a sort that they make others do unexpected things—this is the definition of a mediator" (Latour 2005, 106). Such oppositional concepts between the modern theories of action and Latour's ANT could correspond to that shown in Deleuze's parlance, "the first has 'realized potentials', the second 'actualized virtualities'" (Latour 2005, 59fn.64).

9. See Tanabe (2016, 3–4). And "There is indeed a historical question of the assemblage: particular heterogeneous elements caught in the function, the circumstances in which they are caught up, the set of relationships which at a particular moment unites man, animal, tools and environment" (Deleuze and Parnet 2012, 54).

10. For the characteristic of the voice, see Yamada (2017).

11. See Hewison (2012); Nostitz (2014); Pattana (2011); Pinkaeo (2013); Takagi (2015; 2018; 2019).

12. See also Takagi (2020).

13. See Aranya (2013, 200–203); Takagi (2018, 139–143). For community radio stations in Thailand, see Boonlert (2011).

14. People who talk on the radio are ideally called RJ (radio jockey). But in the case of community radio in Thailand they were usually called DJ (disk jockey).

15. For "coincidence," see DeLanda (2006). "in an assemblage these relations may be only *contingently obligatory*" DeLanda (2006, 11).

16. *Wan Khao Phansa* marks the beginning of the annual, three-month rains retreat for Buddhist monastics, beginning the day after the full moon of the eighth lunar month.

17. See also Takagi (2018, 143–145).

18. See Yamada (2001; 2017). Yamada focused on "acoustic body," resonance or penetration of voice (sound) to body and "symbiotic tuning" (Yamada 2017, 246–250).

19. For social media in Thailand see *Krasuang Diciton Phu'a Sethakit lae Sangkhom* (2019).

20. See also Pinkaeo ed. (2013, 129–163).

21. See also Kanoksak (1985).

22. See also Nishii's Chapter 3 in this volume.

23. See also Kanokrat (2016).

24. Yamada (2017, 93–106) focused on "participatory discrepancies" in live music performance. And Deleuze and Parnet (2012) pointed out the importance of "stutter." "The point is that . . . one can stutter in one's own language, be a foreigner in one's own language, that is push ever further the points of deterritorialization of assemblages" (Deleuze and Parnet 2012, 86).

References

Aranya Siriphon. 2013. "Witthayu Chumchon kap Kankhayaitua khong Khabuankan Prachachon Su'a Daeng (Community Radio and Expansion of Red Shirts Movement)." In *Becoming Red: Kamnut lae Phatthnakan Su'a Daeng Chiang Mai* (Becoming Red: Birth and Development of Red Shirts Movement in Chiang Mai), edited by Pinkaeo Luangramsi, 191–226. Chiang Mai: Chiang Mai University (in Thai).

Boonlert Supadhiloke. 2011. "Creating Citizenship Through Community Radio in Rural Thailand." *Journal of US-China Public Administration* 8(3): 288-297.

Callon, Michel. 1986. "Some Elements of a Sociology of Translation: Domestication of the Scallops and the Fishermen of St Brieuc Bay." In *Power, Action and Belief: A New Sociology of Knowledge?*, edited by John Law, 196–229. London: Routledge.

DeLanda, Mannuel. 2006. *A New Philosophy of Society: Assemblage Theory and Social Complexity*. London: Continuum.

Deleuze, Gills and Félix Guattari. 1987. *A Thousand Plateaus: Capitalism and Schizophrenia*. Translated by Brian Massumi. Minneapolis: University of Minnesota Press.

Deleuze, Gills and Claire Parnet. 2012. *Dialogues II*. Translated by Hugh Tomkinson and Barbara Habberjam. London: Continuum.

Haberkorn, Tyrell. 2011. *Revolution Interrupted: Farmers, Students, Law and Violence in Northern Thailand*. Wisconsin: University of Wisconsin Press.

Hewison, Kevin. 2012. "Class, Inequarity, and Politics." In *Bangkok May 2010: Perspectives on a Divided Thailand*, edited by Michael J. Montesano, Pavin Chachavalpongpun and Aekapol Chongvilavan, 143–160. Singapore: ISEAS Publishing.

Kanokrat Lertchoosakul. 2016. *The Rise of the Octoberists in Contemporary Thailand: Power and Conflict among Former Left-Wing Student Activists in Thai Politics*. Chiang Mai: Silkworm Books.

Kanoksak Kaewthep. 1985. *The Political Economy of Modern Thai Peasant Movement: A Case of the Farmers Federation of Thailand (FFT), 1973–76*. Bangkok: Faculty of Economics, Chulalongkorn University.

Krasuang Diciton Phu'a Sethakit lae Sangkhom (Ministry of Digital Economy and Society), ed. 2019. *Raingan Phonkan Samruat Phlutikam Phu Chai Intoenet nai Prathet Thai Pi 2561* (Thailand Internet User Profile 2018). Bangkok: Krasuang Diciton Phu'a Sethakit lae Sangkhom (Ministry of Digital Economy and Society) (in Thai).

Latour, Bruno. 2005. *Reassembling the Social: An Introduction to Actor-Network-Theory*, New York: Oxford University Press.

Nelson, Michael H. 2010. "Thailand's People's Alliance for Democracy: From 'New Politics' to 'Real' Political Party?" In *Legitimacy Crisis in Thailand*, edited by Marc Askew, 119–159. Chiang Mai: Silkworm Books.

Nostitz, Nick. 2014. "The Red Shirts from Anti-Coup Protesters to Social Mass Movement." In *"Good Coup" gone Bad: Thailand's Political Development since Thaksin's Downfall*, edited by Pavin Chachavalpongpun, 170–198. Singapore: ISEAS Publishing.

Pattana Kitiarsa. 2011. "From Red to Red: An Auto-ethnography of Economic and Political Transitions in a Northeast Village." In *Bangkok May 2010: Perspectives on a Divided Thailand*, edited by Michael J. Montesano, Pavin Chachavalpongpun and Aekapol Chongvilavan, 230–247. Singapore: ISEAS Publishing.

Pavin Chachavalpongpun, ed. 2014. *"Good Coup" gone Bad: Thailand's Political Development since Thaksin's Downfall*. Singapore: ISEAS Publishing.

Pinkaeo Luangramsi. 2013. "Su'a Daeng kap Khabuankan Sang Prachathipathai khong Chonnabot (Red Shirts and Democratizing Movement in Rural Area)." In *Becoming Red: Kamnut lae Phatthnakan Su'a Daeng Chiang Mai* (Becoming Red: Birth and Development of Red Shirts Movement in Chiang Mai), edited by Pinkaeo Luangramsi, 7–31. Chiang Mai: Chiang Mai University (in Thai).

Surichai Wankaew. 1983. "Phanha Sitthi Manutsayachon khong Kasetakon nai Saphawa kan Phatthana Patcuban (Problem of Farmers Human Rights Under the Situation of Develpoment)." *Warasan Thamasat* 12(7): 40–58 (in Thai).

Takagi, Ryo. 2015. "Tai no Seiji-shyakai Undou to Chihou Nousonbu: 1970nendai kara 2014nen madeno Gaikan (Political and Social Movement and Rural Area in Thailand: From 1970s to 2014)." *Kanagawa University Asia Review*, Vol.2: 4–39 (in Japanese).

———. 2018. "Bundan sareru Kokka to Koe de Tsunagaru Komyunithi: Tai niokeru Seijiteki Tairitsu to Chihou Komyunithi Rajiokyoku (Divided Nation and Constructing Community through Voice: Political Conflict and Rural Community Radio Station in Thailand)." In *Teikoku to Nasyonarizumu no Gensetsukukan* (Discursive Space of Empire and Nationalism), edited by Yoshiko Nagano, 125–152. Tokyo: Ochanomizu-shobo (in Japanese).

———. 2019. "Gendai Tai niokeru Seijiteki Tairitsu no Rekishiteki Haikei: 2014nen no Kudeta ni itarumade (Historical Background of Political Conflict in Modern Thailand: Until 2014 coup)." In *Ajia ni okeru Minshushugi to Keizaihatten* (Democratization and Economic Development in Asia), edited by Hiroshi Yamamoto, 159–189. Tokyo: Bunshin-do (in Japanese).

———. 2020. "Tai ni okeru Seijiteki Tsunagari no Kairo: 2019nen Sousenkyo zengo no Hensen to Tai Kouken tou no Seijiteki Atsumari wo Chyusin ni (Politically connected Circuit in Thailand: Some Changes around General Election 2019 and Political Gathering of Phu'a Thai Party)." *Kanagawa University Asia Review*, Vol.7: 12–31 (in Japanese).

Tanabe, Shigeharu, ed. 2016. *Communities of Potential: Social Assemblages in Thailand and Beyond*. Chiang Mai: Silkworm Books.

Tanabe, Shigeharu. 2016. "Introduction: Communities of Potential." In *Communities of Potential: Social Assemblages in Thailand and Beyond*, edited by Shigeharu Tanabe, 1–18. Chiang Mai: Silkworm Books.

Yamada, Yoichi. 2001. "Acoustic Body: Voice Resounding through the Waxei People, Papua New Guinea." In *Traditionalism and Modernity in the Music and Dance of Oceania*, edited by Helen R. Lawrence and Don Niles, 103–112. Sydney: University of Sydney.

———. 2017. *Hibikiau Sintai: Ongaku, Groove, Hyoui* (Sympathetic Resonance Body: Music, Groove, Possession). Tokyo: Syunjyu-sya (in Japanese).

Chapter 3

FOREST MEMORY AND COMMUNITY MOVEMENTS
Hmong Communities in Thailand

RYOKO NISHII

Introduction

After the massacre at Thammasat University on 6 October 1976, many students fled the government crackdown into the forest (*khao pa*) to join the Communist Party. The forest strongholds had already received peasants and ethnic minorities before the students arrived. A large number of Hmong people associated themselves with the Communist movement in Thailand in 1960s.

This paper looks at three Hmong communities to see how their respective memories relate to current movements and circumstances. It may be said that memories drive people to be continuously activated in the present. Conversely, it may be said that memories are not fixed in the past, but are constantly being generated in the present.

The three communities are in different situations. The order 66/23 issued in 1980 to encourage militants to surrender provided 15 *rai* of land and two cows. Implementation of the ordinance was shelved for 30 years, but in 2010, before the government attacked the Red Shirts, the policy was suddenly put into practice,[1] with the government suddenly choosing to give 225,000 *baht* to each household of former Communist Party members instead of land, due to high land prices. This was ironically titled a reward for "those who helped develop the

Thai nation" (*phu ruam phatthana chat thai*). Two communities, Pha Chi and Phu Chi Fa, accepted the payouts. The Hmong of Khao Kho, on the other hand, rejected the money and demanded the return of land.

The relationship between politics and memory has been much debated since Maurice Halbwachs' theory of collective memory. Rather than contrasting individual and collective memory, it is based on the idea that individual memory is also collective and social, that is, that memory is also constituted by the interests and ideas shared by the group. Rejecting the dichotomy between history and subjective memory, which implies rational and scientific knowledge, Lisa Yoneyama argues that the production of knowledge about the past is always caught in the web of the exercise of power and involves elements of repression (Yoneyama 2005: 37). Yoneyama says that the premise of the Hiroshima survivor's testimonial description, "I will not repeat it," gives us a sharp sense of irreversibility, as well as the possibility of an alternative course of history, through the rigorous recounting of what happened there and what can no longer be undone. In other words, from Walter Benjamin's dialectic of memory, she sees the present as a "moment of transformative possibility" that serves as a signpost for collecting and assembling fragments of the past (ibid., 40–42).

When we look at social movements from this perspective, we can see a parallel with the arguments of Melucci, one of the leading exponents of the "new social movements." According to Melucci, a social movement is not the behavior of a subject on the stage of history whose existence and purpose in life are predetermined, nor is it something that is played out in a scenario with a predetermined ending. Such a misunderstanding can be corrected only by rejecting the assumption that collective action is a consistent reality. Only by this rejection can we discover the plurality of perspectives and relations of meaning crystallized in any collective action (Melucci

1997: 15). How can we discover the plurality of perspectives and relations of meaning? A hint of this can be found in Hannah Arendt's method of inquiring into the origins of the present.

Bennett, a political philosopher, notes that Arendt makes the point by distinguishing between "cause" and "origin" in her discussion of totalitarianism. A cause is a singular, stable and masterful initiator of effects, while an origin is a complex, mobile and heteronomous enjoiner of forces. Elements by themselves probably never cause anything. They become origins of events if and when they crystallize into fixed and definite forms. Then, and only then, can we trace their history retrospectively. The event illuminates its own past, but it can never be deduced from it (ibid., 33–34). In fact, what makes the event happen is precisely the contingent coming together of a set of elements. Memory may be said to be the very process of continuing to discover this origin in the present.

Bennett is inspired by Deleuze's assemblage to think about political philosophy, but what is characteristic is that she incorporates not only human but also non-human elements in this assemblage. In her book, *Vibrant Matter: A Political Ecology of Things,* Bennett describes the assemblage as "ad hoc grouping of diverse elements, of vibrant materials" (Bennett 2010: 23). This is different from the way causality is narrated.

This chapter describes how community movements are driven and how they are formed through narratives of the experience of entering the forest. The purpose of this project is to find the process of creative "crystallization" of a community movement that resists and tries to alter the status quo in order to make its own life possible. It is not a social movement based on political culture or class homogeneity, but an ad hoc assemblage formed by chance, characterized by diversity and heterogeneity. This allows us to see the present, as Yoneyama calls it, as a "moment of transformative possibility," and to relativize the existence of the state, rather than seeing it as an absolute, to understand that the state and various institutional structures are also changing while constituting the assemblage. It is the perspective that makes us imagine that there could be another world.

Overview of the Forest Democracy Movement in Thailand: The Communist Party of Thailand and the October 6th Incident

In 1923 the Communist movement in Thailand was started by Thai people of Chinese descent, leading to the formation of the Communist Party of Siam in 1930. It was renamed the Communist Party of Thailand (CPT) in 1942, following the renaming of Siam to Thailand in 1939. With the cooperation of China and the Soviet Union, the First Marxist-Leninist Institute for the Study of Party Members in Asia was established in Beijing, to which Thai Communists were sent. As the CPT recognized the importance of farmers to the revolution, they prioritized local rural operations. In rural areas, Party members were encouraged to marry local women to avoid suspicion. Once infiltrated, the CPT members took up farming: they rented land, grew vegetables and raised livestock. They also distributed medicines to fellow villagers and in doing so gained their respect. Additionally, they trained selected villagers to become future leaders (Takahashi 2014: 304). Study sessions were held in groups of three to five, several times a month, from 7:00 p.m. to 9:00 p.m.. Participants discussed politics, dictatorship, liberties, equality, exploitation, poverty, oppression, and anti-war ideas (ibid., 311).

After the October 6th incident in 1976, the CPT, which had established bases in the provinces, received students fleeing into the forest from repression. In the year and a half after 14 October 1973, until the Kukrit cabinet, formed in March 1975, began a full-scale crackdown, student, worker, and peasant movements were on the rise with freedom of political activity. The purpose of the urban activities of the CPT was to expand its link with the workers and peasants through students and to incorporate the student and intellectual organizations that had been established independently of the CPT. As a result, Sekisan, who was very influential among socialist-oriented student activists, joined the CPT, which chose the path of armed struggle after the crackdown, and went underground (ibid., 32, 35–36). Three alliances of workers and peasants were targeted through the medium of students.

On 19 September 1976, a rally against Field Marshal Thanom, who had returned to Thailand in monk's robes, gained momentum after the assassination by hanging of an employee of the Electric Power Corporation who was holding a poster opposing Thanom's return. Taking advantage of the fact that a satirical play about the assassination was performed at an opposition rally at Thammasat University, a mug shot of the student playing the role of the assassinated official was falsely altered to resemble that of the Crown Prince. This was used as a pretext for the suppression of the students and published in newspapers. On 6 October 1976, a large number of mobilized people surrounded the protesting students and the police and border security police suppressed the protest, resulting in an estimated 530 deaths and 3,084 arrests (Murashima 1982: 39–40), or 3,059 arrested (Kanokrat 2016: 57). (Estimates are from student groups. The government reported 46 deaths.)

In the aftermath, many students fled to the CPT's base in the forest. This incident allowed the CPT to gain over 3,000 new intellectual members and to adopt the stance of defending Thai democracy and culture against imperialism (Marks 1994: 159). In 1979, the Vietnamese invasion of Kampuchea and the Chinese invasion of Vietnam in retaliation worsened the relationship between Vietnam and China and caused a split within the CPT. In 1980, when Prem Tinsulanonda became prime minister, he issued Amnesty Ordinance 66/23 to encourage anti-government fighters in the forest to surrender. Mass surrender and defections from the CPT resulted, and in 1987, the last armed unit surrendered to the government (Murashima 44, Tapp: 76).

Minorities in the forest: Hmong and the CPT

Why were the Hmong people deeply involved with the Communist movement and what was life like in the forest?

In Thailand, the Hmong have borne the brunt of the Thai government's anti-opium campaign. The Hmong in Thailand began contact with the Pathet Lao in Laos in the early 1960s following disputes with local police regarding poppy cultivation. Nicholas Tapp wrote in 1989 that a number of Hmong, alienated by bureaucratic policies targeting them, joined forces with the CPT, and the popular image of them today in Thailand remains one of opium-producing "komunit" (Tapp 1989: 19).

One reason for frequent Hmong border crossings were rumors of the birth of a Hmong "king." These rumors attracted entire Hmong villages to move to guerrilla areas in North Chiang Rai province (ibid., 76). Tapp assumed that Hmong movements on the rumor of a sovereign were motivated by a desire for sovereignty. Otherwise, he wrote: "in order to explicate their own ethnic difference from the members of other majority and more dominant cultures, Hmong have been forced more and more to define their own ethnicity in terms of what it is not, hence, absence of writing, absence of territory, absence of kings and emperors" (ibid., 176).

Prior to the 1960s, the Hmong people had little contact with non-Hmong in the lowlands, living a life of burning fields, growing mustard, and hunting and gathering in the mountains. However, their lives changed dramatically when they became associated with the CPT in the 1960s and 1970s. Many Hmong said that they joined the Party because of economic ruin and problems with the Thai government (ibid., 77).

By joining the CPT, the Hmong community had access to a variety of people with whom they had had no previous relationship, including Chinese Thais in Bangkok, people from southern and northeastern Thailand, and people from other countries, such as Laos, Vietnam and China. Entering the deep forest to join the Communist Party, as opposed to deepening their isolation, brought about cultural, social and political expansion, and trans-national and trans-cultural experience (Baird 2020: 1–2).

Among ethnic minorities in Thailand, the Lafu oppose the CPT, in contrast to the Hmong. Inhabitants of the Lafu village where Kataoka did fieldwork had traversed the Burma-Thai border together with the Kuomintang as they fought Communists. In Thailand, Lafu activities were expected to provide a bulwark against CPT forces and so were largely undisturbed until the CPT collapsed in the early 1980s. Kataoka interpreted the Lafu naming a weed "communist weed (*konchanmu*)," reflecting their harsh experiences with migration. The weed had appeared in the 1950s and rapidly displaced other crops, which paralleled their characterization of Communists as rapidly proliferating alien invaders (Kataoka 2007: 90–91).

In this paper, I would like to shed some light on the Hmong experience of movement through interviews with Hmong people in the location of three former CPT strongholds: Pha Ci (Khet 7),[2] Phu Chi Fa (Khet 8), and Khao Kho.[3]

I visited the Hmong communities of Pha Ci in August 2011 and Phu Chi Fa and Khao Kho in March 2013 with my research assistant, Yai. Yai is a former student who survived being shot in the abdomen at Thammasat University during the October 6th incident in 1976 by entering the forest. His extensive forest network made possible interviews on sensitive issues with Hmong in these three communities. First, I look at how the Hmong people entered the forest and what their experiences were, based on interviews with Pha Ci and Phu Chi Fa. Next, I examine how memory is driving the current community movement in the case of Khao Kho.

Memories in the present: Pha Ci and Phu Chi Fa

Pha Ci (Phayao Province): Cham (56 years old)[4]

Pha Chi was a CPT mountain stronghold. The steep mountain path leading to it was unpaved as of 2011 when I visited. The journey was more difficult in the rainy season as the road became terribly muddy. The name of the village had been changed from Pha Ci to Santisuk (peace) by the Thai government. It was customary after conquering CPT-controlled areas to incorporate words like "peace," "patriotism," "love of country," and so on, into place names. Santisuk consisted of around 200 households. They had been set up to depend on hydroelectric power, but it had not worked for over a month, and while some households had independent generators, most had no TVs or other electric appliances. I interviewed Cham, who was 56 years old in 2011. He was the sixth among eight brothers and sisters.

Cham imagined that his ancestors may have been Mongols or some other peoples from colder lands because funerary rites included the words, "the sky is dark and the ground is cold".[5] From their ancestral lands, many villages had moved to Laos following oracle predictions of where a divine birth may take place. This original myth shared by Hmong villages parallels Tapp's description of modern Hmong migration following rumors of the birth of a Hmong "king."

Figure 1. Cham and his wife left the CPT in 1982.

Cham and his family moved to Laos in 1957 from Doi Yao in Chiang Rai because he was told that the gods would appear there, and many villages had also moved to the village in Laos at the same time. However, life was so difficult that many of them returned to Chiang Mai. Only a few families remained, including his father's. His father built a house and settled there. In 1963, one year after their lives had settled down, Lao anti-Communists attacked them and burned everything. The young Cham and his family escaped into the forest with only the clothes on their backs and found themselves facing starvation.

The whole family joined the CPT. First, his elder sister became a Communist and studied in Vietnam for two years and China for two years. Fascinated by his sister's story of a sea that they had never seen, one elder brother also became a Communist. He also studied in Vietnam and came back to Thailand, but was shot dead with his comrades a year later while scouting Yao village. All family members had become Communists by the time Cham was 13 years old.

Cham was competitive in his studies at the Communist base, as it was his first opportunity at school. In 1972, he was sent to China and fell ill, stranding him there for half a year. His sister was killed by a bomb in the forest when she came back from her second study round in China. Cham was not told immediately, but found out by accident. One day, working as a doctor's assistant, he was asked to exchange guns and saw that his new gun bore scratches from an explosion. He found out later that it was his sister's gun. On realizing that his sister was dead, Cham reported a floating feeling, as if his feet were unable to reach the ground. In 1973, his other sister in Khet 8, Chiang Rai, died in childbirth, which infuriated Cham who believed that the death was preventable. Because the family had already lost three members, in 1978 Cham was assigned a safer post as wireless officer.

In 1979, he married a Hmong woman working as a nurse in the forest. Cham said he chose her because she was good, hoping their life would be better. When I interviewed him, he said in front of his wife that he had made the right choice. Cham's wife said, "I treated you with medical herbs when you were ill. If it wasn't for me you would always be ill. Even now, I massage him before going to bed so that he has a good sleep." His wife gave me some herbs for diarrhea. I recognized the herbs as ones I used to take for diarrhea during fieldwork in Thailand and can confirm they are very effective.

Phu Chi Fa (Chiang Rai Province): Sombun/Saga and Lai

Phu Chi Fa is a tourist spot on the Thai-Laos border known for views of rocks and peaks jutting from thick forest through the clouds. After the rumored suicide of a couple, the Thai government destroyed one rock formation as a preventative measure, to the sorrow of local Hmong who lamented the loss of the prominent landmark (figure 2).

Figure 2. Phu Chi Fa, the tip of the rock has been destroyed

The village was renamed "Rak Phendin (love for country)" after the Thai government drove out the CPT from the area in 1981. By the time I did my fieldwork in 2013, all Thai households had moved away leaving 120 Hmong households with seven different lineages.

Sombun (61 years old)

In 1967, the Hmong villagers grew rice illicitly, having no certificate of residence that would allow them to farm legally. The Thai army burned the village, prompting the Hmong to flee into the forest. Sombun became a CPT soldier at the age of 15 and was sent to Laos for one year to undertake military training and study the politics of communism. His path among Hmong was not rare. His teacher, who had studied in Vietnam and Laos, spoke Hmong to accommodate students like Sombun. In 1975, Sombun studied military affairs in Vietnam for 2 years. After he returned to Thailand in 1977, he married in April, and on 6 June lost his right leg from a bombing. He was sent to China for treatment and returned to Thailand one and a half years later. No longer fit for battle, Sombun engaged in other duties. His artificial leg wore out, so a few years ago he funded a new one with savings and a small subsidy. He put socks and sports shoes on his artificial leg, and on his natural leg he wore thong sandals with the trouser leg rolled up to the knee. I recall his natural leg being quite muscular.

Saga, Sombun's wife (58 years old)

Saga recounted her life as follows. She lost her parents at the age of 13. They had fallen ill, perhaps with malaria, working in the forest in Chiang Rai. She is the eldest among six siblings. One of her younger sisters died at the age of four. She grew up with an uncle who had 12 children. She entered the forest alone and joined the CPT at the age of 15 in 1968. She was sent to Laos for two years to study politics and military affairs. She recalls a Hmong translator assisting students. After coming back to Thailand, she engaged in propaganda work. Two younger brothers joined her in the forest 4 and 10 years later.

She married Sombun in the forest in 1977. Just a few months after their marriage her husband lost his leg. She said mischievously that a normal woman would not keep such a husband. They had two children in the forest.

In December 1981, the family surrendered to the government under the amnesty and left the forest. They subsequently had an additional two children and adopted three children from Sombun's late elder brother.

Lai (55 years old)

Lai's father died while he was still young. In 1967, when Lai was nine, his village of around 20 households was burned by the Thai army, prompting his mother to enter the forest with five of her children and to cross the border to Laos. Two of Lai's sisters had married by this time and did not follow them. In 1970, Lai became a soldier and was sent to China. He came back to Thailand in 1973 and engaged in moving people between Laos and Thailand. In 1974, his mother was crushed to death by a falling tree. In 1976, students fled into the forest and also that year, Lai married and his first son was born. A second son was born in 1979, followed by a daughter in 1980. Lai was caught by the government in 1981 and released after three hours of de-radicalization training. He had four other children after leaving the forest.

Lai regretted sending his first son away to Suratani in Southern Thailand during a crisis in the forest. After 10 years of searching, they found that his son had been raised as the youngest of 6 adopted siblings. His son and adoptive father visited Lai's village in Northern Thailand, but to Lai's dismay, the son preferred to stay with his new family in Southern Thailand.

Lai grieved that in 10 years his son had visited his birth family only with three durians, that he gave no money to his natural siblings, despite having tens of thousands of baht in his wallet, and that he did not give a single cigarette to his birth father. Lai's son's meagre gifts sent the message to his natural siblings that he did not want to be involved with his birth family, and they lost interest in him.

Lai's family tragedy is an example of chaotic forest life separating families. It also exemplifies the formation of networks from north to south via forest zones. However, communication along these networks is slow and mostly on foot.

The importance of *sahai* (comrades) after forest life

Interviews from Pha Ci and Phu Chi Fa shed light on the common importance of *sahai* (comrades).

Hmong villagers assigned land to each household by drawing lots. Cham was lucky in that his allotment was a former paddy field. Some allotments were full of stones or in a river. They had four children: two sons and two daughters. He told me that the youngest Hmong son usually lives with the parents. Cham lived with his second son, whose wife was pregnant with their third child.

Cham said: "If there were no CPT, we would have just been burned, abducted and beaten. To be able to find *sahai* (comrades), to study, that is enough for me." *Sahai* is important for understanding the relationships between those who experienced forest camps. Like "comrade," *sahai* is a title prefixed to an adopted forest name. For example, if a forest camp dweller adopted the name "San," others would call him "*Sahai* San." *Sahai* links and equalizes those who come to live in the forest from disparate backgrounds, be they children of rich bankers and politicians, or unschooled ethnic minorities. Once they enter the forest camp community, they leave behind mainstream societal structures and *sahai* forms their primary relationships. My research assistant who had entered the forest was considered *sahai*, a status we could use to connect to and gain the trust of other *sahai* former forest-dwellers, even if they had not met during their time in the forest. Cham said: "I cannot live without *sahai*. The relationship with *sahai* is much more important than with those of Hmong ethnicity."

Lai told me one precept of Communism: "Face adversity in front, and happiness will follow (*thuk yu na, suk yu lang*)." He said it meant that you should act for others rather than for yourself. My assistant Yai, the student *sahai,* added that there were three qualities required of a revolutionary: courage, virtue and knowledge. However, with only courage, one would be a gangster; with only virtue, one would be a monk; and with only knowledge, one would be a scholar. This balance of requirements made me feel that it was not easy to be a revolutionary.

"*Sahai*" seems to be a magic word connecting people who have entered the forest. It evokes vivid memories of shared struggles, shared ideals and shared status. Lai said to Yai: "Yai's societal status is higher than me because you are Thai. However as you are *sahai*, you are equal to me."

When Lai was asked by a reporter a few years ago why *sahai* were prepared to die together, he replied: "It is because we have an ideal (*udomkan*), we consider ourselves brothers (*phi norng*). When we die, we die together; we suffer together; and if we need anything, we share and eat together." Another Hmong said, "*Sahai* is easy to understand after a short talk." A former student-*sahai* research assistant in attendance said: "It's the same word (*phasa*), the same ideals. People who have gone through the experience of the forest are more likely to understand the experience of living and dying, nature, pain, feuds, life. This is because they have gone through the same thing." The experience of sharing the hardships of forest life has led to a strong sense of camaraderie among *sahai*, allowing it to surpass other statuses like Hmong, student or farmer to this day.

Forest memories and present politics

From the above two communities, we can see that some villagers threatened by the Thai army chose to flee their villages to the Communist stronghold in the forest in order to survive.[6] Many who did so received their first education in the forest. Initially illiterate and understanding only Hmong, they subsequently moved in a network connecting Laos, Vietnam and China, received a basic education, and were trained as soldiers, nurses and correspondents to take on roles in the forest. A radio station set up in Yunnan, China, broadcast in the Hmong language, allowing access to a wide range of information.[7] Although it was limited to what was in line with the Communist Party's policies, it fostered discipline in the forest, ideals of the ideal Communist society, and a sense of camaraderie in pursuing the same ideals.

Sombun settled in Chiang Mai because Saga's relatives lived there. In Chiang Mai, they grew flowers and saved about 150,000 baht with which they built a house in 1997. They then cultivated cabbage, corn and rice in dry fields.

In 2011, the Thai government paid surrendered ex-Communists "Thai national development and compensation money," fulfilling a promise made in 1980 as part of the amnesty deal. Though long-neglected, the promise took on new urgency as Thaksin Shinawatra's "Red Shirt" supporters were growing in power. While in theory every ex-Communist was entitled to a payout, only a subset of CPT members actually received it. Luckily, Sombun received 225,000 baht, although he remarked that the government had promised 15 *rai* (1 *rai* = 1,600 square meters) of land and two cows. The Thai government had allegedly decided that gifting land would be too expensive. Saga did not receive her own payout, ostensibly because she shared a household with Sombun, but Sombun suspected that her entitlement had been pocketed by a corrupt official. With his payout Sombun bought a pick-up truck to carry crops into town. It was immediately useful, and I have met his son returning home with the truck after selling a load of cabbages. However, as I will write later, some ex-Communists — including some Hmong—did not receive compensation and continued their anti-government resistance.

Memory drives the movement—Khao Kho

In Khao Kho, I met with 18 people, including Nom (Phetchabun Province) and Chai (Loei Province).

The Hmong community in Khao Kho is involved in an ongoing land restitution movement. When we arrived at Khao Kho village, we expected to be greeted by the one or two Hmong my assistant had arranged to meet. However, a group of 18 Hmong were waiting to appeal to us to help demand that the Thai government returns their land as promised when they surrendered fighting 30 years ago. Most of them were between 50 and 70 years old, with the youngest aged 49. The site of their original village had been incorporated into a national park. They gave me photocopies of a flier that called on CPT soldiers to surrender, written petitions to various sections of the Thai government, and a 2010 letter acknowledging their petition from the United Nations High Commissioner for Human Rights South-East Asia Regional Office. The Thai government's offer of compensation equivalent to 2 *rai* of land was insufficient to live on, so they had no choice but to continue agitating for the return of their homeland.

What led to them to enter the forest?

They told us how they had entered the forest following government repression, just like the Pha Ci and Phu Chi Fa communities.

A Hmong man told me: "The old government didn't like the Hmong. They despised us and trampled on us. They sent border guards to catch the men and take them to their bases. The soldiers would get out of their cars and walk over, and if they saw a beautiful woman, they would take her as a wife or rape her. We were scared too, and with no other way to escape, we ran into the forest. When the soldiers were gone, we went back and planted fields and raised chickens and pigs. When they came, we ran again. After a few years, we could not come back. The soldiers burned down our house in the 1950s."

Walking through the ruins of the village

Kotaro Takagi's attempt to view human memory not as a process of constructing linguistic representations of past events, but as an act of exploring natural and physical space (the environment), provides a hint as to how the memory of the time when the interviewee entered the forest is connected to the present. I would like to look at this process through the activity of searching for memories while walking with them through the former village of Khao Kho.

Their village is now in a national park. I was told that they would show me its remains, so I met them the next morning and was picked up by a pickup truck full of people in traditional Hmong dress. They were dressed in the same clothes they wore when they were in the forest, which they had worn in the previous year (2012) when they appeared in a movie called "The Heroes of Khao Kho (*wiraburut khao kho*)." In the movie, the hero was with the Thai army and the Hmong were the enemy. A woman who appeared in the movie said it was heartbreaking (*cep cai*) that the Hmong were portrayed as robbers.

To enter the national park, Thai people must pay a 40 baht admission fee. Foreigners pay 200 baht. However, instead of a fee, those of Hmong ethnicity must make a written application, including reasons for entry. The Hmong villagers accompanying us specified on their application that they needed to perform ancestral rituals in the national park. It took five minutes for the attendants at the entrance to check their application. Discriminatory attitudes against Hmong were most visible in the conduct of the gate officers toward our Hmong guides. Gate staff interrogated them in an officious manner, asking: "Where are you going? Are you really worshiping ancestors?" They did not notice me, a foreigner, in the party, and so clearly did not moderate their behavior accordingly. However, we were all allowed to enter at last.

When we entered, we found that the road leading to the former rice paddies that was previously accessible was now closed to us. The Hmong people said it would be better not to get into trouble, even though there was only a small flag marking the road closure, so we took a different road up the barely developed mountain path, from where we could see the rice paddies.

My Hmong companions pointed to land as we passed, making comments like, "whose rice field is that?" and "whose land is that?" Hmong-occupied land had been given to civilians siding with the Thai military on the basis that the land would be ruined in Hmong hands. Much of the land now allegedly belongs to capitalists who had no inclination to maintain the fields. Negotiations for the return of the national park land to the Hmong have so far been unsuccessful. One Hmong said: "This used to be an orchard. It was my grandmother's house. There was a big mango tree. It was destroyed in a fire." The fruit grove that once belonged to the village chief is now the site of a temple.

We got out of the car and walked up a mountain road that eventually led us to an open meadow. Nom, one of our guides, said that American and British helicopters had landed here. He told us: "They came to see Hmong. This was before the revolution. They came to survey the area for development. It was before the Communists, in 1957 or so. There were five or six, and it was also for Christian missionary work."

In 1954, they received a commemorative coin from the royal family that read, "Commemorative Coin for the Mountain People, Phumipon Adunyadet," which they showed us. They also showed us a picture of Hmong representatives gifting a silver collar to the King and a silver hair ornament to the Queen. One Hmong told me that these meant that the Hmong were submitting themselves as servants or slaves (*that*) to the Crown. This was before the Communists came into the country.

We then walked down a few hundred yards from the airfield to the remains of the original village. At the end of the road were the remains of a shattered cauldron with a tree growing through it. Ban Khi Thao (charcoal ash), the name of the village, is said to derive from the whitish soil, which was of good quality and could be used to make white ink. Nom said that the village was burned so many times that it was now exactly what the village was named after. At one point, the village had numbered more than 100 households.

The rice mill's concrete foundations still remains. The village headman, who was a progressive thinker, had bought a rice mill and installed it in his house for use by the villagers. "This is the last evidence that the house belonged to the villagers," said Nom.

An woman aged around 70 who accompanied us was standing quietly. She used to live in this house. "She lost the most," Nom said. As she spoke only Hmong, another Hmong interpreted into Thai for me. The elderly lady was the wife of the village head's second son. In 1968, when the Thai army burned the village, she left behind her possessions—including her house and the mill—and entered the forest with her two children. She stayed in the forest, bearing five more children, until they left in 1982. Her three daughters had since married. She lived with her third and fourth sons, while her two older sons grew vegetables on rented plots in Chiang Mai. Though the Thai government had provided her a small plot of land, it was only enough for her house. Her true hope was to have her own paddy field and vegetable garden so she could be more self-sufficient by raising chickens and pigs and growing rice and herbs, as she used to. She would only have to buy salt and clothes to supplement what she produced (figure 3).

Figure 3. The Hmong woman who lost most, Khao Kho

Ancestral rituals in the national park

A total of 16 people set forth in three vehicles to the field where the ancestral rituals took place. After a while, a car with more than 10 people in camouflage uniforms and guns came up behind the pickup truck. We wondered what was going on, but the Hmong people said the escort was the result of having to notify the authorities in advance. Nom said sarcastically that they would be guarding us. Two more camouflaged vehicles followed, both carrying officials from the forestry department. Chai said that the leader of one escort group had jailed him in 2009. Chai has been arrested three times: in 1989, in 1998 when he took action to return to his original village, and in 2009 on charges relating to an event involving 46 people and the airfield. He was sentenced to six years jail with 20,000 baht bail, but was pardoned with help from the Royal Family (ratchawong).

At the ritual site, our companions lay out the Hmong flag and a curtain listing family names. They placed a plastic rug in front of it, upon which they laid their clothes, as they used when they entered the forest, and related literature. They also spread out old annotated photographs. One Hmong man crouched down to smoke a mortar tube that had been turned into a water pipe. "This is what I do now instead of using narcotics," he said.

Only three Hmong conducted the ancestral rites: a purple-hooded man in his 60s and two assistants in their 40s. In the center of the open field, they made an altar under a tall tree by slashing bamboo with a machete. The man said he chose the tallest tree around, as "this ritual connects heaven, earth and ancestors." They also made bamboo containers to hold offerings of water and rice. The preparations complete, the man started the ritual by praying to the god of the land while burning incense sticks. He then lit incense sticks on the altar, picked up a bell, and bowed his head. He uttered what sounded like "bruuuu," and chanted passages in Hmong. The man then started jumping and ringing the bell. The ritual lasted about five minutes. He was out of breath by the time the ritual finished. Although I couldn't understand the Hmong language, I felt like crying—heartbroken.

The man who presided over the ritual explained to us its dual purpose: to show Hmong customs to me and my assistant Yai, as well as to pray for the land to be returned.

Figure 4. Ancestral ritual, Khao Kho

Conclusion: Memory and posture in the forest— community movements as assemblages

According to Takagi Kotaro, memory is a "special form in which organisms encounter their environment," in which the duality between "past" and "present" differs from ordinary perception. It is in the failure to encounter the environment that memory is born. Takagi analyzes this dynamism in Claude Lanzmann's film "Shoah (1985)," which is composed of interviews with Holocaust survivors. He says that by walking around a site of the past and reuniting with the environment that persists, we recover the same poise that we had when we were in the middle of those past events. The posture of the eyewitnesses that Takagi describes overlaps with the posture of the Hmong people in this chapter as they walked through the ruins of their former village. However, rather than being able to obtain a "direct perception of the event as a fact to be shared," we see an "absent hole" in the environment of a "past event" that is no longer there. This is the discovery of the old event, and at the same time, it is the failure of the endlessly repeated search for absent ones. Accompanying the witness, I "discover the hole of absence through the witness's posture, and look into it with the witness" (Takagi 2006: 55).

The memories of the rice mill, the burned village, the rice fields and orchards, the visits to them, and the repeated ancestral rituals, imprinted on their body have sustained the land restoration movement of the Hmong of Khao Kho for 30 years. The "absent hole" is a failed search in the present environment, but it is not a fixed past event. Rather, it is a constant search that drives the reconstruction of the present movement. The land recovery movement is a continuously generative and changing assemblage on the duality of "past" and "present."

The two terms "double standard (*sorng matrathan*)" and "land for cultivating to eat (*thi thamkin*)" often arose in conversations with the Hmong in Khao Kho. The term "double standard" comes from being treated differently to mainstream Thais. Thai officials frequently do not pay Hmong workers for their work maintaining roads or planting trees in the national park, pocketing their wages instead. Furthermore, when Hmong want to buy cows, they must bribe the officers involved in the transaction. One source told me of a Hmong who lost a part of the proceeds of selling his cow—about 100 out of 600 baht—after being threatened by the officer who brokered the deal when he went to collect the money owed to him. Many Hmong are also angry and frustrated that the land they used to cultivate freely is now owned by others and that they are now forced to pay rent just to continue cultivation. Their current experiences of discrimination, oppression, and lack of ownership over land with which to subsist form the basis of their deprivation, as well as "crystallizing" and driving their campaign.

The connection between memory and the present can also be seen in Hmong narratives from Pha Ci and Phu Chi Fa, in which former forest dwellers could return to and re-occupy villages because they had not been burned. Many of them accepted the 225,000 baht offer in 2010 to exit the forest. We saw many new vehicles in Pha Ci and Phu Chi Fa, and Sombun, whom we interviewed, had bought a pickup truck to transport vegetables to market. Lai had built a new house to live in with his children and grandchildren. Cham of Pha Ci was not sure if the world would have been a better place if the Communists had won. Despite their sense that injustice remained toward the Hmong, they also had a positive view of living within the Thai state.

At the time of the interview, Sombun said that he had never spoken at or attended a demonstration about the conflict between the Red Shirts and the Yellow Shirts, which was dividing Thailand, because both sides were ethnically Thai and he was not. He said that only the capitalists were getting rich and bribes were rampant, expressing his distrust and anger toward politics. Experiences of discrimination and unfair treatment, though not reflected in the form of a social movement like that at Khao Kho, also permeate their individual lives. The insights they gained into society and politics in the forest, as well as their memories of life in the forest, provide a framework for their current view of Thai society and are likely to guide their way forward.

Thus, shared memories of the past in the forest combined with different present circumstances have formed different social movements as assemblages in the three communities. In Khao Kho, the ongoing movement is driven by the repeated renewal over the past 30 years of the memory of a village and a place. In contrast, in Pha Ci and Phu Chi Fa, memory forms the stance with which individuals approach life, rather than a collective movement. Neither is it fixed, but changes with the environment in which it is lived, just as assemblages of community movements transform with present situations.[8]

Another possible narrative of the world might be to find "moments of transformative possibility" in community movements as assemblages in the present. Such a narrative of the present can be seen in the reminiscences of Chai, a central figure in the land restitution movement, and the related notion that collective memory cannot be separated from memory that is deeply connected to individual lives.

Chai says: "For Hmong, entering the forest was a matter of life and death, a measure of survival. Many villages were burned and lost their means of livelihood. By joining the Communist Party, they were fighting on the side opposing the Thai government."

Khao Kho is the site of a major battle between Thai and CPT forces 1968 to 1981. The hall and park memorializing the battle are located where the final shots were fired. Displays in the park include a tank partially melted by trench mortars, a helicopter with a gaping hole, and the firearms that destroyed the helicopter. In the memorial basement, there is a map alongside a description of the battle and an eerie mannequin soldier wearing the uniform from that conflict. The monument lists the names of roughly 1,200 Thai soldiers killed in the battle, a battle in which many Hmong comrades also died.

When we visited the monument with the names of the Hmong dead, Nom said: "This is the place where the names of the dead killed at Long Kha are inscribed. And over here are the names of those who died in Khao Kho, Phu Kat and also Long Kha including. My name could have been in here by now. Quite frankly, I was lucky; I'm not dead yet. My mother and father's names are here, too, so I come here when I miss them. I was still a small child when my father died. Hmong never lived here. I really wanted to put it at Ban Khi Thao (where the ruins of the village are at present), but they wouldn't let us, so we had it built here."

No doubt Thailand would be different if the CPT had triumphed. If the Communists had overrun Thailand, it would have been a different world. Hmong villages may have remained intact,[9] but Nom and his comrades may have been killed by one side or another. However, Nom is still alive. This is the "hole of absence = the dead" that leads to the potential of another world that could have been, and is the starting point that drives the community movement to make a better life in the present. I understand his words in this way, as I accompanied him around the ruins of the village and the monument of the dead. It may be said that I discovered the "hole of absence" through the words and posture of Nom, and tried to look into the hole with him.

Endnotes: Forest Memory and Community Movements

This paper is based on fieldwork conducted in 2011 and 2013, and supplementary research conducted afterwards. I would like to thank the people of Hmong for their willingness to be interviewed, and Phi Yai for being a bridge to them and always supporting my research. I would also like to thank Shigeharu Tanabe and Kwanchewan Buadaeng for constructive and perceptive comments on a draft of this paper.

1. The struggle that divides Thailand into two groups, the Red Shirts and the Yellow Shirts, began in 2006 with the formation of the People's Alliance for Democracy (PAD), an anti-Thaksin organization. As the protest coincided with the 60th anniversary of the King's reign, people wearing yellow shirts, which signified the celebration of the King, gathered at the protest, which came to be known as PAD (Yellow Shirts). On the other hand, the Thaksin faction formed the United Front for Democracy against Dictatorship (UDD) in 2007 and began wearing red shirts. The policy of the Thaksin administration is that former student movement leaders who joined the Communist Party in 1976 and "went into the forest" are involved in policy making, and by implementing policies that benefit the grassroots public one after another, the government has won elections even when the royalists, the military and the bureaucracy have staged coups or used their judicial power to intervene in politics. The anti-Thaksin regime, in order to win the elections, had to capture votes in the rural areas, so it continued the healthcare system and policies to promote rural areas that Thaksin had implemented.

2. Strongholds or bases were called *Khet*; the Phu Ci Phu Chang area in Pong District, Phayao Province called Khet 7; the Doi Yao Mon area in the mountains of Thaeng and Wiang Kaen Districts Chiang Rai Province called Khet 8; and the Khet 3 Changwat area, which initially included two liberated areas (Khet 10 and 15) on the border between Phetchabun, Phitsanulok and Loei provinces in the Kho-Khao Ya and Phu Hin Rong Kla areas; and later the Phu Mieng and Phu Khat areas (Baird 2020: 6–7).

3. There have been many publications in recent years on the history and memory of people, including Hmong, who entered the forest and joined the CPT in these areas (Canthana 1993, Khunphon 2005,2009, *Kamakan cat gan ramlwk phu sia sala khet 7* 2006, Noparat 2011, Urai 2015, etc.).

4. Names of people in this chapter are pseudonyms. Age is at the time of the interview.

5. There are many theories as to where the Hmong came from. Urai introduces the theory that they entered China from Siberia and the north, from Europe to Mongolia (Urai 2015: 37–38). Anne Fadiman also referred Hmong's northerly roots found in their rituals citing Marie Savina, a French apostolic

missionary, who wrote that a Hmong homeland "was perpetually covered with snow and ice; where the days and nights each lasted for six months; the tree were scarce and very small"(Fadiman 1997: 13-14).

6. Hmong people commonly report similar experiences: (1) the lowlanders' predatory and unfair taxation; (2) the lowlanders' racialization of Hmong people; (3) unwanted sexual advances on Hmong women and sometimes the subsequent abuse of younger and married Hmong women; and, (4) the security forces' killing of pigs and chickens for food without asking permission or providing compensation, etc. (Baird 2020: 5).

7. "The Voice of the People" by the CPT based in Kunming, was reportedly broadcast in Thai, Isan (Northeast Thai area), and White Hmong in the 1960s. The station was shut down by the Chinese government in July 1979 (Baird 2020: 10).

8. On how an assemblage is transformed in the political context, see Tanabe and Takagi in this volume.

9. Baird sees the possibility that the CPT might have committed similar human rights abuses and killings as the Khmer Rouge committed in Cambodia (Baird 2020: 15).

References

Baird, Ian G. 2020. "The Hmong and the Communist Party of Thailand: A Transnational, Transcultural and Gender-Relations-Transforming Experience." *TRaNS: Trans-Regional and – National Studies of Southeast Asia* (2020), Cambridge University Press: 1–18.

Bennett, Jane. 2010. *Vibrant Matter: a Political Ecology of Things*. Duke University Press.

Canthana Fongthale. 1993. *Cak doi yao twng phu pha ci* (From Doi yao to Pha Ci). Bangkok: Wi parin co. limited (in Thai).

DeLanda, Mnuel. 2006. *A New Philosophy of Society: Assemblage Theory and Social Complexity*. Bloomsbury.

Fadiman, Anne. 1997. *The Spirit Catches You and You Fall Down: A Hmong Child, Her American Doctors, and the Collision of Two Cultures*. Farrar, Straus and Giroux.

Kamakan cat gan ramlwk phu sia sala khet 7. 2006. *Rao tang ma cak thua thuk saratit: Pha Ci* (We've come from every direction: Pha Ci). Chiang Mai: Ming Muang Chiang Mai (in Thai).

Kanokrat Lertchoosakul. 2016. *The Rise of the Octoberists in Contemporary Thailand*. New Haven: Yale University. Southeast Asia Studies.

Kataoka, Tatsuki. 2007. "Lafu no i ju: Kurashi no nakano kingendai seijishi (The Migration of Lafu: Modern Political History of Daily Life)." *Shizen to bunka soshite kotoba* (Nature, Culture and Language) 3: 85–95 (in Japanese).

Khunphon. 2005. *Phu Wae Phu Payat* (Phu Wae Phu Payat). Bangkok: Art Et kraffik (in Thai).

Khunphon. 2009. *Phu Wae Phu Phayat lem 2* (Phu Wae Phu Payat 2). Bangkok: Art Et kraffik (in Thai).

Marks, Tom. 1994. *Making Revolution: The Insurgency of the Communist Party of Thailand in Structural Perspective*. Bangkok: White Lotus.

Melucci, Alverto. 1989. *Nomads of the Present: Social Movements and Individual Needs in Contemporary Society*. London: Hutchinson Radius.

Murashima, Eiji. 1982. "1970 nendai no taikoku ni okeru akusei undo to kyosanshugi (The Student Movement and Communism in the 1970s)." *Ajia Keizai* vol. 23. no. 12: 24–49 (in Japanese).

Nopharat Lamun. 2011. *Rao ko pen cao khong phendin:prawatisat, niwet, wattanatham doriyao doiphamon* (We are also the owners of the land: history, dwelling and culture of Doi Yao and Doi Phamon). Bankaetmuangnorn co. limited (in Thai).

Takagi, Kotaro. 2006. "'Kioku kukan' shiron (A Study of 'Memory Space')." In *Shakai Kukan no jinruigaku: Materiariti, Shutai, Modaniti* (Anthropology of Social Space: Materiality, Subjectivity, and Modernity), edited by Ryoko Nishii and Shigeharu Tanabe. Kyoto: Sekaishirosha (in Japanese).

Takahashi, Katsuyuki. 2014. *Ajia reisen ni idonda heiwa undo: Tai Kyosanto no toitsu sensen katsudo to taishusanka* (The Peace Movement during the Early Cold War Years in Asia: The Development of the United Front of the Communist party of Thailand and the Participation of Multiple Actors). Waseda University Press (in Japanese).

Tapp, Nicholas. 1989. *Sovereignty and Rebellion: The White Hmong of Northern Thailand.* Oxford University Press.

Urai Yangcheepsutjarit. 2015. Kan chuang ching khwam songcam tang sangkhom nai chumchon mong (Contesting Social memories in Hmong Community of Doi Yao – Doi Phamon). Master thesis, Chiang Mai University (in Thai).

Yoneyama, Lisa. 2005. *Hiroshima: Kioku no politikusu* (Hiroshima Traces: Time, Space, and the Dialectic of Memory). Tokyo: Iwanami Shoten (in Japanese).

Part 2

The Community Movements Today: State, Religion, and Education

Chapter 4

TEACHER TRAINING WORKSHOPS AS AN OPPORTUNITY FOR SELF-TRANSFORMATION
The Dhamma School Movement in Myanmar[1]

KEIKO TOSA

Introduction

In the study of social movements, "new social movements" have attracted attention since the 1980s. Previous social movements, according to scholars of new social movements, reflected class contradictions between workers and managers in industrial society. Contrariwise, the emergence of new types of social protests indicates the transition to a qualitatively new type of society, the post-industrial society. Touraine (1985) argued that "the displacement of protest from the economic to the cultural field has been linked with an opposite tendency, the privatization of social problems, an anxious search for identity and a new interest for the body, demands which can lead to the definition of new social norms or, in an opposite way, to an individualism which excludes collective action" (1985: 784).

However, there is a set of implicit assumptions in the study of social movements, including those of Louis Pierre Althusser and Alain Touraine. These studies have focused on liberal social reforms, such as civil society or prodemocracy movements. In contrast, Melucci (1996: 30–32), by comparing new social movements with traditional ones, identified new methods and objects for consideration.

Up to this point, literature on social movements, my own work included, has been mainly devoted to oppositional movements, revealing an explicit bias of the majority of students of collective phenomena. With some important exceptions, much less attention has been paid to what we can call *reaction*, that area of collective action where solidarity is employed to defend social order, even by breaching the system limits (Melucci 1996: 31),

Melucci then discusses studies treating right-wing movements and movements with conservative tendencies. Nash's book on social movements also takes into account these directions and includes several articles dealing with right-wing and conservative movements (Nash 2005). For example, Bowie (2005) provides an extreme example of a right-wing social movement that was directly created by the Thai state. She points out that the Village Scout movement is "a clear-cut case of a state-sponsored initiation ritual deliberately designed to manipulate its participants" (Bowie 2005: 59). Takagi (2012) also focused on the Village Scout movement and, in comparison with the Royal Birthday Ceremony, successfully demonstrated how the community was reconstituted as moral and ethical targets and how the art of governing was extended to individual bodies through rituals.

This chapter focuses on the establishment of Buddhist Sunday schools, which have mainly been understood in connection with Buddhist exclusivist movements in Myanmar. After half a century of military rule, with the first general election of 2010, the Union Solidarity and Development Party (USDP), close to the military, was elected as the ruling party. USDP chose U Thein Sein as president. However, he promoted greater democratization than expected, and as a result, the National League for Democracy (NLD) led by Daw Aung San Suu Kyi, decided to participate in the by-election in 2011. As the economic sanctions imposed by Western countries were lifted, the market economy became active with strong foreign investment. However, the clash between Rohingya and Rakhine Buddhists in 2012 led to a widespread religious conflict between Buddhists and Muslims across the country. The religious conflict also vitalized the 969 movement, with anti-Islamic tendencies among some Buddhists, and led to the formation of the Association for the Protection of Race and Religion (MaBaTha). Since the anti-Muslim movement and the establishment of Buddhist Sunday Schools appeared around the same time, the latter movement has been overlooked or simply considered part of the anti-Islamic movement. For example, articles mentioning Sunday Schools have stated that MaBaTha founded the schools (e.g., Crisis Group 2017, Walton and Hayward 2014, Walton et al. 2017). However, these articles fail to capture the complex social context. Walton, an expert on Myanmar religion and politics, has written a short online article focusing on Buddhist Sunday schools, questioning whether they are to be interpreted as an innocent example of imparting religious values to the next generation or another worrying indication of the insidious spread of anti-Muslim nationalism in Myanmar (Walton 2014). He places two institutions, the Dhamma School Foundation, which conducts religious education, and MaBaTha, an anti-Muslim movement, at the two ends of a spectrum, stating that this makes it "even more difficult to know how to respond and intervene." Walton's view of Sunday Schools is significant in the sense that he focuses on two aspects: educational promotion and nationalism. However, he seems to assume that "Buddhist Sunday School" is a single entity. Rather, I would propose to regard the diffusion of Buddhist Sunday Schools as community movements.[2] Tanabe (2016) defines the recent movements in Southeast Asia as new "community movements." The community he assumes here is not the classic theories of community and communality that have often assumed "integrity and tradition in the shaping of the core identity of its members," but "a kind of alliance or communality, including a variety of networks developed through the Internet and social media" (Tanabe 2016: 1). He points out that many contemporary community movements take on a complex form of "assemblage" (*agencement*)," inspired by some works of Gilles Deleuze and Félix Guattari's works. Such an assemblage consists of "a configuration of heterogeneous forces, institutions, individuals, groups, things, and nature where its constituent parts have significant roles and retain a certain autonomy" (Tanabe 2016: 3).

There might well be skepticism about considering the activity of founding Sunday schools as movements. As the Dhamma Schools (DSs) aim at education, the core organization creates basic textbooks and teaching guidelines and spreads them in the countryside; it thus has many features of a top-down movement. In terms of promoting education in accordance with standardized textbooks and prescribed guidelines, it can be understood as a much more rigid form of activity than recent community movements. However, DSs could not be expanded by founding them from the top down, because the core organizations do not have enough funds or human resources to expand their movements in this way. Rather, it is the sort of movement observed in many communities, where various actors decide to participate in this activity to establish DSs. People interested in the activity participate as founders, supporters, volunteer teachers, students and parents. The extent of membership is not clear, as members enter and leave the organization frequently. For this reason, it might be meaningful to consider the activity as community movements. Hereafter, the activity is referred as the Dhamma School Movement (DSM).

Such functions as "impart[ing] religious values to the next generation" and "the insidious spread of anti-Muslim nationalism" to which Walton (2014) refers seem to be linked with the purposes of the respective core organizations. First, this paper aims to examine how the DSM is spread and interacts with the political-religious situation in Myanmar.[3]

We should also note that DSs are founded for "(religious) education." The abovementioned articles view DSs as a tool for spreading MaBaTha ideology. Some authors presuppose that the religious education offered is merely pedagogical imposition or a rote memorization of the canons, similar to secular education in Myanmar. The second aim of this paper is to clarify what participation in DSM means to its supporters and the experience they gain by participating in its activities.

The establishment of the core organizations

There are several core organizations of the DSM. The first organization to be founded was Hitadaya Young Men's Association (Hitadaya), followed by the Dhamma School Foundation (DSF), which has spread more widely across the region than Hitadaya. Although a few other organizations are involved, they are smaller and more regional.[4] I focus on the first two organizations.

Hitadaya (Hitadaya Young Men's Association)

Hitadaya was founded by Rev. Wimalabiwuntha at Mahamyaing Pariyatti Monastery in Mawlamyaing City on 16 January 2011.[5] Before founding Hitadaya, some monks in Mahamyaing Monastery, considering that religious education indispensable for children, began to teach children about the life of the Buddha and basic knowledge of Buddhism every Sunday. This activity gradually became known by school teachers and neighbors. Hoping to expand this kind of Sunday

School throughout Mawlamyaing City, supporters founded the Hitadaya Young Men's Association based in Mahamyaing Monastery. As they had already started religious education, the association quickly created a syllabus, a textbook and teacher guidelines. On 11 April 2011, they started DS activities. At first, the monks at Mahamyaing Monastery were in charge of education (*thindanhmu*). However, finding that the number of teachers was insufficient as DSs expanded outside Mawlamyaing City, they sought to establish a system to train teachers.

Establishment of the DSF in Yangon

Subsequently, another organization, the Dhamma School Foundation (DSF), was established in Yangon through the initiatives of monks and nuns who had studied abroad. Recently, the possibility of earning a master's degree or doctorate of Buddhism has spread widely, and monks who have obtained sufficient funds have started to study abroad, mostly in India, Sri Lanka and Thailand. At the time, Buddhist monks and nuns studying in Sri Lanka were inspired by the teachings of Christian Sunday Schools as well as by the Buddhist Sunday Schools in Sri Lanka, and one day organized a meeting. The attendees, concerned about the future of Buddhism in Myanmar, concluded that the establishment of a Buddhist Sunday School was urgent. However, they also noted that they were too young to hold much influence among the monks and laypeople in Myanmar. Therefore, they consulted their mentors or influential monks and requested their cooperation.

The foundation was established on March 14, 2012. The organization comprised 5 monks appointed to an honorary advisory board, 23 monks on advisory committees, and 17 monks on central working committees. The first honorary advisors were the most established monks in Myanmar.[6] As the foundation could not afford to own its own building, it rented office space in the Meikkya Monastery, Yangon.

The DSF was characterized by the adoption of advanced educational methods unavailable in national schools at the time. Among the founding monks was a disciple of Rev. Nayaka, Phoungdawoo Mandalay, who founded one of the best monastery schools, which serves as a model in the country. Phoungdawoo School has also been famous in promoting a Child-Centered Approach (CCA) with strong support from overseas. In light of the current situation, Rev. Nayaka strongly advised adopting the latest teaching methods for religious education and facilitated the cooperation of educationists working with international organizations. Several educationists and scholastic monks from famous Pariyatti monasteries were appointed to write textbooks. While adopting the CCA, they held detailed discussions of what should be taught from the Buddhist scriptures, doctrines and religious practices, based on which they edited original textbooks and teaching guidelines. The compilation of textbooks and teaching guidelines for the first three grades was completed in March 2013. The Foundation also started a teacher training workshop using this textbook. In addition, starting in October, teacher training instructors (*nibya saya/sayama*) began to be trained by inviting applicants from early participants in the teacher training workshop.

Expansion of Dhamma Schools

Hitadaya expanded mainly in Mon and Karen States. In 2017, there were 350 DSs in Chondo Township, 30 in Hlaingbwe Township, Karen State, three branches (approximately 90 schools) in Mon state, and some schools in Yangon Division.[7] Schools of DSF, meanwhile, spread across the country in a few years. The DSF reported that

6,233 schools had been established in all divisions and states and in Naypyidaw Union Territory in 2018. In fiscal 2014–15, there were 36,410 elementary schools, 4,860 junior high schools, and 3,134 high schools in Myanmar (Ministry of Education 2014–15). In other words, the number of DSs has reached about one-sixth of the current number of national elementary schools, which attests to how widely DSs have spread.

The rise of DSM and its social background

When I asked the officers and monks of the core organizations, the founders and supporters of each DS why they established DSs, I received a variety of answers. However, they can be summarized under four basic reasons: the need to protect Buddhist traditions, fear of Islamic expansion, reflective awareness of Buddhist habitus, and anxiety about educational collapse. These answers sometimes overlap with the aims of founding the organization and the central discourse of DSs. In this section, I first introduce popular narratives and consider the social background of this movement.

Anxiety about the disappearance of Buddhism tradition

When asked why the DS was founded, most participants expressed concern about the disappearance of Buddhist values and traditions. As adult Buddhists, they stated that they naturally acquired such values within their community, but children today do not have the opportunity to learn such Buddhist values and traditions. In addition, they observed that some children seemed not to know how to speak to monks, elders and teachers. They behaved "barbarically" (*yain*).

This concern had spread before the movement during a period of rapid social changes. President Thein Sein (2011–2016) promoted political reform and achieved greater democratization than expected. As a consequence, Western countries lifted economic sanctions and gradually began economic assistance. Overseas investment also increased. This trend continued after the National League of Democracy (NLD) led by Aung San Suu Kyi took power in 2016. These economic policies and the influx of a market economy caused fluctuations in Myanmar, especially in Buddhist society. Under these circumstances, younger generations in particular have gained employment opportunities, become familiar with new consumer lifestyles and begun to distance themselves from traditional Buddhist values. This concern reflects the anxiety of the older generation in the face of rapid changes in habitus among the young.

Fear of Islamic expansion

Along with the abovementioned anxiety, fear of Islamic expansion is also mentioned. One typical statement is as follows: "Among the world religions, only Islam expands. On the other hand, Buddhism has already declined in its original birthplace, and the population of Buddhism continues to decline." In order to stop this, the next generation, expected to inherit Buddhism, should be brought up through DSs. In fact, this narrative seems widespread in the anti-Muslim movement; indeed, the early DSM in some regions was deeply linked to anti-Islamic nationalism.

The anti-Muslim movement in Myanmar refers to the 969 movement and its derivatives, the "Association for the Protection of Race and Religions" (MaBaTha), with a more defined organization and purpose. The influx of immigrants from South Asia during the British colonial period triggered anti-Indian, particularly anti-Muslim, movements, which appeared, for example, in the anti-Indian riots in 1930 (Walton and Hayward 2014, Kuramoto 2020). On the other hand, even during the military regime, some Buddhists claimed that Islam was a threat, and the term "969," a symbolic figure created based on the nine special attributes of the Lord Buddha, the six special attributes of his Dharma, or Buddhist Teachings, and the nine special attributes of the Buddhist Sangha (community of monks), started to be used during this period in opposition to 789, used to refer to Islam in South Asia. In the early 2000s under the military government, U Kyaw Lwin, then Director General of the Department of the Promotion and Development of Buddhism, mentioned the 969 principles in lectures at the State Pariyatti Sasana University[8] (Tosa 2019). Since then, the concept has been spreading.

After religious conflicts in 2012, the anti-Muslim discourse that has long existed has come to the surface of society.[9] Ashin Wirathu agitated the audience in this direction and has been criticized by the international community for his radical remarks. These Buddhist nationalists moved further to enact laws and formed MaBaTha for the purpose of enacting marriage laws in 2013. During the military regime, gatherings of five or more people were prohibited by law, but Buddhist preaching was allowed as religious activity. For this reason, preaching ceremonies can function effectively as a medium for certain movements. Under the military regime, there were many messages of support for democratization. On the other hand, anti-Muslim thoughts related to the 969 movement were conveyed in a way that aroused emotions through SNS (social networking service) and Buddhist preaching.[10] As mentioned above, many articles refer to DSs as an anti-Islamist tool sponsored by MaBaTha, in part perhaps because the core monks at both Hitadaya and the DSF include many proponents of and prominent figures in the 969 movement. I return to this point later.

Reflective awareness of Buddhist habitus

DS participants often reflect on their practices of traditional Buddhism in comparison with other religions. For example, Christians and Muslims have established an excellent system for providing religious education to children and encourage them to go to churches and mosques. On the other hand, many Burmese Buddhists leave their children at home when they go to the monastery because they are afraid that their children will be too noisy and interfere with the meditation and preaching of the monks. This is a very common narrative told among the participants of DSs that might have been spread through pamphlets or preaching concerning DS. In any case, it is understood that Buddhists established DSs after realizing that they did not give children an appropriate opportunity to understand Buddhism deeply and searching for a system to impart to children as much understanding of Buddhism and Buddhist ethics as possible. In this sense, the DSM is reflective of their own religious habitus.

Anxiety over education

The collapse of education has long been a major concern of the people of Myanmar. The people who participated in the founding of DSs also often showed such anxiety. This was widely understood to be due to military rule. When the military government took power to suppress the pro-democracy movement in 1988, the military regime closed the universities for several years because college students were the driving force behind the movement. In the meantime, the regime has shifted the core function of universities to suburban campuses and has strengthened control over university staff, professors and students. In addition, education itself has been neglected. In fact, textbooks for basic education (elementary, junior high and high school) have not been revised so much, since the socialist period. Rote memorization was promoted, under the military regime. Under these circumstances, there was a popular saying: "The government seems to think that it will not be threatened if it brings up the nation blindly obeying authority. That is why the government is trying to weaken education." Therefore, the NLD government cited "education reform" as a top priority.

Meanwhile, with the cooperation of UNESCO, the Ministry of Education has made efforts to increase the enrollment rate in primary education. In this context, the new policy of reopening the monastic schools started in cooperation with the Ministry of Religion. In Myanmar, monasteries traditionally taught reading and writing to novices as well as lay children; however, with the spread of schooling during the colonial period, monastic schooling was banned. However, in 1992 the relevant legislation was amended and monasteries were allowed to establish monastic schools (*Pondawgyi Thin Pinnya Kyaung*). The aim was to support children from needy families and orphans, but it also raised the possibility of open schools based on existing monasteries in the community. As a result, monks became increasingly interested in education, while the laity has also affirmed the connection between monasteries and education. These concerns about education and the reaffirmation of the connection between monasteries and education were a major basis for the spread of DSM.

Process of DS establishment

In this section, I introduce rather early cases of the establishment of DSs to show how local people were introduced to the movement and how they founded DSs.

The case of Pyi School (Karen State)

This is a case study that I observed at Pyi Township (pseudonym) in September 2013. This was, to be precise, in the middle of the founding of a DS. The main participants were approximately 20 lay members.[11] Some belonged to the same religious network, through which they supported monasteries. Most of them were financially well-off. For example, one of them started a business by smuggling cloth, which had been popular in Mawlamyaing since the Ne Win period, and opened a store there. He is now a wealthy business owner with several large stores along the Thai border and in Mawlamyaing. Another runs a restaurant where meetings are often held. They felt that the Muslim population had increased considerably in Karen and Mon states.

Some members had a chance to attend Hitadaya teacher training courses. During this period, special lectures concerning the anti-Muslim 969 movement and MaBaTha were held in association with the course. The lecturers and organizers seemed to participate both in the 969 movement and in Hitadaya. However, this does not mean that all attendants participated with dual aims. Rather, it was an opportunity for people interested in religious education to encounter the 969 movement or the activities of MaBaTha. At the seminar, attendants were warned of the threat of Islam's expansion and keenly felt the need for religious education for children. After the course, they proposed the establishment of a DS to their acquaintances. One member told me about the need for a DS as follows: "Children today have few opportunities to learn Buddhism or practice Buddhism properly. Therefore, young Buddhists have few religious bases and are easily converted to other religions." They sought to organize a committee that included people they were originally close to, as well as regional leaders. In addition, they asked Ashin Wunna (pseudonym), the chairman of the Township Sangha Maha Nayaka (TSMN), to support them as an advisory monk of the Committee. They then founded a DS Preparatory Committee on 9 June 2013. The committee consisted of 35 laymen and 8 monks.

They first bought land for the DS and were going to apply for permission to build an auditorium, at which point Rev. Wunna received notification that the Sangha should monitor the political use of 969 by the anti-Muslim movement. Interestingly, Wunna Sayadaw is a member of the MaBaTha and a beloved disciple of its chairman, Tilawkabiwuntha Sayadaw. However, he showed an ambivalent attitude toward DSs because of his administrative position. Moreover, he treated the DS circle as almost equivalent to the 969 movement. He gathered the Committee and suggested that they stop the DS movement and see how things go. They were dismayed and, at the same time, resentful that their movement had been misunderstood, but were eager to overcome any difficulties. Incidentally, all the supporters bought the monthly magazine published by MaBaTha, which had just been established at that time, and they eagerly recommended it to me. In other words, the DSM, the 969 movement, and MaBaTha activities were viewed by the participants as having the same purpose, and they participated in the activities of all three.

The case of Nang School (Shan State)

I participated in a teacher training workshop held in Shwe San Township (pseudonym), Shan State in 2019, and during this workshop I learned how local DSs are set up. There are many tourists in this area, and the residents are mainly ethnic minorities, such as Intha and Danu. Lan Monastery was the first in this area to open a DS. The Sayadaw running the monastic school became interested in DSs because of that. Around 2013, during the early years of the foundation, teacher training workshops were held only in Yangon. They sent two female volunteers to a DSF workshop in Yangon, and then started a DS with the help of the two teachers. However, they soon married and were unable to teach at the DS because of the need to care for their children. Therefore, the DS at the Lan Monastery was suspended.

Conversely, in Nang Monastery, near Lan Monastery, the chief monk Rev. Nanda (pseudonym) and his leading assistant monk thought that religious education was necessary for children, and they had been holding a Buddhist Culture Class (*Yinkye Leinma Thindan*) for about three years from around 2014. The Buddhist Culture Class was started under the leadership of the State Sangha Maha Nayaka Committee (SSMNC) during the military government. The class was held once a year for about one month during the summer vacation. Since the content is the same every year, children who attended the class once did not participate again, so they felt it was not very effective. They gradually became interested in DSs as, following Lan Monastery, some neighboring monasteries began to host DSs. Further inquiries revealed that a friend of Rev. Nanda who had studied at the same monastery was now one of the core members of the DS working committee. In 2017, he sent three monks to the teacher training workshop. After that, four lay teachers and another four in the following year were dispatched to the training class. Currently, they manage a DS with eight teachers in charge of education.

There were about 90 students up to the fifth grade. According to them, there were senior students in the fifth grade or higher. However, as they could not afford enough teachers for the intermediate curriculum, so they taught the fifth, sixth, and seventh graders together in the fifth-grade class. Once they had sent new teachers to the intermediate teacher training workshop, they planned to teach junior high school courses by separate grades. Rev. Nanda also recommended the DS on various occasions, such as donation and preaching ceremonies. Although most of the parents agreed on the necessity of a DS, it was difficult for children to attend because of distance. The monks thus sometimes prepared a bus for transportation. The students of Lan School mentioned above now attend the DS classes at Nang School.

Educational Practical Training, 2019 Aug.

Teacher Training Workshop, 2019 Mar.

The early DS movement

Both cases are early examples of the movement to establish DSs, in the case of the Pyi School by Hitadaya and Nang School by the DSF. In both cases, teacher training workshops were not held in rural areas, so teachers had to participate in training courses held at centers in Yangon or Mawlamyaing. In addition, the Pyi School was established mainly by lay believers, while Nang School was established mainly by monks. There is a tendency for monks to lead the establishment of DS in rural areas, while the laity seems to lead to the establishment of DS in urban areas. However, there is no fixed pattern.

On the other hand, the case of Pyi School is characterized by a sense of fear about the disappearance of Buddhism or Buddhist tradition and a shared anti-Muslim discourse. This might be because the Hitadaya movement coincided with the 969 movement and MaBaTha activities as a feature of this region and period.

In fact, the ratio of Muslims in the Karen and Mon states is rather high, even in national terms (Census 2014). Some monks, including Hitadaya founder Rev. Wimalabiwuntha, describe common regional experiences as follows: When there are Muslim communities in a village, they usually coexist without much problem. However, problems arise when Buddhists marry Muslims. For example, in a marriage between a Buddhist and a Christian, it is possible to continue to follow one's own religion after marriage. On the other hand, Muslims require Buddhists to convert to Islam, which causes problems. Many monks in this region have seen many laymen who hastily consult with monks after their children marry Muslims and say they will convert.

Among the monks sharing this perception, preaching monks formed the Thathana Para Ghandha Wasaka Network. They began to promote their ideas through preaching, which led to the rise of the 969 Movement in Lower Burma. Indeed, the monks who played a key role in the founding of Hitadaya DS are at the core of the 969 movement as well as MaBaTha activities. In other words, these core monks were trying to mobilize different strata with different framings for one purpose.

Given these circumstances, it is possible that the Hitadaya DS course often included 969 lectures in its activities.[12] Although both activities have often been identified, the two are different things as movements. One issue is that the participants are not shown the whole picture. Rather, it should be noted that the core advocates in Hitadaya used one movement as a medium for other activities. An examination of Hitadaya textbooks and distribution materials shows that anti-Islamism is not included in the activities and instructions. However, the advocates conducted two activities at the DS workshop, as indicated above. In other words, the participants unintentionally participated in other activities through the Hitadaya DSM.

Nang School, on the other hand, is based on the education method of the DSF and has not given any special lectures. The chief monks decided to establish a DS because of the need for Buddhist ethics education and educational reform. In particular, Lan Monastery, the first to participate in the event, originally ran a monastic school and learned about DS activities through its network. In addition, it commonly occurs that once a new DS is established in one location, the neighboring communities quickly learn about it and seek the opportunity to establish a new school. Even if one school is shut down, like Lan School, the children can continue to attend the neighboring school. This trend was observed in the other regions.

However, as Walton shows, DSF is sometimes considered an activity of MaBaTha. This might reflect the fact that some participants of the 969 movement and MaBaTha have worked as advisors for the Foundation. For example, Rev. Tilawkabiwuntha, the president of MaBaTha, worked as an Honorary Advisor, and Rev. Dhammapiya, a MaBaTha controversialist, as a member of the Executive Committee.

In fact, when I interviewed the monks and the laity among the core founders of DSF, I found that most of them distanced themselves from or clearly opposed the anti-Muslim movement. When I asked why they had appointed some members of MaBaTha to important posts, they replied that they were appointed based on their mentorship, not their activities in the anti-Muslim movement. In monastic society, the teacher–student relationship is crucial. As the Pariyatti Monastery (specified in Learning Canons) has an essential educational function in a monastic career, the abovementioned monks, principals and chief priests of the famous Pariyatti Monasteries have great influence on monks in Myanmar.

DSM during the Aung San Suu Kyi period

MaBaTha lobbied the ruling USDP to enact four Marriage Laws in 2015. During the 2015 general election, some members of MaBaTha tried to promote support for the USDP, but unintentionally pushed rather many supporters to leave it. There are three possible reasons for this. First, the marriage laws were enacted, so MaBaTha's original goal had been achieved. Second, the criticism of Daw Aung San Suu Kyi provoked the antipathy of pro-democracy supporters and invited criticism that monks showing their opinion in party politics were too secular and inappropriate. Third, as a backlash against anti-Muslim discourses, the argument began to emerge that such criticisms deprecating others were not suitable for Buddhists. Meanwhile, Rev. Wiratu and others continued to make hate speeches and were banned by the State Sangha Maha Nayaka Committee (SSMNC), which issued a Sangha Order in May 2017 declaring that it would not recognize

MaBaTha as a Sangha activity. This was in effect a dissolution order, and MaBaTha was forced to dissolve.[13]

Under these circumstances, the Dhamma School Foundation (DSF) has clearly defined its distance from politics and MaBaTha. In 2015, for example, it added a fourth line to the Foundation's three principles: "To be completely independent of party politics." In addition, Rev. Tilawkabiwuntha resigned from his position as advisor during the third term in 2018. At the same time, the mainstream DSM became centered on the DSF. For example, although Hitadaya expanded around Karen State and Mon State, some DSs have changed from Hitadaya to the DSF system in Karen State. Ms. Nun, a teacher training instructor living in Karen State, told me that they changed the system because some members perceived the political movement as improper and others preferred the curriculum and textbooks of DSF.

Education at Dhamma Schools and internal change

Considering DSs as a movement, this section examines it from the participants' point of view. Participants here include children, teachers and supporters who helped to establish and manage DSs. Although the changes in children attendees should also be analyzed, this paper focuses on volunteer teachers as mediators of the movement. Focusing on the teacher training workshop, I clarify what kind of educational effect to expect from DS and how adults themselves change by participating in the training course.[14]

Outline of teacher training workshops

Teacher training workshops are held for seven days for elementary and junior high school courses and for five days for kindergarten courses. The number of participating teachers was set at 50 for junior high school courses and 100 for elementary school courses.[15] The following is based on a teacher training workshop for junior high school courses observed in Shan State in September 2019. All of the instructors and volunteer teachers stayed overnight, making it a kind of training camp.[16] In this case, one monastery was the host, which took care of all the expenses and prepared the venue and meals for the attendees. Usually, three or four teacher instructors are sent from the Foundation, and each attendee receives one textbook, one set of teaching guidelines and a certificate of completion. The necessary equipment, such as microphones, PCs and projectors, are lent out by the Foundation. The host should pay for expendable items, such as large paper and markers, as well as shipping costs.

Most DSs in the neighborhood are operated at monasteries. When they receive the news that a teacher training course will be held, monks select teacher candidates among their high school graduates (10th grade) or above to register the course. At the course I attended, there were over 50 attendees including 4 monks (novices). Although they varied in gender and age, most attendees were female, with two males and four monks (novices), and they were mostly young people who had just finished 10th grade, with some elderly persons in their late 50s. Several active and retired school teachers participated. Even though there is a restriction on the number of participants from the same community, the host community had many participants. This is an advantage for the host community, but also they actually need people to help with the meal provisioning for the workshop. Thus, only a few people from each of the other communities participated. Many of the participants in the workshop were unacquainted with each other.

They have a tight schedule with classes and practical training from 8:00 to 17: 30, except for lunch time and tea break, and preparation for practical training was sometimes required after dinner.

On the first day following the opening ceremony, the instructor began to teach the basic concept of the CCA and the basics of the junior high school course. Then, using the fifth-grade textbook, the instructor gave model classes and taught theoretical subjects. After that, she selected some important lessons for the fifth grade and the attendees prepared mock classes. The class was divided into two groups, and each group was divided into several subgroups. They prepared a mock class in accordance with the teaching guidelines, while consulting with others in the group. The team could decide who delivered the class, or the instructor could draw lots, so that in the end all the attendees take a mock class. It was easy for attendees to get along with each other because in the course new groups were constantly divided. I participated as an observer, but it was easy to make friends and become close, as people in the same group asked me to sit next to them. On the last day, the attendees took photos together and exchanged Facebook addresses.

Classes and comments

Although there are several characteristics of DS workshops and educational policies, I focus on the introduction of a mutual comment system in this section. There are many opportunities to comment or make peer reviews during workshops on teaching practices. When we met at 8 a.m., everyone was required to talk about what he/she learned and how he/she felt the previous day. Turning to the microphone one by one, everyone was supposed to speak. When similar and general comments, such as "I learned a lot by doing the mock class for the fifth grade" followed, one person would make more specific comments, such as "Yesterday, I learned the way of exchanging opinions as *thandaman nyi* (diplomatic system)." Gradually, the attendees began to prepare to express their own impressions. At an early stage, as a teaching method the attendees learned two evaluation methods, namely, *apyu thabaw* (positive response) and *apyet thabaw* (negative response), and practiced how to convey the same content to children with positive comments.

Commentators were always appointed to mock classes. The remaining attendees entered the class as "students," while the commentator watched them from outside. After the class was over, the commentator made comments on the entire class based on a check sheet for loudness of voice and comprehensibility, and the person who gave the lecture responded to the comments. The commentator pointed out whether the summary written on the *simili* paper was good, whether their handwriting was clear and easy to understand, and whether their voice was loud or unclear. Sometimes, the commentator added suggestions for improvement. I observed that one commentator, a young novice, gave incisive comments such as, "It's good to look at the students who are answering and observe their facial expressions" or "You do not respond to the children when they say something, but you should comment on their answers; that would motivate them." I was impressed by his keen observation, profound insight and deep understanding of children's habits. Active and retired school teachers participating in the workshop stated that they had had no experience listening to and commenting on their own classes in national schools. I also attended this workshop with the intention of conducting research, but I ended up feeling that it was more useful than the faculty development seminar at my own university.

More interesting are the attitudes of attendees who played the role of students. At first they did not shed their adult habits and tended to give only correct answers to the teacher's questions. However, as they gradually became used to the situation, some began to grumble, "*Sayama* (Teacher!), I want to pee!" based on children's habits. Alternatively, they began to predict what the children were likely to answer. For example, one section teaches a story about a classmate who provokes a fight. When asked how to deal with a quarrel or other problems, an attendee answered cheerfully, "I'm angry, so I'll get back at him!" and received great applause from the "children" around him. The person who played the role of teacher asked back, "Well, I understand your feeling, but what else are you supposed to do? Can you think about other choices?" These "imitations of a child" and expectations of the child's behavior were based on their own childhood and experiences as a teacher or adult, and ultimately provided the other person with practice in dealing with them. Such deep consideration was gradually fostered within the class.

In addition, there are various devices to ensure that everyone speaks equally. For example, as I mentioned above, at the morning meeting, they used a microphone. At first I did not understand why the microphone was used, for the assembly was held in a circle in the auditorium, and we could hear well at that distance without using a microphone. However, those who had not worked as teachers and had just graduated from the 10th grade had almost no experience speaking in public. At this workshop, I noticed that one young woman never used a microphone, but others got used to it quickly. In this sense, a microphone serves to make people express their opinions. In other words, the microphone is an agency to make the person who holds it speak out in front of others. In addition, handing the microphone to the next person identifies the next person to speak.

A ball was also used instead of a microphone, where the person holding the ball represented the person to give feedback, who then threw it to the next person to give feedback. In this case, the ball serves to make people express their opinions. Although the ball was thrown at random at the beginning, people who had not expressed their opinion began to be targeted, and those who already expressed their opinion took care not to take the ball. In other words, the ball became an object to be manipulated so that everyone could express their opinion.

Using a microphone at Teacher Training Workshop, 2019 Aug.

Becoming teachers of the DSF

The participants of the DS Workshop at junior schools were DS teachers engaged in primary education and volunteers interested in DSs. The participants came from a variety of career backgrounds. Some were young people who had just graduated from high school, and others were farmers and merchants. Except for the teachers and monks, many of the participants said they had never expressed their opinions in public. At the workshop, however, with the help of positive comments from the instructors, they gradually gained experience expressing their opinions and collaborating with others. At the end of the training session, they were asked again whether they had achieved their own goals and how they felt after participating. In other words, participants had the opportunity to think reflectively on their self-transformation at the end of the workshop. I heard many conversations among the participants during the workshop, in which many said that they had learned to speak in front of people and gained experience in expressing their opinions. In DSF workshops, teachers train themselves to express their opinions. In addition, they are supposed to learn to observe other people's behavior, praise their good points, and suggest what they should improve in an acceptable way.

The development of human resources capable of appropriately expressing criticism and opinions is recognized as an issue for Myanmar society as democratization progresses. Under the military regime, politics usually proceeded in the form of "rule" imposed from above, and there were few opportunities to express opinions from below. School education originally had an important function of human resource development; however, in the classroom, it became common for students to only memorize everything a teacher said or answer with the "correct answer" when asked something. With the progress of democratization and the spread of SNS, there have been more opportunities to express opinions. The next goal might be not only learning to express opinions, but also to avoid one-sided criticism and to express opinions appropriately. One of the major characteristics of the DS Workshop is that it provides opportunities and training for participants to express their opinions appropriately and to listen to other people's opinions and make comments.

There are many problems with mutual auditing in the education field (see Strathern 2000). However, in view of the political situation in Myanmar, the introduction of mutual reviews and training in expressing opinions and criticisms in consideration of the person being evaluated should be promoted. Incidentally, elementary school principals and vice-principals, and several teachers from the nearby community also participated in this workshop for the second time. The CCA method has only started being implemented in national schools under the NLD government; however, according to the principals, it is not going well. In this sense, the DSM is trying to complement secular education, taking into account the problems of educational methods. The DSM was originally founded for religious education so that the children would be taught to understand Buddhism clearly. However, as far as I observed the workshops or learned from textbooks, DSs seem to avoid excluding others and teach social cooperation. The workshops and textbooks include ethics education targeting the issues of living in a wider society.

Conclusion

In this paper, I described the establishment of DSs as community movements. When DSM, especially the early Hitadaya movement, emerged, it overlapped with religious and political movements, such as the 969 movement and the activities of MaBaTha. Although there have been arguments conflating the two, I analyze the situation in the early days as one of different movements being initiated by the same promoters. In other words, it is true that MaBaTha supporters participated in the DSM. In this context, MaBaTha monks seemed to view founding DSs as a means of achieving their goals. However, as described in this paper, the DSM itself had multiple directions in connection with the various actors. Meanwhile, the National League for Democracy came to power in 2016 and MaBaTha was dissolved in 2017. Against such a background, DSs have come to be expected to promote the education based on child-centered approach or improve Buddhist ethics education.

I also examined what attendees would gain by participating in DSs through teacher training sessions. A DS is not a medium for transmitting ideology that the core organization holds. Participants in the workshop had the opportunity to practice speaking in public, as well as expressing their opinions, commenting on others and sharing their impressions of comments. In that sense, they learned how they cooperate with each other by participating in the workshop. Interestingly, most of the teachers and adults who have participated to improve children's education became aware of their changes by participating in teacher training workshops and continuing to teach as DS teachers. This change might be one of the important characteristics of this movement.

Endnotes: Teacher Training Workshops as an Opportunity for Self-transformation

1. This paper focuses on the multi-directional community movements to reform education concerning religious ethics before the coup d'état in Myanmar on February 1, 2021. At the moment, it might be difficult to analyze how things will change. However, the reform of education and the reform of religious ethics education have been major issues in Myanmar. I am sure that understanding the situations of communities before the coup d'état will be indispensable to understanding the current social situation.

2. The participants also regard the activity of founding Sunday Schools as "*hlokshahmu* (movement or activity)".

3. Research on the two core organizations has been conducted since 2017 at more than 20 Dhammma Schools in Yangon, Mandalay, Zagaing, Magwe, Mon and Karen Shan. I also attended the Teacher Training Workshops three times (Ayadaw Ts., Zagaing, Nyaungshwe Ts., Shan State, Magwe). I would like to express my sincere gratitude to all the related monks and lay persons for allowing me to participate in the training course and ask some questions about the schools. I am grateful to Apinya Feungfusakul, Ryoko Nishii and Tanabe Shigeharu for their suggestive comments on the draft.

4. For example, Buddha Dhamma School in Nay Pyi Taw. According to Rev. Mya Nan, there are also Yankin Thissa Dhamma School and Kuthasa Dhamma School.

5. I did research in Karen State and Mon State on September 15–16, 2013, and in September 2017.

6. The members are as follows: Dr. Kumarabiwuntha, Chairman of the State Sangha Maha Nayaka Committee; Dr. Nandamalabiwunta (Rev. Professor), President of International Buddhist Mission University; U Tilawkabiwuntha at Ywama Pariyatti Monastery; Tipitakadara Yaw Sayadaw; and Rev. Myakyauk.

7. According to Rev. Mya Nan (31 August 2017).

8. According to my interview in Karen State in September 2013.

9. Many brochures for the 969 movement include reprints of old documents. See also Saito (2015) for details.

10. Several studies have already pointed out that anti-Muslim discourse spread through social networking service (For example, Schissler 2016; McCarthy and Menager 2017). In addition, we should pay attention to Buddhist preaching celemonies. Some prominent monks of the 969 movement excelled in preaching, and they held the preaching celemonies mentioning about the crisis of Buddhism. In fact, anti-Islamic sentiments often grew through such preaching celemonies (Tosa 2020).

11. Most of the laity came from local NGOs or religious associations; there were 9 members from DS, 6 members from a free clinic, 4 members from the Young Buddhists Association, 6 members from three welfare associations, 3 members from Friends of Buddhism (Thathana Nokhgaha), 1 member from the Free Funeral Services Society, and 10 members from two Buddhist donation associations.

12. According to my source in Karen State, he participated in a Hitadaya DS course held in a different township, and found that the anti-Muslim lectures were held (Interviewed September 2013).

13. MaBaTha changed its name and formed a new association of its lay supporters, the "Buddhist Dhamma Charity Foundation," on 15 July of the same year.

14. The impact of Dhamma School on children needs to be analyzed. At present, educational reforms are under way in Myanmar, and we should reconsider the characteristics of DS in terms of educational methods and moral education.

15. I participated in teacher training workshops as observer three times, at Ayadaw Township, Magwe Region, in March 2019, Nyaungshwe Ts, Shan State, in August 2019, and Indo Ts, Zagaing Region in March 2020.

16. The size of the workshops varies according to the host. They sometimes have more than 150 participants, including observers. Although the rice and ingredients are largely donated by the local community, around 1.5 million and 3 million kyat is needed to host one workshop. In addition, the host should prepare every meal for the attendants and instructors, so a large support staff is needed.

References

Bowie, Katherine A. 2005. "The State and the Right Wing: The Village Scout Movement in Thailand." In Nash ed. 2005, 46–65.

Buddhism and State Power in Myanmar. Asia Report N°290 (5 September 2017). https://www.crisisgroup.org/asia/south-east-asia/myanmar/290-buddhism-and-state-power-myanmar (2020/8/28)

Census. 2014. *The 2014 Myanmar Population and Housing Census: The Union Report. Religion Census Report Volume 2-C.* Myanmar: Ministry of Labour, Immigration and Population Crisis Group. 2017.

DSF (Dhamma School Foundation). 2013a. *Bokdha Bhatha Thinkhansa (Patama Tan) Kyang Tha Kain* (Textbook for the 1ˢᵗ grade). Yangon: DSF.

———. 2013b. *Bokdha Bhatha Thinkhansa (Patama Tan) Hsaya Lanhnyun. Kyang Tha Kain* (Teacher Guideline for the 1ˢᵗ grade). Yangon: DSF.

———. 2015. *Thon Hnit Pyi Hnitpatle Asiyinhkansa* (Annual Report of the 3ʳᵈ Aniversary). Yangon: DSF.

———. 2016. *Le Hnit Pyi Hnitpatle Asiyinhkansa* (Annual Report of the 4ᵗʰ Aniversary). Yangon: DSF.

———. 2018a. *Dhamma School Foundation (Baho) Akyaung Thikaungzaya* (Memorandumo of the Dhamma School Foundation). Yangon: DSF.

———. 2018b. *Bokdha Bhatha Thinkhansa (Athama Tan) Kyang Tha Kain* (Textbook for the 8ᵗʰ grade). Yangon: DSF.

———. 2018c. *Bokdha Bhatha Thinkhansa (Athama Tan) Hsaya Lanhnyun.* (Teacher Guideline for the 8ᵗʰ grade). Yangon: DSF.

———. 2018d. *Nga Hnit Pyi Ahtuhtok Meggazin* (Annual Report of the 5ᵗʰ Aniversary). Yangon: DSF.

Kuramoto, Ryosuke. 2020. "Bukkyo wo kessetsuten toshita "tsunagari" to sono henyo ("Relatedness" based on Buddhism node and its transformation)." In Tosa and Tamura eds. 2020, 141–164 (in Japanese).

MaBaTha. 2013. *Thathana Wunthapala Ahpwe Myawadimyo, Myawadi Hkayain.* (Thathana Wunthapala Association), unpublished.

McCarthy, Gerard and Jacqueline Menager. 2017. "Rumours and the Muslim Scapegoat in Myanmar's Transition". *Journal of Contemporary Asia* 47(3): 396–411.

Melucci, Alberto. 1989. *Nomads of the Present: Social Movements and Individual Needs in Contemporary Society.* (edited by John Kearne and Paul Mier). Philadelphia: Temple University Press.

———. 1996. *Challenging Codes: Collective Action in the Information Age.* Cambridge: Cambridge University Press.

Nash, June. ed. 2005. *Social Movements: An Anthropological Reader.* Malden, Oxford, Carlton: Blackwell Publishing.

Ohnmer Tin and Emily Stenning. 2016. *Situation Analysis of the Monastic Education System in Myanmar* (Final Report). Yangon, Myanmar Education Consortium. https://mecmigration.files.wordpress.com/2016/05/mec-monastic-education-analysis-report-july-20151.pdf

Saito, Ayako. 2015. "Myanma syakai niokeru musulimu: Minshuka niyoru kitai to genjo (Muslims in Myanmar: Expectations for Democracy and Current Situation)." In *Posto gunse no Myanma: Kaikaku no jitsuzo* (Post-Military Myanmar: Substance of the Reforms), edited by Toshiharu Kudo, 183–204. Tokyo: Institute of Developing Economies (in Japanese).

———. 2020. "Minshuka niyoru aratana shiren to musulimu komyunitii (New Trials of Democratization and Muslim Communities)." In Tosa and Tamura eds. 2020, 165–184 (in Japanese).

Schissler, Matt. 2016. "New Technologies, Established Practices: Developing Narratives of Muslim Threat in Myanmar". In *Islam and the State in Myanmar: Muslim-Buddhist Relations and the Politics of Belonging.* edited by Melissa Crouch, 213–233. Oxford: Oxford University Press.

Strathern, Marilyn ed. 2000. *Audit Cultures: Anthropological Studies in Accountability, Ethics and the Academy.* London and New York: Routledge.

Takagi, Ryo. 2012. "Kokkatochi no katei to komyunitii: Tai no kokuoutanjobi to sonmin sukauto kensyu no sougokoui (The Process of State Governance and Communities: Thai King's Birthday and Interaction of Village Scouting Training)." In *Jissen toshiteno komyunitii: Ido, Kokka, Undo* (Community as practice: Mobility, Nation and Movement), edited by Kyonosuke Hirai, 187–217. Kyoto: Kyoto Daigaku Gakujutsu Shuppankai (in Japanese).

Tanabe, Shigeharu. ed. 2016. *Communities of potential: Social Assemblages in Thailand and Beyond.* Chaing Mai: Silkworm Books.

Tosa, keiko and Katsumi Tamura. eds. 2020. *Tenkanki no Myanma wo ikiru: "tosei" to koukyosei no Jinruigaku* (Living in Myanmar at a Transition: Anthropology of "control" and public sphere). Tokyo: Fukyosha (in Japanese).

Tosa, Keiko. 2016. "Bukkyoto to Islamukyoto no Kyouzon no Kanousei (Possibility of Coexistence of Buddhists and Muslims in Myanmar)." In *Myanma: Kokka to Minzoku* (Myanmar: The Nation and The Ethnicity), edited by Kuniaki Asomura and Ryuji Okudaira, 578–594. Tokyo: Kokon Shoin (in Japanese).

———. 2019. "Shukyo to "Seigi": Myanma niokeru Bukkyotojoseikoninho wo megutte (Religion and "Justice": Myanmar Buddhist Women's Special Marriage Law)." In *Globalukasuru "Seigi" no Jinruigaku: Kokusaisyakai niokeru hokeiseito lokariti* (Anthropology of Globalizing "Justice": Legal Formation and Locality in the International Community), edited by Hiromi Hosoya and Yoshiaki Sato, 309-337. Tokyo: Showado (in Japanese).

Tosa, Keiko. 2020. "Seppoukai wo kakutosuru Bukkyo koukyosei (Buddhist Public Sphere developing through Preaching Ceremonies)." In Tosa and Tamura eds. 2020, 185–225 (in Japanese).

Touraine, Alain. 1985. "An introduction to the study of social movements". *Social Research* 52(4): 749–787.

Walton, Matthew J. 2014. "What are Myanmar's Buddhist Sunday Schools Teaching?", *East Asia Forum* (16 December 2014). https://www.eastasiaforum. org/2014/12/16/what-are-myanmars-buddhist-sunday-schools-teaching/

Walton, Matthew J. and Hayward, Suzan. 2014. *Contesting Buddhist Narratives: Democritization, Nationalism, Communal Violence in Burma.* Policy Studies 71. East-West Center.

Walton, Matthew J., Ma Khin Mar Mar Kyi and Aye Thein. 2017. "Ma Ba Tha", *Mekong Review* 2(3): 14–15.

Chapter 5

MUSLIMS AS CITIZENS OF MYANMAR

Education in the Muslim Community[1]

AYAKO SAITO

Introduction

This study focuses on education in the Muslim community in Myanmar, which, in addition to typical religious education, is particularly conscious of what life as a Muslim in Myanmar entails. Myanmar mainly comprises ethnically Burmese Buddhists, and a number of riots have occurred against the religious and ethnic Muslim minority,[2] triggered by conflict in the Rakhine State in May 2012 and the anti-Muslim movement led by radical monks and lay believers. While this anti-Muslim movement somewhat deescalated in 2020, anxiety among the Muslim community still persists, with a fear that violence will flare up again. Against this backdrop, the Bamar Muslims,[3] as they call themselves, have long held Islamic training courses for students from elementary school to university level, especially during the summer holiday period, covering such subjects as "Muslims in the History of Myanmar." These courses aim to instill students with a consciousness of being "indigenous Muslims."

Bamar Muslims view these Islamic education courses as important, and if they are canceled for any reasons, this group ensures that the courses are restarted quickly thereafter. However, a recent desire has been voiced to prioritize such skills as vocational training that can be linked to employment, with many parents enrolling their children in English and computer classes during the summer break, rather than the Islamic summer schools. Notwithstanding this tendency, the question remains as to why people continue to have these summer schools outside of their regular religious education.

While investigating the reasons, first the status of the Muslim population in Myanmar since the country's democratization is considered. Subsequently, using information gathered from interviews and various documents, the reasons why Bamar Muslims desire such courses is explored. Finally, specific examples of training courses, including interviews with instructors, are introduced to show that each organization is conducting unique activities for the benefit of children. This paper primarily deals with case studies and interviews conducted in the cities of Yangon and Mandalay.

The Muslim community after democratization: Facing the anti-Muslim movement

Following Myanmar's transition to a democratic government in 2011 after a long period of military junta rule, there was an explosion of anti-Muslim sentiment that had hitherto not surfaced to any great extent. Under military rule, rights to freedom of speech and assembly were limited; and while it cannot be said that there were no anti-Muslim sentiments, access to information was limited, and due to the prompt dispatch of the military, any such expressions were quickly quashed. However, with the move toward democracy, several restrictions were gradually eased. Through a simultaneous expansion in telecommunications infrastructure and the lowered cost of mobile devices and telephone charges, a larger group of people had the potential to obtain, produce and share a wide variety of information.

Thus, in late May 2012, violence emerged between the Buddhist Rakhine and the Rohingya[4] population, in the wake of an assault on a Rakhine woman. Initially, the Myanmar government labeled this violence a "conflict between ethnic groups"[5]; however, several factors, including that the Rakhine people were largely Buddhists and the Rohingya largely Muslim, ultimately, led to the anti-Muslim movement expanding beyond the Rakhine State and throughout Myanmar. From 2013 to 2016, several violent riots broke out, ranging from smaller fights to larger incidents involving many fatalities and injuries. Since then, the violence has been limited to small-scale skirmishes; however, there have been instances of various other forms of harassment, such as the obstruction of religious events and prayer during Ramadan. By 2020, the situation had calmed, perhaps owing to the coronavirus pandemic.

Under the military junta rule that began in 1988, the people were unable to voice their concerns regarding the government and lived with their troubles. The Bamar Muslims, thus, were dissatisfied with the various forms of discrimination they experienced, despite adopting Myanmar's culture and strongly believing themselves to be ethnically indigenous to the country. In the interview-based survey conducted by the author, respondents shared stories of lived experiences in which even if one became a civil servant or joined the military with the aim of working for the nation, they would not be promoted owing to their religion or would be forced to contribute to a Buddhist event; if one did not, they would receive a negative performance review. Moreover, even if one held citizenship, because Islam itself was viewed as foreign, they would not be accepted as indigenous.

However, with the transition to democracy in 2011, Muslims expected a guarantee of their human rights, that discrimination based on beliefs would cease to exist, and that the hardships experienced under military rule would gradually disappear. Unfortunately, the expansion of the anti-Muslim movement from 2012 ran contrary to these expectations. Moreover, while the period around 2019–2020 marked a significant increase in the number of people who disapproved of the actions of the radical monks and lay believers, Muslims still felt that they could not act freely and needed to be cautious, especially with older Muslims struggling to control the dissatisfactions of the younger members of their community. The rising anti-Muslim sentiment was a particular source of worry for Bamar Muslims who, despite consistently being, up until this time, a part of Myanmar society and maintaining cordial relationships with non-Muslims, began to worry that even their friendly relationships might collapse.

The anti-Muslim movement and accompanying riots were the results of a long-hidden anti-Muslim sentiment rising to the surface, spurred by the eradication of censorship and the acceptance of both rights to free speech and assembly, with the emergence of democracy. This democratic development also made opportunities for interfaith dialog and peace gatherings possible; such events involved Muslim organizations or individual practitioners in a new initiative. In addition, restrictions on organizational activities were lifted; thus, organizations that were originally engaged in welfare activities, as well as newly formed organizations, were able to begin operations in their local communities or to expand.

A wide variety of organizations run by Muslims involved in various activities, attempted to quell discrimination. For example,[6] some Muslims suggested that tours of mosques be held, after fake pictures and information were shared through social networking sites indicating that weapons were being hidden in a mosque. To further mutual understanding, Muslim organizations also held events, inviting members of the public, monks, leaders and clergymen from the Buddhist, Christian, Hindu and Muslim traditions to visit mosques, churches, Hindu temples and pagodas to hold dialogues at each place of worship.

In another example, the C Fund Trust,[7] which conducted a range of initiatives, such as free vocational training (computers, sewing), cram schools, English tutoring, health clinics and support for medical costs, has opened activities to all people living in the local area, the singular exception being a women-only elderly care home that only admits Muslims. The organization is run exclusively by Muslims, with operating expenses paid for by membership fees and donations, and appears to be unaffected by the anti-Muslim movement. Myanmar has many people, not only Muslims, still living in poverty; therefore, it is the organization's policy that unless a particular activity cannot be separated from religion, people will be accepted regardless of faith or ethnicity. The proportion of Muslims participating in the organization's free vocational training is comparatively high, while other programs have seen 60–70% Muslim participation, indicative of other non-Muslim participation. Further, the organization has installed water purifiers in such places as public schools and Buddhist monasteries.

In a more recent example, a volunteer group operating out of a mosque in the city of Yangon has provided food to people who are hospitalized or quarantined due to COVID-19, as publicized by the domestic media.[8] Even outside of the current pandemic, when someone is hospitalized in Myanmar, meals are distributed individually. Since September 2020, the social support organization at Nway Aye mosque has been engaging in volunteer work whereby it delivers halal food on request to different hospitals and quarantine centers. Regardless of whether this began as a conscious decision, the organization responded to calls from people of all ethnicities and religions who were in need and delivered each person three meals a day (including a simple breakfast) in hospitals, quarantine centers and other facilities, including Buddhist monasteries. As of December 2020, they delivered meals for over 1600 people a day, with as many as 100 volunteers involved in the preparation and packaging. All free meals are donated, and these donations are posted to Facebook. While the details of the donor's religion are not shared and therefore remain unknown, they include Buddhists. Further, when responding to media reports, the organization has said that it will deliver to anyone who is struggling, regardless of religion or ethnicity, including those in Buddhist monasteries. By contributing to the local area and helping those in need, this activity may ultimately lead to a reduction in prejudice and discrimination against Muslims.

Though increasingly anxious in the face of a buoyant anti-Muslim movement, Muslims in Myanmar eventually avoided acting collectively or opposing this movement with further violence. It is fascinating to see how they have conducted themselves in their attempts to promote understanding about their religion and how, by visibly contributing to their local area, they have managed to create and maintain cordial relationships with their neighbors. To carry out their initiatives quietly and calmly without being fazed by the anti-Muslim movement, Muslims themselves have had to understand Myanmar's culture and its society.

The significance of educating children outside of religious schools: Blending in with a Buddhist-majority society

Many school-aged children attend public elementary schools in the daytime; while in the evening, they attend religious schools (called Arabic schools) that have been set up in residential districts to learn the Koran. Depending on the region, such religious schools may be found inside mosques. These classes begin at 5 p.m., ending somewhere between 7: 30 p.m. and just after 8 p.m., during which time children are taught how to read the Koran, its meaning, and the traditions and culture of Islam. Essentially, children are educated to be good Muslims.

Almost all Muslim children attend these religious schools. However, the Bamar Muslims believe that this is not enough. One of the reasons for this is revealed in the below extract from the introductory speech at the 15th Summer School for elementary students held at the Islamic Center of Myanmar in 2019. This center was originally established in 1964 with the primary aim of spreading Muslim education in the Burmese language. It hosts lectures on weekends about Islam, and other classes teaching people about Islam in English. During the summer vacation, it holds Islamic Summer Schools, which are directed at students from elementary school up to university levels.

> If one looks at the subjects we teach in the Islamic Center, one sees that they are not so different from those taught at other religious schools. What we would like parents to know is that, just as you learn about the religion of Islam from religious texts such as the Koran, Hadith and Taaleem ul Islam (Teaching of Islam) in other religious schools, at the Islamic Center students also learn by quoting and taking excerpts from the Koran and other religious texts. However, what is different here is the teaching method. The method we use at our center is called the Participatory Learning Approach and involves the children learning through participation. Here, we leverage teaching approaches, such as religious songs, rhymes, styles of play, and biographies of prophets that are appropriate for the age of the child, as well as what are known as audiovisual materials, that

is, materials such as videos that are more memorable for having been experienced aurally and visually. We also use PowerPoint for learning. (Speech Draft 2019)

Thus, students attend the center and relearn things they have already been taught in religious school because they experience a different teaching method, which involves learning in a fun, actively participative way, instead of simply listening to the teacher as they would in regular religious school. The textbooks consist of writings about Islam; however, students will often be practically instructed and practice the target of the lesson together. For example, the lesson may involve learning about hygiene and health: how children should line up at the sink to wash their hands before eating or how they should throw away waste. One source of minor concern was conflicting views regarding the insertion of colorful pictures into textbooks; the teachers were divided; however, it was said that such pictures should not be used in religious schools. Depending on the region, religious schools hold competitions in Koran recitation, while the Islamic Center holds religious song contests, poetry and story contests, as well as summative examinations on coursework for elementary school students, with outstanding performers awarded prizes. The center aims to teach children that they should try their best to win prizes in areas in which they have talent and not simply memorize content; it aims to train children to understand and internalize the teachings of the faith in a true manner.

Education received by university students has been addressed in another article (Saito 2014: 34). It is also states in the foreword to the textbooks used at the center that its courses aim to foster students' ability to explain the teachings of Islam to non-Muslims. The author was unable to obtain the revised texts introduced post-democratization. However, on examining the contents of the textbooks used in the university student course that were published in 2007, the content infers that they are conscious of Myanmar, covering Myanmar-style translations of Islamic culture, the first Bamar Muslims, the Islamic Center, and Myanmar and Islam. It is clear that the course textbooks taught at the Islamic Center not only take a religious perspective, but also teach about the relationship between Myanmar and Muslims.

The Islamic Center's policy emphasizing course content in the context of Myanmar, as well as the pedagogical strategies it employs to teach children, is similar to that of courses offered by other Bamar Muslim groups. There are several reasons why Bamar Muslims offer this type of education, if only during the summer holidays. Many Bamar Muslims are concerned about the conservative education offered in religious schools, particularly that their style of instruction has remained almost entirely unchanged. The author spent only a short time observing such a school, but witnessed students who arrived late being whipped on the hand, though only lightly.

Muslims whom the author interviewed shared their dissatisfactions about religious schools.[9] Most schools involved students sitting on the floor, gathered around a small table, and reciting the Koran and listening to their teachers. Despite being able to afford them, they simply did not use desks and chairs. Moreover, while in other countries many different textbooks and modern styles of teaching are used, content in Myanmar has remained unchanged since colonial period, as have the teaching methods, perhaps because teachers have no desire to introduce new practices. Teachers are also generally unfamiliar with secular education, and while there are universities in Myanmar that train Islamic intellectuals, the number of teachers who have studied at regular universities is very small.

In addition, while the whipping mentioned earlier has somewhat reduced in the education of children, the style of educating through fear is still very prominent. One Muslim stated that his wife still believed things that she was taught in a religious school; for example, the idea that Muslims should not participate in the Water Festival held in Myanmar at the start of the year. She was told that something bad would happen if she was struck by the water that is thrown around at this festival. Of course, if the Water Festival was without trouble, there would be no reason not to participate in it. In reality, there have been many cases of young people getting drunk and causing trouble at the festival in recent years, so students are told that "something bad will happen" as a threat to discourage them from participating. The interviewee stated that people believed entirely in what the teachers said at the religious schools, and the manner of education caused parents to worry about sending their own children to these schools. He believed that a religious school that taught children in the style of the courses held by the Islamic Center should be open all year round.

Despite these expectations, for a variety of reasons it has not been possible for Bamar Muslims to open a religious school that operates year-round. One major reason is that Bamar Muslims are themselves a minority within the Muslim community. Many mosques and religious schools have inherited the conservative management style of the colonial age immigrant tradition, and it is not easy for the opinions of Bamar Muslims to gain traction. While they may be called conservative Muslims, when questioned about having studied abroad, they responded that a small number were gradually changing their thought processes after returning to Myanmar and finding jobs in mosques or religious schools. However, the vast majority inherits the same teaching strategies and sermon content unless a more senior person signals a wish to reform. This means that education in religious schools and the content of sermons do not change to any great extent.

How Bamar Muslims educate their children

In the previous section, the Islamic Center course aims and the reasons for seeking education outside religious schools were explored with reference to the thought processes of Bamar Muslims. In this section, case studies of organizations that educate children are examined.

As mentioned earlier, most children in Myanmar attend standard public schools in the daytime and religious schools in the evening. Consequently, independent courses are largely held for elementary school to university levels during the summer holiday period (from the end of March to May). These annual courses are run by a small number of organizations and, depending on circumstances, may be canceled for a time. The branches of some organizations may run preexisting courses independently, although there are also cases of organizations developing new courses. The Islamic Center does not have any branches outside of Yangon; however, people who support its approach request that the faculty visits their local areas to hold courses. The course content discussed here is based on information gathered in an interview-based survey.

In 2010, an organization called M, headquartered in Yangon, established a summer school for children titled, "Children Who Are Good Muslims." Owing to the expansion of the anti-Muslim movements, this course was canceled for two years. However, it has been held annually thereafter. The course is free and targets children from the ages 10 to 15 years, who come together as part of a small group of 10–20 persons (one or two people from each township in Yangon, with larger numbers of girls participating). It lasts for four to five days and is essentially focused on religion. On the final day, participants go on an excursion. The theme changes slightly each year and includes teachings about how to behave as a Muslim, morals (like those taught in public schools), and natural disasters.

In 2019, sex education was incorporated, led by a doctor. There are no examinations at the end of the course. The courses are offered to children from 10 years of age because younger children would not be able to listen to people speaking for such long periods. Nevertheless, the leader of the course was originally a primary school teacher and would also like to run a course for children younger than 10.

Organizers plan the course dates so that they do not overlap with that of other organizations, and they hold arts and literature contests for elementary to university level students. There are three types of contests: a speech contest (from a set list of topics), a religious song contest and a short essay contest (also from a set list of topics). Groups are separated into elementary school, middle school, high school and university school students (up to the age of 25), with the top five in each section being recognized for their achievements. No limit is placed on the number of participants, with over 100 taking part. The religious song contest is particularly popular with children. The children and grandchildren of members of the organization also participate, and the judges are commissioned externally. However, there are cases in which the children and grandchildren of these judges participate in the contests, so careful attention is paid to ensure that participants and judges are not related to one another.

The next example involves a course that is slightly different than the abovementioned types, and involves an organization that provides free education to poor Muslim children. As this organization also operates on weekends, the author observed these children being educated several times when carrying out the survey.

This new organization, called W,[10] began its work dedicated to improving education and lives in March 2014 in Mandalay City. While teaching the children regular subjects, it also focuses on imparting the necessary knowledge that they need in their daily lives. There is no charge to students for classes, and management costs are covered by donations. However, the organization's space is rented, and in an unfortunate development, when it relocated to a space just outside of the poorer residential ward in 2019, some children could no longer attend the classes.

During the summer holidays, from March to May, for five mornings a week (not including Thursday and Friday), a summer course is run with a higher number of students than usually accepted. While the number of students varies from year to year, 100 participants enrolled between 2019 and 2020, with ages ranging from 8 to 15. On weekend mornings (Saturday and Sunday) during the school term, 70 students are taught by the organization. On some weekend afternoons, sewing classes are run for women above the age of 15. The organization places particular importance, both at weekends and during the summer, on teaching ethics and discipline, as well as Burmese (composition), English (using foreign textbooks for practical English), mathematics (calculus and mathematical thinking) and painting. When the author visited the school, the teacher did not simply read a book to the students—the students themselves also took turns at reading books and explaining why they had chosen them. While this course is intended for Muslims, W is not a religious school, and the teaching style is not based on religion. Ms. N, the primary teacher at the school, was originally Christian but converted to Islam upon marriage and ordinarily teaches at a middle school. Two close friends of Ms. N who assist her in the weekend activities are non-Muslims who work at the same middle school.

In addition to the aforementioned subjects, activities that may be of interest to the students are carried out in the classroom, depending on the current circumstances, such as social studies tours of the neighborhood and activities aimed at improving the local environment, like picking up litter. Once, after the children read the Burmese-language edition of the Japanese book by Testsuko

Kuroyanagi, *Totto-chan: The Little Girl and the Window,* they stated that they would like to go on a field trip with lunch of "something from the sea and something from the mountains." While it might be different from Japanese food, Ms. N prepared dried fish from the sea and *lahpet* (dishes made with pickled tea) from the mountains, and they all left the classroom, eating outdoors as if they had gone on a field trip. This course is run only in the mornings and targets poor children. It does not offer lunches and requires donations to fund its management costs. However, the idea of "something from the sea and something from the mountains" is useful in terms of thinking about nutrition, and the children were happy "to do something that is done in Japan." Thereafter, they introduced occasional "Bento Days." However, there are some families who cannot provide lunches for their children, and the organization thus provides rice and *lahpet*.

Few organizations have continued their initiatives in this manner, and in reality the efforts of people such as Ms. N, who plays a central role in teaching at the W organization, have made a difference. Many poor Muslim families would prefer traditional religious schools, where whips are used, and do not see the value in things like painting pictures or singing songs. Why would they allow their children to attend these schools? It would appear that they cannot look after their children themselves during the summer holidays. People outside of the Bamar Muslim community are also critical of the fact that even though W is a Muslim organization, it does not center its activities on Islam. However, in an interview Ms. N stated that when students who had enjoyed painting at W won a prize at a competition held by their public school, both the students themselves and their parents were very happy and finally seemed to understand what the organization was trying to do. These activities are innovative initiatives that differ from the types of courses managed by religious institutions and are important and worthwhile endeavors.

In this section, only two specific examples are given. There are other individuals and organizations that offer such courses for children, but few of them seem to be continuing their activities for various reasons. Some reasons are that before democratization, it was difficult to obtain permission, and after democratization, individuals were busy with their own work and did not have time for volunteer activities, or the activities of the organization increased. In addition, because these courses are for children, many of them are taught by women, which is probably a big difference from religious schools.

Conclusion

This paper presents an aspect of education for the Muslim community in Myanmar. Muslims, who make up less than 5% of the total population, have faced a nationwide anti-Muslim movement since democratization, which has made them realize anew how difficult it is to live in a Buddhist society. However, rather than expressing their grievances, Muslims seem to be taking advantage of the fact that democratization has enabled them to engage in a variety of organizational activities and contribute to the local community in order to gain a better understanding of themselves. In doing so, it is necessary for Muslims themselves to understand Myanmar's society and culture, and they are seeking ways to establish good relationships with others through religious education.

Education that incorporates new methods, especially for Bamar Muslims, as well as education that fosters understanding of Myanmar's society and culture, can be seen as a new movement in the Muslim community. However, most religious education in the Muslim community is still conservative, and it is difficult to say that the movement is expanding rapidly. Alternatively, with the spread of cell phones and access to a wide range of information since democratization, as well as increased opportunities to study and work abroad, Muslims are now able to relativize the Islam they have studied and the Muslim community in Myanmar society. It may not be said that the anti-Muslim movement has completely died down, and an increase of Muslims who are aware of the necessity of teaching and understanding others from an early age to survive in Myanmar's society can be expected.

This paper focuses on religious education for Muslim children, but there seem to be signs of a gradual change from the conservative educational methods of the past in the content and methods of religious higher education for to train intellectuals.[11] How leaders are being trained to provide religious education to children is also an important, issue for the future. In addition, in February 2021, a coup d'état in Myanmar put the military back in power. In response, the people of Myanmar, regardless of ethnicity or religion, have come together as one to oppose the military authorities and it is necessary to continue to monitor the position of Muslims in Myanmar.

Endnotes: Muslims as Citizens of Myanmar

1. This study focuses on education in the Muslim community in Myanmar before the coup d'état in February 2021. It is very difficult to guess how the future political situation will affect the Muslim population. In fact, religious education during the summer vacation, which was the subject of this study, was cancelled this year. On the other hand, there is a situation where the majority Burmese and ethnic and religious minorities are beginning to cooperate with each other again and I hope that the current political unrest will settle down soon so that new analyses can be conducted in the future.

2. According to the 2014 census, inclusive of estimates, the population of Myanmar was 51,486,253, with Buddhists comprising 87.9%. Muslims comprised 4.3% of the population, the third highest group behind Christians at 6.2%. Many Muslims currently living in Myanmar are descendants of immigrants who came to the country during colonial times from every part of British-controlled India, or the descendants of immigrants and indigenous ethnic Burmese. There are also descendants of migrants who settled in Myanmar from places such as South, West, and Central Asia who were merchants, soldiers and prisoners of war during the country's dynastic period. In addition, there are converts from other religions, as well as Chinese and Malay Muslims, although these comprise only a small subset of the total population.

3. "Bamar Muslims" is the name by which many Muslims who live in Burmese society, understand the culture of the country, and maintain cordial relationships with non-Muslims, refer to themselves. However, there are also Muslims who prefer the name "Pathi," which was in use during Myanmar's dynastic period. "Bamar" refers to the Burmese ethnic group that makes up the majority of Myanmar's population.

4. The government of Myanmar takes the stance that there is no such ethnic group as the Rohingya, with many of its members calling them "Bengalis" and believing them to be illegal immigrants from Bangladesh. In June 2016, the government attempted to change the group's name to the "Muslim community of Rakhine State." However, it ultimately abandoned this plan in the face of criticism, particularly from the ethnic Rakhine.

5. The Burmese version of the riot investigation report (Republic of the Union of Myanmar 2013b, 1) refers to it as an ethnic conflict (*Lumyoyei adigayoun*). On the other hand, in a press release dated 21 August 2012 the government stated that the conflict was neither inter-religious nor ethnic.

6. For more details, see Saito (2020: 172–173).

7. Interviewed in G township, Yangon, on 26 August 2017.

8. Media coverage includes BBC Burmese Facebook Page and RFA Burmese Facebook Page.

9. Interviewed in T township, Yangon, on 23 February 2020.

10. The organization's activities originally began in Yangon, but were unable to continue there; instead, they are conducted in Mandalay as of 2020, primarily by people who empathized with the efforts of the group in Yangon.

11. In 2020, various face-to-face activities were restricted due to the new coronavirus infection, but during this period, there have been attempts to conduct activities online, and even after the coup in February 2021, there have been calls on social networking sites for participants in online Islamic courses for children and university students using the latest educational methods.

References

BBC Burmese Facebook Page dated 12 Dec 2020. https://www.facebook.com/BBCnewsBurmese/posts/3675207429201782 (Accessed on 14 May 2021)

Department of Population [DP]. Ministry of Labour, Immigration and Population. 2016. *The 2014 Myanmar Population and Housing Census, The Union Report : Religion, Census Report Volume 2-C.* https://myanmar.unfpa.org/sites/default/files/pub-pdf/UNION_2C_Religion_EN.pdf (Accessed on 24 January 2021)

The Islamic Centre of Myanmar. 2007a. *Nwe Yathi Iksalam Yeya Pochahmu Asiasin. Ahtettanhsin Iksalam Thinkhansa* (Summer Islamic Course, Higher Education Level Textbook), Vol.1, Yangon.

———. 2007b. *Nwe Yathi Iksalam Yeya Pochahmu Asiasin. Ahtettanhsin Iksalam Thinkhansa* (Summer Islamic Course, Higher Education Level Textbook), Vol.2, Yangon.

Ministry of Foreign Affairs. Press Release, 21 August 2012. https://www.burmalibrary.org/sites/burmalibrary.org/files/obl/docs14/NLM2012-08-22.pdf (Accessed on 14 May 2021)

Republic of the Union of Myanmar. 2013a. *Final Report of Inquiry Commission on Sectarian Violence in Rakhine State.* https://www.burmalibrary.org/docs15/Rakhine_Commission_Report-en-red.pdf (Accessed on 14 May 2021)

———. 2013b. *Yakhain pyine patipetkha myā sonsān sikhsēiyēi kawmashin asiyinkhansa* (Final Report of Inquiry Commission on Sectarian Violence in Rakhine State). https://www.mypilar.org/sites/mypilar.org/files/publication-files/rakhine_investigation_commission_report_myanmar_version.pdf (Accessed on 14 May 2021)

RFA Burmese Facebook Page dated 13 Oct 2020. https://www.facebook.com/watch/?v=634995137377920 (Accessed on 14 May 2021)

Saito, Ayako. 2014. "The formation of the Concept of Myanmar Muslims as Indigenous Citizens: Their History and Current Situation." *The Journal of Sophia Asian Studies* No.32: 25–40.

———. 2020. "Minshuka ni yoru aratana shiren to musurimu komyunithi (The New Challenges of Democratization and the Muslim Community)." In *Tenkan ki no Myanma wo ikiru: Tousei to koukyousei no jinruigaku* (Living in Myanmar at a Transition: Anthropology of "control" and public sphere), edited by Keiko Tosa and Katsumi Tamura, 165–184. Tokyo: Fukyosha.

Speech Draft. 2019. *15 kyein myauk Nwe Yathi Iksalam Acheikhan Pochahmu Asiasin Ahsint 1 Thindan Phwintpwe Akhanana Twin Thintanhmu ka Shinlintinpyachin* (The introductory speech at the 15th Summer Islamic Basic Course, The Islamic Centre of Myanmar.) Obtained on 22 February 2020.

Chapter 6

ETHNIC LANGUAGE EDUCATION AND STATE-BUILDING IN MYANMAR
Community Movement of Kayah (Karenni)[1]

TADAYUKI KUBO

Ethnic issues in Myanmar

After Myanmar's democratic reform in 2012, several Ethnic Armed
Organizations (EAOs) signed a nationwide ceasefire agreement with
the Burmese government, but the process of building a nation that
respects ethnic diversity is still incomplete. The fate of the country
is further unclear after the coup in 2021. This chapter explores the
ethnic community movement in Kayah State, Eastern Myanmar,
where a sense of belonging remains a core issue. Specifically, the
Burmanization of minorities has been the subject of controversy,
especially as the cultural and language policies centering on Burman
have led to EAO conflicts. Previous studies addressing Myanmar's
ethnic issues have focused on ethnonationalism and resistance
movements against the military government led by the Burmese
people, revealing that ethnic minorities have also been defined
by comparison with the Burmese.[2] However, throughout Burma's
modern history, ethnic languages remained, even under the policy of
Burmanization. Some nationalities could develop and promote their
cultures and languages as long as their activities did not undermine
national unity. The socialist government was not against the idea of
ethnic minorities possessing multiethnic identities (Kyaw Yin Hlaing

2007, 162). Textbooks were published by the Ministry of Education in Mon, Shan, Paw Karen, Sgaw Karen, Chin and Kachin languages (Khin Khin Aye and Sercombe 2014, 158).[3]

Both Buddhist monasteries and Christian churches in ethnic areas continued to offer language courses after school and during the summer holidays throughout the socialist period. Ethnic cultural and literary organizations have also been active at the state and township levels, as well as in universities and colleges (Thawnghmung 2013, 147–149). Like the socialist government, the Burmese junta permitted both indigenous and foreign minority groups to promote the teaching and studying of their own languages as long as it did not violate the policy. Ethnic minorities were further impelled to promote their own languages when the Junta held the National Convention in 1992 to draft a new constitution. Referring to the language requirement for statehood proposed by Aung San in 1947, many ethnic groups tried to emphasize the uniqueness of their languages when they presented their causes at the convention. Since then, some minority groups have tried to revive their languages. However, the scarcity of use of the Kachin State's Red Shan written language culminated in the ignorance of many Red Shan of the existence of their written language. Although the National Convention has been stalled since 1996, minority political parties have continued to promote their languages in a more aggressive manner than they did in the 1970s and 1980s. In the meantime, the military government did not have a clear definition of "Myanmarness" other than the fact that Myanmar represented all the ethnic groups in the country (Kyaw Yin Hlaing 2007, 168–169).

In discussing Myanmar's state-building, it is important to clarify the relationships among languages, ethnic groups and sense of belonging. Thawnghmung's (2013) notion of "The other Karen" argued that someone who identifies themselves as Karen may only speak Burmese, not Karen, indicating that language and identity do not always match. In other words, even though these individuals are called Karen, their actual identities vary. Thus, analyzing the situation in terms of ethnic groups resisting Burmanization is rather simplistic, so it is necessary to clarify the notion of ethnic affiliation or communities that are not a dichotomy between assimilation and resistance.

This chapter explores a new type of assembly community consisting of heterogeneous forces, institutions, individuals, groups, objects and nature, in which the constituent parts have significant roles and retain a certain autonomy (Tanabe 2016, 3). Group affinity, rather than solidarity, unity or collective identity, characterizes this community, which forms unstructured interrelationships among people and contains individuals who are assembled by contingency. As this grouping can be examined in relation to power arrangements and governance, this chapter analyzes the latter two concepts within the Burman-centered state by discussing the status of minority languages. Furthermore, minority languages have not only been oppressed, but also used as a tool for anti-government movements. Hence, this chapter also explores the process of language and literature education, which is primarily the heart of political movements, but also has consequences beyond political intentions. Among various ethnic groups, the standard ethnic language is not the mother tongue, and there is a problem of which language(s) should be used in schools. Salem-Gervais and Raynaud (2020) indicate that the "dominant" ethnic language of the school should become the language of instruction. This paper examines the case of Kayah.

Lastly, contingency, defined as an asymmetrical relation between abstract objects that are inevitable (e.g., nation, economy and order) and concrete objects that are experienced in one's daily life, characterizes this community assemblage. Hall (1996) pointed out that anaphora relations between abstract and concrete objects, which do not necessarily correlate, are vulnerable and nonessential. In other words, the gap between the abstract idea of governance and people's concrete behaviors constitutes an unstructured assemblage community. Overall, the purpose of this chapter is to examine state-building in contemporary Myanmar by focusing on the community movement of ethnic language education that began in 2013. Particularly, it considers the case of Kayah State in Eastern Myanmar where the civil war seeking independence and autonomy occurred, as the Karenni have remained in this region for many years.

In the remainder of the chapter, Section 2 discusses the politics of ethnic languages, examines the invention of the Karenni script in the context of anti-government movements and ethnonationalism, and clarifies the form of governance in relation to ethnic languages. Section 3 addresses the process for approving the Karenni script, as the official Kayah language, and highlights the various actors who are committed to the new script's dissemination. Although ethnic language education is related to politics and leads to building a nation or community, the learning process in this context reveals a lack of political consequences. Finally, Section 4 examines the state's building of contemporary Myanmar. Some researchers have noted that language education leads to political national reconciliation, but this paper reconsiders this through comparisons with the Mon and Kachin cases and by discussing the community of the Kayah (Karenni) society assemblage.

Resistance movement and script politics

Invention of the Karenni script

Kayah State, the smallest state in Myanmar, has a population of 286,627, accounting for only 0.56% of Myanmar's total population according to the 2014 Census. In addition, 75% of the population lives in remote areas (The Republic of the Union of Myanmar 2015). This state was formerly known as "the Karenni States" during the British colonial era, and the Karenni States were subsequently incorporated into the Union of Burma as the "Karenni State" when the country gained independence from the British Empire in 1948. The state name Karenni is composed of the English term for the associated ethnic group "Karen" (Kayin in Burmese) and the word "ni" (red in Burmese). In other words, Karenni means "red Karen," but the related ethic group calls themselves the "Kayah" (meaning human).

On 4 January 1952, the Burmese government changed its name to the Kayah State, as the residing majority were the Kayah, and to distinguish people from the separation and independence movement, known as Karenni (Bamforth, Lanjouw, and Mortimer 2000, 11). On that note, the Karenni National Progressive Party (KNPP) pursued the state's separation, independence and subsequent autonomy, and carried out armed anti-government agitations that resulted in many refugees crossing the border to Mae Hong Son in Thailand. KNPP redefined the word Karenni, originally referring to Kayah, as a collective term that incorporates all ethnic groups within the state, including the Kayah, but also the Kayan, and others. In other words, to achieve its political goal of opposing the Burmese government, separating and gaining independence, the KNPP tried to form a political unity between ethnic groups within the state under the term Karenni.

As a result, the Karenni script emerged as one of the core foundations of the Karenni Nation. During his time at Rangoon University during the latter half of the 1950s, the former KNPP Chairman, Khu Hteh Bu Peh (1937–2011), created the script with the help of his friends. He was motivated to create the new alphabet when he discovered that the pronunciations and tones of his Kayah language could not be expressed correctly with the English or Burmese alphabets. Thus, while some consonants have similar shapes to Thai letters or Burmese scripts, they are pronounced differently. He also created unique notation rules for his Kyebogyi village's Kayah dialect and announced it in Loikaw, Kayah's state capital. However, under the 1960s socialist regime, so-called Burmanization was promoted, and ethnic minorities' languages and cultures were limited as the Karenni involved in anti-government activities. Thus, Khu Hteh Bu Peh and his friends began an underground movement to teach the new script in the KNPP dominated areas. After a textbook was created in 1980, this script and writing system were taught in the Thailand-Burma border area and refugee camps in Thailand. In the 2000s, computer fonts were created, with the help of US linguists, and today the Karenni script is used on social network services (SNSs), such as Facebook.

As refugee camps have been the locations for disseminating KNPP's political ideologies since the 1990s, the Kayah language script was gradually explained and eventually recognized as the Karenni language within the camps. However, the Kayah language, defined as the Karenni language, did not function as the common language shared by ethnic groups within the refugee camps. For example, as the Kayah and Kayan people could not converse with each other using their mother tongues, their common language was Burmese. Even among the Kayah, it was sometimes difficult to converse, as each village had its own dialect. Overall, for decades, the Karenni script had little social impact considering that it was not taught in Burma and even the use of the name Karenni was prohibited, as it implied the anti-government movement. As such, the Karenni name and script became a symbol of the KNPP political movement.

Script politics

In Kayah State, there are three Kayah language writing systems: the Romanized alphabet, the Burmese script adapted for transliteration, and Khu Hteh Bu Peh's script. Eighteenth century missionaries were the first to transcribe the Kayah language into the roman alphabet, but the first attempt to create an original Kayah writing system was in 1951 using Burmese script. Although U Aung Min completed this writing system employing the Burmese script in 1956, it was difficult for people to understand, because it was based on the Daw Tamawgyi and Daw Nyeku villages' dialects. In 1968, U Mii Reh invented another writing system using the Burmese script that was officially approved by the Burmese government in 1979 as the Kayah script (Meeting Minutes 2013). It was based on Burmese characters to ensure that it was easy to learn for the Kayah people who were already familiar with Burmese. Some of these characters match Kayah pronunciation, while others maintained their original pronunciation (Moe Moe Htwe 2011, 348). According to my investigations into the scripts in Loikaw between September 2014 and August 2017, Mii Reh created the Kayah alphabet based on the documents Khu Hteh Bu Peh wrote after he escaped to Thailand, probably because both scripts use the same writing rules. However, this script is presently only used in some music VCDs and the Bible.

Furthermore, in Thailand's refugee camps, which provide Karenni literacy education, some of the younger generation easily mastered the Kayah language. Thus, some non-Kayah people speak the Kayah language. On the contrary, it seems that no Kayah people speak a non-Kayah language, except Burmese. This is parallel to the majority-minority relationship seen in Myanmar: some ethnic minorities speak Burmese, but no Burmese speak the languages of the ethnic minorities. Although Karenni is the ideology opposing the Burmanization that has suppressed ethnic minorities, it also includes the power relationship between majority (Kayah) and minority (non-Kayah), and involves the notion of nationalism: KNPP and the government share Kayah-centrism. Specifically, the collective name Karenni stresses KNPP's ethnonationalism centered on Kayah, while Myanmar nationalism stems from the state's claims of being "multiethnic," justified by its positioning of the Kayah people as its members. It should be noted that Karenni nationalism includes Kayah ethnonationalism and Myanmar nationalism, which empowers Karenni nationalism centered on the Kayah (Kubo 2021).

Overall, language plays an essential role in governing states and building nations (Anderson 1983). This case demonstrates that the language of ethnic minorities leads to two contradictory consequences: while opposing the hegemony of a state as Karenni, it also contributes to the state's governance centering on the Kayah. After the democratic reform and once the KNPP began to negotiate a ceasefire with the government, the script was officially approved as the standard Kayah script, not as Karenni, but as the Kyebogyi script for all Kayah people in the state. This recognition appeared to be an opportunity to end conflict and begin reconciliations.

Script recognition and literature education

Script recognition

There have been many twists and turns in the process of acknowledging the anti-government Karenni script. It was accepted as the Kyebogyi script for all Kayah people at a meeting held on 20 April 2013 and subsequently confirmed on 29 May 2013. During the meeting, the participants agonized over what the script should be named. One government official objected to calling it Karenni, because even though the term can be used at some public ceremonies, the KNPP is still an unofficial party so the use of Karenni was not favorable for officials. As Karenni was rejected, delegates from the KNPP advocated for calling it the all-people's script in Kayah State instead. Finally, on 18 July 2013, the Kayah National Literature and Culture Committee (KnLCC) (*kayâ amyôuthâ sapei hhi' yincêihmu komiti*) released a statement noting that Khu Hteh Bu Peh's script would be the official script in the state.[4] The statement declared that:

> ... throughout the years, a variety of Kayah scripts have been used among the Kayah people, and this lack of one writing system has created obstacles toward the standardization of one script. A one-script solution, instead of detracting from our Kayah national unity, will support it. For this reason, the many representatives of our people, along with the Literacy and Culture Committee, have thoroughly discussed and reached a compromise regarding the future development of our literature ... we will use one national script for the development of our national literature, the maintenance of our culture, and most importantly, the steadfastness of our unity. As of 20 April 2013 and 29 May 2013, the majority community has agreed that Kyebogyi Script will be the standard script for the Kayah.[5]

The statement recognized the script for all people in Kayah State, rather than casting it as Karenni characters. The KnLCC used the term "Kyebogyi" for the characters, because the latter term is the state's former capital and Khu Hteh Bu Peh's birthplace. The Kayah State Assembly, held on 8 September 2014, approved the teaching of this Kyebogyi script in elementary schools within the state. And the 2008 Constitution stipulates the right to develop an ethnic language in both Articles 22 and 354. Specifically, Article 22 in Chapter I of the Constitution declares the Basic Principles of the Union, noting that it "shall assist to develop the language, literature, fine arts, and the culture of the National races," while Article 354 specifies that:

> every citizen shall be at liberty in the exercise of the following rights, if not contrary to the laws, enacted for Union security, prevalence of law and order, community peace and tranquility or public order and morality . . . (d) to develop their language, literature, culture they cherish, religion they profess, and customs without prejudice to the relations between one national race and another or among national races and to other faiths. (Ministry of Information 2008, 150)

Ethnic language education approval can be positioned as part of this cultural right defined in the Constitution. However, the executive members of the KnLCC were more concerned with preserving the mother tongue than constitutional rights.

Separating script from politics

During the meeting, held on 20 April 2013, the 29 attending representatives, including politicians, township heads, religious leaders and KNPP representatives, changed their opinions regarding the script's name and decided to change "Karenni" to "Kyebogyi." Daw De De Paw, the KNPP's Minister of Literature, who is also Khu Hteh Bu Peh's wife, organized this meeting. Although the KNPP assembles its own political structure as a government, this Ministry of Literature is unofficial in Myanmar, as the KNPP is still considered an unofficial political organization and it cannot, as a result, put up candidates for elections. The meeting also included two other KNPP delegates, including the vice-chairman. In short, they all agreed to eliminate the confusion of having three Kayah script types, because it represented an obstacle for the development of Kayah culture and literature. They also needed to prepare for ethnic language education, which was approved for public schools. During the meeting, the participants recognized that other languages, such as Kayow, were quickly approved and their related educational systems were rapidly established, while Kayah was still lagging, because the standard script was not decided.

To inform all the state's districts, they also agreed to distribute the meeting minutes, describing the historical backgrounds of the invention of various scripts, as well as the difficulty in developing literature in accordance with the political situation.[6] The representatives at the meeting agreed to use Khu Hteh Bu Peh's script as the Kayah national literature (*kayâ amyôuthâ sapei*) and reorganize the literature and culture committee that had been inactive for a long time.

At the beginning of the meeting, the minutes recorded the opinion of a Buddhist monk, who highlighted that Burmese works with the latest computers and is currently the best common language to use among the white Karen, red Karen, Shan, Mon, Rakhine. On the other hand, he also noted that it would be preferable to change the present situation, but this would take time to make it acceptable for people of all religions. One particularly noteworthy participant comment was a statement by U Toh Reh, a representative of Loikaw (the Kayah State capital), claiming that "literature is not politics (*sapei dhi naunngan yêi mahou*')," as a nation that needs writing and conducting party politics are different matters. He also noted that "since this is a matter of nation (*amyôuthâ ye keisa*) and we are all Kayah, we should have a frank discussion here" (Meeting Minutes 2013, 4).

The participants confirmed that the situation of the Kayah language was complicated, as it is sometimes called Kayah and sometimes Karenni, though both languages are the same. This confusion not only stems from the two names, but also from their political implications. As most people are tired of referring back to the hidden message behind the names, U Toh Reh said "literature is not politics" to separate the script from the associated political issues. At least the participants did not perceive the script and ethnic language education discussion as a phase of political national reconciliation. Rather, they tried to avoid the political implications as much as possible by using the name Kyebogyi, which is neither pro-government Kayah nor anti-government Karenni. However, no matter how much the script is depoliticized, the state's governing mentality is still present, due to the governing power's notion that one nation should have one language.

Literature education: Textbooks

The literature and cultural committees (*sapei hhi' yincêihmu komiti*) of each ethnic group organizes language education through teacher training and textbook editing, among other aspects. Salem-Gervais and Raynaud (2020, 112) pointed out that the literature and cultural committee names, both in Burmese and English, are slightly misleading. Among a variety of cultural activities that they carry out, their focus tends to be on literacy rather than literature. This is partially correct, as these committees mainly implement language education, but the statement undermines their role by implying that their focus is mainly on literacy education. For instance, on 18 July 2013, the KnLCC noted that "from ancient times, the Kayah nation has had its own literature (*sapei*) and culture, and from generation to generation they have sought to preserve it without a suitable writing system." They used the term literature beyond teaching script and language, as it involves more than writing and reading.

In 2013, just after the script was approved for teaching, the committee prepared a Kyebogyi script textbook by translating Burmese textbooks that were used in elementary school Burmese classes (Fig. 1). However, this was not an easy process, as the order of consonants is different, making it impossible to translate the text entirely. Also, once the fully translated text was available for students, they found it boring because they had already learned all the stories in the Burmese class textbooks. Thus, the new textbooks contained original stories and instructional guides (Fig. 2). For instance, a famous lake in Kayah State replaced the sea in one of the stories, due to the land-based nature of the state.

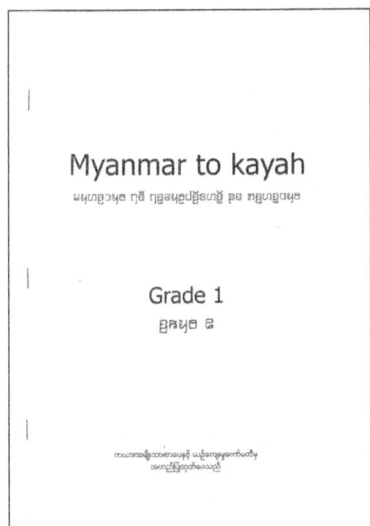

Figure 1. Textbook translated from Burmese.

Figure 2. Newly compiled textbook.

Before the script's official approval, it was unofficially taught using textbooks brought from refugee camps in Thailand (Fig. 3). Refugees who voluntarily returned to their homeland provided training to voluntary participants for approximately two weeks. The Finnish Refugee Council, a Finnish NGO that supported the refugee camps from 2011 to 2014, sponsored the campaign and played a crucial role in developing the procedural knowledge to teach the script and textbooks to the refugees (Finnish Refugee Council 2015). This knowledge was imported to Kayah State, and teachers were trained to develop the appropriate skills and capabilities to teach the Kyebogyi language. One of the training textbooks used was *Kayah Li Heritage: Kayah's Proverbs, Classic Songs, and Dances* (Richard Thu Ra Htu and Tin Nilar Aye 2018), written in Kyebogyi, Burmese and English, and edited based on field research interviews with the Kayah elderly, as well as the intellectuals in Kayah State and Thailand. It was published by *Deeku,* a term that derives from a traditional Kayah festival held in August or September, in which the people pray for a good harvest to pacify spirits. It is also celebrated as a Karenni traditional festival in refugee camps in Thailand to strengthen family unity and Karenni togetherness.

Deeku was established in the United States, where most of the Karenni refugees resettled from the camps in Thailand. These resettled refugees formed the organization after the collapse of Lehman Brothers in 2008 that caused high unemployment rates among the Karenni refugees. At that time, volunteers among the Karenni community in Texas sought an opportunity to build solidarity and to find ways to help each other. On 1 January 2011, 30 representatives from Dallas, Austin, Amarillo, Houston, San Antonio and Fort Worth first met in Houston for a two-day conference and formed the Karenni Community of Texas (subsequently renamed *Deeku*). The organization's first purpose is to help Karenni families living in Texas and Karenni (Kayah) State, and the second is to preserve, promote and build the Karenni identity. As with many resettled refugees, the Karenni were uprooted, suffered a loss of identity and questioned who they were. This sense of marginality also overlapped with the situation in their homeland, the smallest state in Myanmar. Although they self-identified as Karenni-Americans, the term Karenni was just a political consciousness constructed in the refugee camps in Thailand, another place were they felt uprooted and could not call home. For these reasons, their imagined homeland was Kayah State and evidently not the refugee camps.

Figure 3. Karenni textbook used in refugee camps in Thailand.
(*right*) **Figure 4**. Training textbook published by *Deeku*.

With regard to the aforementioned textbook, for refugees resettled in the United States it is used to maintain the political and collective identity of the Karenni, who remain in a marginal position.

Specifically, as the first generation of resettled refugees is concerned that the next generation will forget their ethnic origins, the textbook is expected to help children to remember their origins and maintain a sense of belonging to the Karenni people.[7] For the Kayah people in Myanmar, the textbook's aim is literary education, including reading and writing, as well as learning culture and traditions and Kayah songs, dances and old stories.

Learning one's own language

The Kayah language is largely divided into eastern and western dialects, but there are also differences among villages. Although teachers can verbally communicate, they must practice and master Kyebogyi pronunciation and its standard form. Thus, the teachers hold regular training sessions to practice pronunciation and writing the Kyebogyi language, as not all instructors are familiar with these notions. While they have a sense of belonging as Kayah, when it comes to language education they need to master the specific Kayah language by repeatedly practicing reading aloud. As one of the goals of language education, they hope to use their mother tongue in the classroom to explain what they have learned, but to teach, practice and embody the language requires significant efforts on their part.

As in the case of Karen, over the years scholars have pondered who the Karen are (Keyes 1979) and the sense of belonging as a Karen, as their linguistic diversity sometimes results in differences between language and ethnic identity. Establishing and teaching a particular language for a particular ethnic group takes place in the context of political ethnicity-building, such as the KNPP's emphasis on producing an education system for the Karenni language. However, this movement to accept a specific dialect as a standard language does not include political purposes, at least for the participants, even though it may have a political impact. At this time, the script and language do not represent the core of the nation-state, as discussed by Smith (1991), but new inventions.

For subsequent generations, this script might become a Kayah *ethnie,* defined as a human population or a collective cultural unit with shared ancestry, myths, histories, cultures, territories and solidarity; and representing an emotion, a form of expression, an identity, a symbol and a code for communicating that precedes modern national units and emotions (Smith 1991, 14). What is clear at this time is that even though this is their own ethnic language, it is still in the practicing and embodying phase, as if they were learning a language stemming from other ethnic groups. Thus, the anaphora relationship between formulated language and specific language acquisition does not necessarily correlate. Furthermore, as discussed in the next section, the language does not constitute one nation and is not linked to the national reconciliation. The Kayah community, illustrated by this script movement, is constitutively heterogeneous. Therefore, becoming an *ethnie* is their far-reaching dream.

Ethnic language and state building

Ethnic language education and national reconciliation

Ethnic language education is expected to extend rights to non-Burman ethnic groups that have been suppressed in the name of the Burmanization policy and to lead to national reconciliation, the provision of educational opportunities, and the preservation of minority languages and cultures (Pon Nya Mon 2014; Wong 2017). It should also empower marginalized ethnic minorities and facilitate their political participation, while retaining their languages and cultures. Salem-Gervais and Raynaud (2020, 12) noted that improving ethnic minority children's access to education would not only preserve linguistic and cultural diversity, but also contribute to national reconciliation.

However, such a reconciliation would essentially be based on defined nations or ethnic groups. This imagined ethnicity, from the perspectives of the ethnonational elite, only partially reflects the complex realities. Researchers must examine the situation not only in terms of its political nature, but also in accordance with the local context. Accordingly, Myanmar's nation-building is often discussed on the political basis of reconciliation between the government and the EAOs, but as demonstrated above, the local people do not perceive ethnic language education as a phase of national political reconciliation.

Culture is used politically, but not every culture has a political character. In fact, the people who worked on the script's dissemination had tried to separate it from politics. At least at this point, ethnic language education has no political reconciliation power, but merely holds a symbolic meaning, as it is in its development phase and is permitted on the basis of the Burmese language's predominance. As the EAOs have not reached a peace agreement and are still seeking an equal relationship with Burman organizations, it is clear that language education does not bring about political reconciliation. Indeed, it is too early to determine the consequences, but the situation can be referred to as diversity domesticated by the government.

The position of minority languages

Previous case studies of other ethnic groups, Mon and Karen, suggest a particular language education model. Lall and South noted that the Mon National School system might be a model for a more decentralized and federalized approach to education (Lall and South 2014; South and Lall 2016). In contrast, they highlighted that the Karen education regime has been associated with armed opposition groups so needs to be reconsidered, and suggested that they follow the Mon education system (Lall and South 2014). Throughout its history, Myanmar has experienced the linguistic hegemony of the Burman language and culture, particularly over the past half-century. The current reform period represents a possible counter-hegemonic movement, as previously marginalized ethnic groups seek to advance within the field of education and language (Lall and South 2018).

Similarly, Kelly (2018) argued that the invention of ethnic languages can be a resistance resource. This notion was based on Scott, who asserted that hill people rely on slash-and-burn agriculture and hunting, and have no shame in their illiteracy, because they intentionally do not follow the norms of civilization in lowland states and become "barbaric" of their own accord. This enables them to distance themselves from state power, geographically and culturally, and to escape from the state and have social autonomy. To be illiterate, or abandon letters, is also a part of this art of not being governed (Scott 2009).

Kayah people, like other ethnic groups, such as the Karen and Lafu, have myths that emphasize the "backwardness" of illiterate minorities that do not have their own letters. Specifically, the Kayah, as well as other ethnic groups, have a myth about a lost book that goes as follows: There once was a leather book containing words written by God. However, a dog ate it and then the chicken ate the dog's droppings. At that time, persons could communicate with animals. When one individual asked about the lost book, the chicken replied that God's words were embedded in the bones of its feet. Therefore, when Kayah people have to make a decision on something important, such as the date of traditional festivals, they use chicken bones for fortune telling. Losing books with knowledge also represents the backwardness of these people. The traditional chief in Kayah State, called *Sopya* (*Sawbwa* in Shan), came from outside the Kayah community and had literacy skills. Reading, writing and a knowledge of letters were the sources of the leader's charismatic power (Lehman 1967).

Scott (2009) interpreted this "backwardness" positively as an artful way of not being governed, but Kelly (2018) argued that Scott's provocative suggestion overlooked multiple examples of "found writing" from within those same Zomian populations. In fact, among the upland groups of Southeast Asia, stories of lost writing are occasionally given narrative resolutions through inspired rediscoveries of indigenous literacy. Thus, Kelly highlighted that the documentary records reveal no fewer than nine reinventions of writing in Zomian Southeast Asia since the 1840s: the Lake script of Karen, the two Kyebogyi scripts, the Pau Cin Hau script of Chin, the Khom script of Jruq, and the four Hmong scripts. In almost all cases, the reinvention of writing took place at the hands of charismatic leaders with radical political agendas, founded on the revelation and diffusion of new scripts. These new state-like configurations allowed them to be recognized as literate entities, while the language remained illegible to the states they opposed. As a resistance strategy, the introduction of rebel scripts gave impetus to the new movements, investing their advocates with authority and rendering marginalized languages visible (Kelly 2018, 3).

These writings were strategically reappropriated among other markers of statehood to build new visions of society that were recognizable, yet illegible to their lowland antagonists (Kelly 2018, 14). Scott used the term "legibility" to refer to the state's assessments of the population and way of grasping them as human capital, while at the same time controlling the land and appropriate crops. Kelly paraphrased Scott's perspective and argued that script revival makes minorities recognizable as ethnic groups with their own scripts. At the same time, the scripts are illegible for the state, because the majority are illiterate in these particular scripts, and as a result cannot assess, grasp, control and appropriate minorities' minds and literature.

Overall, the arguments that the Mon case can serve as a model for other ethnic groups to follow, that ethnic languages are "counter-hegemonic," or that they can serve as a resistance resource against the state, do not apply to the Kayah case. Compared to the relatively homogeneous Mon language, Kayah contains large dialect differences, even among the same Kayah, as they must practice the Kyebogyi dialect. Furthermore, considering the entire state, various literature committees have begun to provide ethnic language education not only in Kayah, but also in Kayan, Kayow, Bwe and Yintale.[8] Thus, it is difficult to simply adapt the Mon situation as a model (Kubo 2021).

Although Kelly (2018) also discussed the Kyebogyi script as an example, he overlooked that Kyebogyi is neither Karenni nor Kayah, but a depoliticized ethnic language. Therefore, it cannot be clearly positioned as being counter-hegemonic. He focused only on the resistance aspect of ethnic languages and ignored the naming process of Kyebogyi. Also, as this script is recognizable, yet illegible for the state, it symbolizes the people's autonomy with regard to state governance. However, from a local perspective it is also recognizable, yet illegible, for the Kayah, as most are illiterate in this alphabet. As Scott used the terms "legible" and "illegible" to describe a form of state control and a mode of escaping this control, respectively, it is more accurate to refer to the Kayah situation as illiteracy, not illegibility. This script is a language that must be acquired through training.[9] A script's political, cultural and personal meaning is heterogeneous, but all constitute and characterize an assemblage of the Kayah community.

In abstract and symbolic aspects, it can be analyzed as an element of political reconciliation, a resistance resource, or a source of ethnic autonomy. On the other hand, at the individual and concrete levels, literature education, which is conducted separately from politics, is a starting point, but neither are those who perceive language as apart from politics free from the state's governance imposing "one language to one nation."

Kayah (Karenni) Community as *communitas*

To conclude, this chapter examines the type of community assemblage formed by the Kayah (Karenni) people. The Kyebogyi script is neither completely inclusive of nor resistant to the state, because the movement's created communities are *communitas* (Turner 1969). Accordingly, Tanabe (2016, 14) considered two ideal models of community movements: *communitas* and reflectivity. Some communities and community movements emerge at the confluence of liminality and *communitas* that arises from the marginality of a larger structure under a current political, economic and cultural context. Marginality could be one of the conditions from which an assemblage of individuals or component parts arise (Tanabe 2016, 9). With regard to the present context, the KNPP political movement initially constructed Karenni identity as an anti-structure-oriented movement. The experience and condition of being a refugee, neither Thai nor Burmese, empowered the Karenni movement, but it lost its political legitimacy when it crossed the border to its homeland, the Kayah state. While the symbolic political importance was lost, as in the case of *Deeku,* the Kyebogyi language textbook shows that it remains important for refugees resettling in third countries. Even after resettlement, people who are put in a marginal position still have their Karenni identity, but this identity is characterized by liminality, existing neither here nor there.

In recent years, the script has been used online. In fact, as many refugees are resettled in third countries, such as the United States, Australia and Finland, SNSs have become tools for connecting refugees dispersed around the world, as well as linking them to their homeland, the Kayah state. It remains a question whether cyberspace will create a new type of imagined community.

On the other hand, the current movement to promote the Kyebogyi language reveals a process of retransforming antistructure into structure. The Kyebogyi script was incorporated into the state as one of the official ethnic scripts. While the script symbolizes the autonomy of Kayah people and is recognizable yet illegible to the state, most of Kayah people are still illiterate. Therefore, the script does not serve to form a single community within the state. Overall, this chapter has discussed the asymmetric relations between ideals and practical events that arise in the process of this restructuring, clarifying the Kayah's community assemblage formed by group affinity.

Acknowledgement

I would like to express my appreciation to all people in Thailand, Myanmar and third countries resettled from refugee camps in Thailand. I would like to pay special thanks to them for their hospitality during my fieldwork.

Endnotes: Ethnic Language Education and State-building in Myanmar

1. This paper discusses an aspect of state-building before the coup d'état in Myanmar in February 2021. It discusses the community movements that have emerged since the previous military regime and following the democratic reform in 2011. It is impossible to predict how the situation will change in the future. However, the following two points will remain central issues to discussions on Myanmar: how people confront state power and the relationship between the ethnic Burman majority and other minorities. This paper will hopefully contribute to the consideration of these issues.

2. Although earlier studies have examined ethnic and religious diversity, these studies have not considered relations within the ethnic groups themselves. One exception is Sadan's work on Kachin (Sadan 2013). The author examines intra-ethnic relationships of Karenni (Kubo 2021). The prospects for peace negotiations between the government and the EAOs became increasingly bleak following the coup d'état by the Myanmar Army in February 2021.

3. However, the languages of smaller ethnic groups were taught only in Buddhist monasteries and Christian churches since some local state governments in minority areas dominated by major ethnic groups did not care to promote the cultures of smaller groups (Kyaw Yin Hlaing 2007, 156).

4. KnLCC provides language education in Kayah State. In refugee camps in Thailand, the Karenni Relations and Culture Development Committee (KnRCDC) has been trained in the script. The KnRCDC had been teaching the Karenni language informally in the Kayah State even before it was approved as an official script. The KnRCDC's counterpart in the state was the Kayah Literacy and Culture Committee (KLCC) (Finnish Refugee Council 2015), but the organization's English names are not consistent; KnLCC and KLCC are likely to be the same organization. This organization is sometimes translated as The Kayah Nationalities Literacy and Culture Committee or Kayah Literature and Culture Committee.

5. The author obtained this statement during a survey conducted in 2013. The statement was released in three languages: Burmese, Karenni and English. For the full statement, see Kubo (2021).

6. The meeting minutes also clarified that the government approved Mii Reh's script, based on the Karenni script, and that the letters and tone symbol replacements, invented by Khu Hteh Bu Peh, created the writing system (Meeting Minutes 2013).

7. For the Karenni identity of the refugees who have resettled in the United States, see Duran (2017).

8. A project to translate the Bible into the languages of various ethnic groups has been implemented in the Kayah State. This project has nothing to do with ethnic language education. The Old Testament and the New Testament are translated into Kayah, Kayow, Manumanow and Yintale languages. The Seed Company in the United States, which facilitated translation of the Bible into languages around the world, supported this project.

9. The case of the Shan script also indicates that many peasants were illiterate, and it is important to consider disjuncture between nation-building projects and the notion of local people (Ferguson 2008).

References

Anderson, Benedict. 1983. *Imagined communities: Reflections on the origin and spread of nationalism.* London and New York: Verso.

Bamforth, Vicky, Steven Lanjouw, and Graham Mortimer. 2000. *Conflict and Displacement in Karenni: The Need for Considered Approaches.* Bangkok: Burma Ethnic Research Group.

Duran, Chatwara Suwannamai. 2017. *Language and Literacy in Refugee Families.* London: Palgrave Macmillan.

Finnish Refugee Council. 2015. *Final Report for Thailand intervention (2009–2014).* Helsinki.

Ferguson, Jane M. 2008. "Revolutionary Scripts: Shan Insurgent Media Practice at the Thai-Burma Border." In *Political Regimes and the Media in Asia*, edited by Krishna Sen and Terence Lee, 106–121. London: Routledge.

Hall, Stuart. 1996. "Introduction: Who Needs Identity?" In *Questions of Cultural Identity*, edited by Stuart Hall and Paul du Gay, 1–17. London: SAGE Publications.

Richard Thu Ra Htu and Tin Nilar Aye, eds. 2018. *Kayah Li Heritage: Kayah's Proverbs, Classic Songs, and Dances.* Loikaw: DeeKu.

Kelly, Piers. 2018. "The Art of Not Being Legible. Invented Writing Systems as Technologies of Resistance in Mainland Southeast Asia." *Terrain-Anthropologie & Sciences Humaines* 70: 1–24.

Keyes, Charles F., ed. 1979. *Ethnic Adaptation and Identity: The Karen on the Thai Frontier with Burma.* Philadelphia: Institute for the Study of Human Issues.

Khin Khin Aye and Peter Secombe. 2014. "Language, Education and Nation-Building in Myanmar." In *Language, Education and Nation-Building: Assimilation and Shift in Southeast Asia*, edited by Peter Sercombe and Ruanni Tupas, 148–164. London: Palgrave Macmillan.

Kubo, Tadayuki. 2021. "Ethnocentrism or National Reconciliation: Rethinking Ethnic Relations and the History of Karenni." *Journal of Burma Studies* 25(2): 155–191.

Kyaw Yin Hlaing. 2007. "The Politics of Language Policy in Myanmar: Imagining Togetherness, Practising Difference?" In *Language, Nation and Development in Southeast Asia*, edited by Lee Hock Guan and Leo Suryadinata, 150–180. Singapore: ISEAS–Yusof Ishak Institute.

Lall, Marie and Ashley South. 2014. "Comparing Models of Non-State Ethnic Education in Myanmar: The Mon and Karen National Education Regimes." *Journal of Contemporary Asia* 44(2): 298–321.

———. 2018. "Power Dynamics of Language and Education Policy in Myanmar's Contested Transition." *Comparative Education Review* 62(4): 482–502.

Lehman, Frederic K. 1967. "Burma: Kayah Society as a Function of the Shan-Burma-Karen Context." In *Contemporary Change in Traditional Societies.*

Vol. 2 *Asian Rural Societies*, edited by Julian H. Stewart, 3–104. Urbana, IL: University of Illinois Press.

Meeting Minutes. 2013. *Hkùhni' epyila 20 ye'ne nanne' 10:00 nayiahkyein kayâhpû hni'hkyîn athîntotwin pyulou'dhô kayâ amyôuthâ sapei paûnsîmu nyihnaîn asîawêi hma'tân* (Meeting coordinated by Kayah Literature Association, held in Kayah Baptist Association at 10 AM on April 20, 2013).

Ministry of Information. 2008. Constitution of the Republic of the Union of Myanmar. https://www.wipo.int/edocs/lexdocs/laws/en/mm/mm009en.pdf

Moe Moe Htwe. 2011. *Karenni Sekai, Syuukyou, Sinkou* (Religion and Faith in Karenni). In *Myanmar Gaisetsu* (Overview of Myanmar), edited by Toshikatsu Ito, 354–368. Tokyo: Mekong.

Pon Nya Mon. 2014. Education Reform and National Reconciliation in Burma. https://www.salweeninstitute.org/uploads/1/2/6/3/12630752/ed_reform_and_national_reconciliation_1.pdf.

Sadan, Mandy. 2013. *Being and Becoming Kachin: Histories Beyond the State in the Borderworlds of Burma*. Oxford: Oxford University Press.

Salem-Gervais, Nicolas Salem and Mael Raynaud. 2020. *Teaching Ethnic Minority Languages in Government Schools and Developing the Local Curriculum: Elements of Decentralization in Language-in-Education Policy*. Yangon: Konrad-Adenauer Stiftung, Ltd.

Scott, James. 2009. *The Art of Not Being Governed: An Anarchist History of Upland Southeast Asia*. New Haven: Yale University Press.

Smith, Anthony D. 1991. *The Ethnic Origins of Nations*. Oxford: Blackwell Publishers.

South, Ashley and Marie Lall. 2016. Language, Education, and the Peace Process in Myanmar. *Contemporary Southeast Asia* 38(1): 128–153.

Tanabe, Shigeharu. 2016. "Introduction: Community of Potential." In *Community of Potential: Social Assemblage in Thailand and Beyond*, edited by Shigeharu Tanabe, 1–18. Bangkok: Silkworm Books.

Thawnghmung, Ardeth Maung. 2013. *The "Other" Karen in Myanmar: Ethnic Minorities and the Struggle without Arms*. Lanham: Lexington Books.

The Republic of the Union of Myanmar. 2015. *The 2014 Myanmar Population and Housing Census-Kayah State Census Report* Volume 3-B. Myanmar: Department of Population, Ministry of Immigration and Population.

Turner, Victor. 1969. *The Ritual Process: Structure and Anti-Structure*. London: Routledge and Kegan Paul.

Wong, Mary Shepard. 2017. "Linguistic, Religious, and Ethnic Identities as Pathways to Peace: Views from Eight Lisu, Karen, Kachin, and Chin Seminary Teachers in Myanmar." *Asian Englishes* 19(3): 211–227.

Part 3

Networks and Globalization: Land, Life, and Movements

Chapter 7

THE INTEGRATED AGRICULTURE AND COMMUNITY MOVEMENT IN NORTHEAST THAILAND

NOBUKO KOYA

Introduction

Looking back on Thai agricultural policy over the past several decades, two aspects are to be keenly grasped: modernization/industrialization under the influence of foreign multinational entities, and pursuing alternative agricultural methods. The former has been implemented on a nationwide scale with political backup since the 1960s, while the latter has mostly appeared in a sporadic/spontaneous manner in rural areas since than the 1980s. In general, the former trend contributed to national economic growth, but it has brought about many other problems directly to local farmers, such as uncertainty in their lives due to monocultivation of cash crops that depend on the market economy and degradation of land and forest. In this situation, a movement to transform "agriculture for selling" into "agriculture for living" has occurred among villagers and local non-governmental organizations in Northeast Thailand.

The following sections explore the rise and expansion of integrated agriculture in Inpaeng Network as a community movement. The concept of a community movement is conceived in the form of "assemblage" (Deleuze and Guattari) that "is a dynamic and contingent configuration that emerges through articulation of diverse forces" and "consists of a configuration of heterogeneous forces, institutions, individuals, groups, things, and nature where its constituent parts have significant roles and retain a certain autonomy" (Tanabe 2016, 3). With this in mind, particular attention is paid to the word "assemblage" in actual involvement and engagement of people, things and circumstances in the course of that specific agricultural movement. As such, agricultural practice in Inpaeng is considered as a community movement in the multi-layered nexus of local, regional and state entities and the actors in the global capital market.

Integrated agriculture in Thailand

From agriculture for selling to agriculture for living

Scholarly works on Thai agricultural policy in the second half of the 20th century have generally referred to the shift toward more industrial and export-oriented development in the 1960s, which opened the pathway for multinational corporations to expand their business through single-crop plantations (Darlington 2019, 2; Delcore 2004, 36; Seubsman et al. 2013, 57).

Since the 1980s, the trend has accelerated, and contract farming has rapidly become popular in Thailand (Suehiro 1993, 161). With this type of farming, farmers have contracted to sell their products to export trading companies or processing manufacturers (e.g., broiler production, shrimp raising, or cultivation of sugarcane and pineapple for canning). Contract farming has been brought about by agribusiness groups that have received political support from the government, financial support from local commercial banks, and support from multinational companies and foreign trading companies for technical aspects and market development. In addition, such farming has led to the growth of agribusiness groups in the short term. With regard to political support, during and after the 4th National Economic and Social Development Plan (1977–1981), the Thai government began to encourage investment in the agroindustry for exports and offered tax benefits to agribusiness groups (Suehiro 1993, 158–160). However, this resulted in an increase in risks related to farm management, with farmers concentrating on particular kinds of production.

These business actors, who promoted unsustainable modernized agriculture, pushed Thai farmers into globalized commercialization of agriculture. The farmers were subjected to an elaborate mechanism of exploitation. Susan Darlington mentions agro-chemical companies as actors that "provided farmers with seeds, fertilizers, herbicides and pesticides often as loans to be repaid at harvest . . . Seed corporations set strict standards for the quality of the produce they would buy from farmers to whom they lent seeds and fertilizers. If farmers could not meet these standards, they slipped into severe debt" (Darlington 2019, 3). In particular, this vicious cycle was damaging to the ecology in northern and northeastern Thailand because farmers with heavy debts tended to cut down forests to expand their fields (Darlington 2019, 10).

In these circumstances, a movement to transform "agriculture for selling" into "agriculture for living" developed among villagers and local non-governmental organizations. Integrated farming and the idea of developing a village based on "community culture" have spread and have been actively practiced since the late 1980s. The Inpaeng Network, the focus of this chapter, also began its activities around that time.

New theory farming or sufficiency economy

In parallel with the undesirable effects of modernization and globalization of Thai agriculture, since the 1980s local NGOs have expressed concern over the official direction of farming and advocated an alternative way.

Henry Delcore notes the concept of alternative agriculture (*kasetakam thang lueak*) that subsumes terms and ideas of agroforestry (*wannakaset*), integrated agriculture (*kaset phasomphasan*), and other ecological farming methods in the context of the rural work by Thai NGOs (Delcore 2004, 36–37). The term sustainable agriculture (UNDP 2012, 26) can also be included in this group. The primary drive of the NGOs inclined toward these movements was a general dissatisfaction with "state-led capitalist development." Therefore, the objectives and principles of the NGOs' alternative projects stood opposite to mainstream formal agriculture.

In this context, the word "integration" is explained as "the intensive and diversified cultivation of a limited area of land with environmentally friendly methods and reliance on domestic labor" (Delcore 2004, 37). In technical terms, "integrated farming" refers to combining the production of crops, fruit, vegetables and livestock. Delcore notes that the significance of diversification is the interconnection between different activities (ibid.).

The desirable goals of these activities were the use of domestic resources, avoidance of debt and production of "household consumption with only a secondary emphasis on commercial production" (ibid.). The background principles that supported these methods and goals were such ideals as "environmental awareness, emphasis on household self-reliance, a wariness of the market, and the struggle against the perceived atomization of village society caused by commercialization and competitive individualism" (ibid.).

Curiously, the set of principles or objectives of alternative agriculture, which are anti-authority in essence, has been officially stipulated and adopted in a passionate manner since the mid-1990s. This broad shift in policy orientation was traced in the 8th National

Economic and Social Development Plan (1997–2001) and the drafting of the 1997 constitution, "both of which conceded greater political autonomy and the sustainable management of natural resources to local communities" (Rado 2019, 9). From a macro perspective, this period was acknowledged as a severe economic crisis from 1997 onward.[1] This disastrous blow from the global economy severely impacted the Thai collective consciousness, both of policymakers and ordinary citizens who lost their jobs and had to return to their homes in rural areas.

In such social context, on the day before his birthday on 5 December 1997 during the economic crisis, His Majesty King Bhumibol (1927–2016) showed the direction the Thai people should take by presenting the philosophy of a "sufficiency economy" (*sethakit pho pian*). The word "sufficiency" has been explained as "moderation and due consideration in all modes of conduct, as well as the need for sufficient protection from internal and external shocks" (Mongsawad 2010, 127) and "resilience through risk reduction and management . . . ability to endure shocks and adjust to external change, sometimes translated as 'self-immunity'" (UNDP 2012, 25). Protection, resilience and self-immunity against negative shocks and risks brought about by rapid globalization, clearly suggest the social context in which the King's word was symbolically accepted by various actors, ranging from local farmers to government officials in that period.

However, the King seemed to have predicted the economic outbreak during the preceding years. In 1994, he unveiled a model of a self-reliant family farm and began experimenting with the model on a small plot in Saraburi Province. The model was based on a 2.4-hectare holding, which was the median for smallholders in much of the country. This was divided into four zones: 30% for a pond to store 19,000 cubic meters of water for cultivation in the dry season and to raise fish; 30% to cultivate sufficient rice for year-round home consumption; 30% for other crops and fruit; and, 10% for housing, animal husbandry and other activities. Soil fertilization and weed and pest control were carried out by natural methods (UNDP 2007, 28).

At first sight, this model farm appeared to be a rejection of the market, but this was far from the case. The model farm was expected to create a surplus beyond household consumption, and this surplus could be exchanged in the local market (ibid). The model of farming suggested by the King was called the "New Theory (*thitsadi mai*)" in Thailand. According to the work of Misui et al. (2008), in which they reported on the food self-sufficiency and income of farm households engaging in New Theory farming in Singburi Province, many people were using their land for crops and fruit following the concept of agroforestry. They also reported that the main technique was organic farming with circulation of organic resources on the same farm, although New Theory farming does not promote the adoption of any particular farming techniques. (Various farming techniques, such as organic, modern and "natural," could be adopted under New Theory farming) (Misui et al. 2008, 47).

Since the economic crisis of 1997, New Theory farming has been largely promoted, taught and practiced in elementary and junior high schools in Thailand. It could be said that this way of farming was not new, as it mirrored agriculture by the subsistence method in the late 1980s. The promotion of integrated farming was an extension of attempts by dedicated farmers and development monks (Suehiro 2009, 136–137).

In adopting the sufficiency economy approach, practical guidelines have generally shared the following three stages (UNDP 2012, 26): (1) developing a self-reliant family farm to supply enough food for the family's own consumption; (2) selling surplus through community cooperatives to gain greater efficiency in production and marketing; and, (3) proper implementation of stage 2 in each community, with interaction among communities in larger-scale activities, such as selling commodities and gaining bargaining leverage with middlemen and end markets.

After the King's speech, the sufficiency economy idea was included in the 9th National Economic and Social Development Plan (2002–2006) as a guiding principle for national development and management. Furthermore, in 2005 the Ministry of Interior adopted the philosophy of sufficiency economy as a basic framework to set up development programs based on the "bottom-up approach," which constitutes cutting down on domestic expenses, increasing income by supporting local enterprises and industries, encouraging local saving, promoting local leadership and community-based programs, protecting and preserving the environment, and promoting social capital, such as local welfare programs and cooperatives (UNDP 2012, 30). Rado (2019, 11) compared the concept of the sufficiency economy with earlier National Economic and Social Development Plans, pointing out that the sufficiency economy weighed more than earlier plans on the significant role of traditional wisdom in achieving holistic and long-term growth and acknowledging rural communities and farmers as autonomous actors.

Technically, these types of agriculture are primarily called alternative agriculture, sustainable agriculture, integrated agriculture or New Theory farming. They share the same essence. All these methods focus on the farmers' autonomous subsistence and recovery of the natural environment. The following sections address the works and principles of the Inpaeng Network, which arose in a larger orientation toward alternative methods of agriculture in late 20th century Thailand. This chapter posits that these types of agriculture, which pursue self-sufficient food systems as well as a sustainable environment, including agroforestry, are recognized as a community movement, and examines how they embody assemblage in their practice.

Inpaeng Network

Ethnographic Background: Geographical Features and Ethnicity

The Inpaeng Network covers a wide area in which people have had close relations with the Phu Phan Forest. Today, a large area of the forest is a national park. The Phu Phan National Park is located in the Muang, Phanna Nikhom, Kut Bak and Phu Phan districts of Sakon Nakhon Province and in the Somdet and Huai Phoeng districts of Kalasin Province in Northeast Thailand. In 1972, this area of 669 square kilometers was marked as the seventh national park in Thailand. Later exclusions decreased the total area of the forest to 664.70 square kilometers in 1982 (Office of National Park 2017).

The ethnic population living in this area includes the Tai Yor, Yoy, Lao Isan, Kaloeng, Thai and Phu Tai Tai-speaking groups, and the So Mon-Khmer speaking group. There are also Vietnamese and Chinese residents. The Inpaeng Center is in Bua Village in the Kut Bak district of Sakon Nakhon Province, where almost all villagers are Kaloeng.

According to Schliesinger (2001), Kaloeng is classified as a southwestern branch of the Tai-Kadai language group within the Austro-Tai language family. Although little is known about the origin and history of the Kaloeng, they have adapted to Lao Isan culture. The Kaloeng people tend to live in matrilineal family units. After marriage, the groom moves to the house of his bride's parents. Inheritance is split equally among children, and those who care for the parents in their old age inherit the house. They are Buddhists, but also believe in spirits (Schliesinger 2001, 1–6).

Establishment, development process, and activities

The following description is primarily based on first-hand data from my field research between 2015 and 2019, supplemented by the secondary materials from existing literature on Inpaeng Network by Rado (2013, 2019) and Suksudaj (2010), which were important groundwork for this network. Literature by Istvan Rado thoroughly covers the fiscal and institutional aspects of various activities in the Inpaeng Network. Suksudaj reports the details of both the network's values and its activity in light of the intersection between food security and the local welfare system. In comparison, the following sections provide notes on the direct experiences of Inpaeng members, focusing on their practical wisdom and efforts for autonomy.

In 1986, Mr. A, one of the leaders of the Inpaeng Network, came to Bua Village to study the ethnic culture of the Kaloeng as a college student. This occasion encouraged villagers to talk about their culture, their traditional relationships with the forest and some of the problems they face. According to one villager, around the time that the leader came it became difficult to collect anything to eat because the forest near their village had disappeared. With regard to agriculture as livelihood, they faced such problems as decline in land fertility and increased cost of chemical fertilizers, which were consequences of the monocultivation of such cash crops as cassava.

Some villagers with common problems formed a small group with Mr. A and local scholars and began to change their farming methods. They started integrated farming (*kaset phasomphasan*) to produce food for family consumption and tried to plant rattan (*wai*) in their fields using seeds brought from the forests. Mr. A himself has also engaged in integrated farming in the village and played an important role in the Inpaeng Network.

The term Inpaeng combines the name of the Hindu god "Indra" (In) with *paeng* (to establish). Thus, the term Inpaeng connotes "land or area that has been established by an Indic deity" (Suksudaj 2010, 22). According to Suksudaj (2010, 22), "the name was given in 1990 to this network by Mr. Boasri Srisung, the chair of the Thai-Isaan Foundation. Mr. Boasri visited the network near the Phuphan mountain range and was very impressed by its fertility; the land is incredibly fertile as if it were created and blessed by Lord Indra."

In 1992, the founding members established the Inpaeng Center in Bua Village as an activity center. Inside the meeting hall of the center are the following words: "Phu Phan is life; all friends are power; self-reliance is hope; Inpaeng is for everyone." Local people have used the forest resources of the Phu Phan for generation after generation. Living in the forest is an important part of their identity. Inpaeng, from the outset, was conceived to coalesce ethical orientation, pragmatic agriculture and local identity through generations. It can be viewed as a contemporary agricultural movement that fits well within the frame of community movement.

The Inpaeng Network has gradually expanded and spans four provinces, around 900 villages, and more than 100,000 members (UNDP 2007, 38), who are not only Kaloeng, but also from other ethnic groups.[2] It features a vague contour of membership identity, as Rado (2013, 187) noted: "It is hard to make a clear distinction between Inpaeng members and non-members: whereas many formal members follow similar livelihood patterns as others in the village, some of those stating not to be involved in the network exhibited views close to the Inpaeng philosophy or entertain relationships with the network." Given the unique and flexible autonomy of the members in the network, further investigation of the Inpaeng way of life remains for inquiry.

The activities of the Inpaeng Network can be divided into four categories: agriculture; the processing and sale of agricultural products,[3] activities concerning learning,[4] and mutual aid funds or savings. In addition, activities include occasional health-related events and a community radio station. Each activity group operates independently, even though the members have cooperative relationships with other groups under the Inpaeng Network.

In the following two sections, I focus on agriculture as a basis of the Inpaeng Network and the processing and sale of agricultural products as one of its activities.

Collaborations with outside institutions

In the 30 years since its inception, the Inpaeng Network has collaborated with many institutions that have financially supported its projects. In terms of large-scale projects, the "Phu Phan Conservation Project" was conducted with funding of 5 million baht over three years, from 1996 to 1998.

Today, the network has its own funds, commonly called "Inpaeng Bank," that supports members' activities. According to Mr. A, the funds provide financial support for each activity through 58 groups, which are located in about 30 sub-districts (*tambon*). Activities include maoberry juice processing, indigo dying and weaving, and rice milling. Of those, 12 to 15 groups have comparatively high profits, and 20 groups have moderate profits. Some groups, however, end in debt.

The profitable groups return some of their earnings to the fund, in which money is saved as benefits for the Inpaeng Network's leaders. Approximately 200–240 people have the right to receive benefits when they are ill or in the event of death. These beneficiaries perform many roles, such as dealing with visitors from outside the network, so the fund serves as compensation for the network's leaders. The secretariat of the Inpaeng Network does not order or require the groups to do anything as part of their management; instead, they give advice and help as needed. The issue of accepting new members also depends on each group.

Regarding the question of which institution was the most important to the Inpaeng Network for these 30 years, Mr. A referred to three types of institutions: those that provide support by building the network's foundations (for example, the Agricultural Land Reform Office (*Samnakngan kanpathirup thidin phuea kasetakam: So.Po.Ko.*); those that support specific subjects during a particular period (for example, the SCG Foundation); and those that collaborate with a particular activity depending on the current situation (for example, Ratchamongkon University for herbal medicine, and Biodiversity-Based Economy Development (BEDO) for activities with potential to be developed for business, such as indigo cloth and maoberry juice).

On the other hand, some leaders explained that they had not recently received any financial support from outside institutions because they needed to spend time on paperwork and were more or less dedicated to institutional, although they would prefer to practice their own agricultural programs freely and autonomously.

Integrated farming

Agriculture is the dominant activity of the Inpaeng Network. Villagers make organic fertilizer, grow saplings and trees from seeds collected from the Phu Phan Forest. The members practice integrated farming (or agroforestry), in which they grow various kinds of plants collectively,[5] following the nature of the forest. Some people have stopped the monocultivation of cash crops, such as cassava, which is "agriculture for selling" (*kaset phuea setakit*). They receive everything they need from their integrated fields, such as food, medicinal herbs and timber for constructing houses, and they can generate income by selling extra products. Their efforts are regarded as a successful cases consistent with the philosophy of the sufficiency economy, and many people have visited the Inpaeng Center to learn from them (UNDP 2007).

Here, I record the views and experiences of some of the integrated farming pioneers.

Beginning of the practice "make to live, make to eat": The case of Mr. B

Mr. B is in his 70s. He is one of the initial 13 members of the Inpaeng Network and its first representative. When I asked him why he started the Inpaeng Network, he told me about the situation at that time. Farmers were suffering from debt so planted cash crops, such as kenaf, sugarcane, cassava and rubber. They sold their products according to prices determined by the buyer.

Mr. B himself planted kenaf for three years and subsequently planted cassava for the same amount of time. He incurred debts to grow cassava, spiraling to 40,000 baht in three years because the price of cassava fell, and for fertilizer that was needed for the fields. Moreover, it had become difficult to collect food from forests because of their degradation due to cultivation. If there was not enough food, he needed to earn money to purchase commodities. When money was not available, he had to borrow. For this reason, Mr B decided to begin integrated farming. He began to "make to live, make to eat (*het yu, het kin*)" in the same way as his parents and grandparents used to. In this way, he could provide basic goods, housing and herbal medicines in addition to food.

Thus, the Inpaeng Network was initiated to solve these problems. The prerequisite to join the group was to plant at least 20 kinds of crops to secure food. Since the late 1980s, Mr. B sometimes goes to the Phu Phan Forest to gather seeds with his children and has planted them in his field. Now, one of his daughters has succeeded her father and grows many kinds of saplings to sell at home.

Mr. B's story shows a typical case of how the Inpaeng leaders were aware of the surrounding problems so took the initiative. They sought to solve their problems and find alternative ways of living by rethinking traditional knowledge and their relationship with nature. He said, "We are not rich; however, we are not poor either (*bo ruai tae bo chon*). We do not own a lot, but are not in poverty because we can eat properly. This is the point. You first need to change your basic way of thinking (to move into such a new agriculture). This is very difficult to determine... We should belong to the mountain and follow what our ancestors did. Following others led us to suffering."

Experience of integrated farming: The case of Ms. C

By describing the case of Ms. C, I intend to highlight the characteristics of integrated farming in this community. She is in her late 60s. She met Mr. A in 1987 and then visited a rattan nursery in the Waritchaphum district of the province. After the field trip, 13 of the 30 participants formed a group, which led to the establishment of the Inpaeng Network, and they began to work together.

They gathered the fallen rattan seeds in the forests and planted them in their nursery beds, and then transplanted the seedlings to black plastic pots after approximately six months. The Inpaeng Network supports the cost of plastic pots. She also sold rattan saplings to other people. Ms. C said it was very difficult to raise rattan and that their income was low in the beginning, but the rattan she grew later provided enough money to feed herself. Rattan can be sold throughout the year. Her income from selling rattan shoots varies from day to day. Ms. C simply sells rattan to people coming to her garden and not at any particular outlet. Moreover, she sometimes exchanges agricultural products with her friends in the Inpaeng Network. When her friends bring her rice, she gives them rattan, maoberry and other products from her garden in return.

According to Ms. D, who was one of the leaders of the Inpaeng Network and visited Ms. C together with the author, such exchanges of rattan and other items has been taking place for years. Villagers in Bua sometimes bring rattan from the forest and receive rice in return. Their choice to raise rattan as a source of income in the Inpaeng Network is based on tradition.

Young rattan shoots are used in soups and salads, whereas large ones are mainly used for furniture. Rattan is a relatively expensive agricultural product and is sold for 25–30 baht per bundle. The skin is stripped, and the soft interior is used for food. Rattan soup or *kaeng wai* is often made and served for guests from outside the village as a major local food in this community.

Ms. C said that farmers could plant whatever they wanted in integrated farming. Currently, many kinds of vegetables and fruits grow in her garden for self-consumption, such as bananas, mangos and guava, while rattan and maoberry are harvested as income sources. As for livestock, she currently raises chickens. She used to raise pigs, but quit because the work was tough. Moreover, she is interested in medicinal herbs and plants. For example, she collects a herb called *kamlang suea khrong* (*Ziziphus attopensis Pierre*) from the forest, which is renowned for its efficacy as a revitalizer. She drinks a decoction of it every day.

Ms. C cultivated cassava before planting rattan and engaging in integrated farming. However, it was difficult for her to grow cassava of sufficient value because of invasive grasses. She could not gain enough income from selling cassava. She earned only about 1,500–2,000 baht in the beginning, although she had invested 10,000 baht in cassava cultivation. Ms C earned a maximum of 7,000–10,000 baht. The monocropping of cassava led to poor soil quality, which resulted in insufficient growth. However, she did not want to use chemical fertilizers or herbicides. While seeking an alternative to agriculture for selling or monocropping, Mr. A and Mr. B asked her to go on a field trip with them to observe the rattan nursery in the Waritchaphum district described above. Currently, she never uses chemicals and practices organic farming in her garden, which features rattan and other crops.

According to Ms. C, people growing cassava face many problems today, such as poor soil, stunted growth and the increasing cost of chemical fertilizers. She said, "The more money we put in, the poorer we become. We are not poor when practicing integrated farming. I am free of uncertainty. I am satisfied and happy on an income of 100 or 200 baht per day. I feel free (*sabai chai*). I do not need to seek outside work and I can feed myself throughout life."

Integrated farming is "*kaset phasomphasan*" in Thai. "*Kaset*" means "farmland" or "farming," and "*phasomphasan*" means to "integrate" or "mix." In the members' words, Inpaeng's farming methods literally enacts the concept of assemblage with pragmatic motives. Through long practical research, each farmer finds and creates a unique assemblage of products ranging from grains, vegetables, fruits, herbs and trees to fowls. The assembling pattern is not governed by the network. They plant and raise whatever they want, including various kinds of crops (more than 20 kinds during the early period). Farmers base their choice on their own practice and successive interactions with other farmers.

When I asked Ms. D on the way home from Ms. C's garden about the mixture she features, she mentioned planting wild plants from the forest (*khong pa*) with domesticated plants in the village (*khong ban*) and various kinds of other plants. One of the outstanding features of integrated farming in this community is the ability to acquire a source of income by raising rattan and maoberry, in addition to achieving self-sufficiency. These products from the forest have high value. This is agriculture for living (*kaset phuea chiwit*) based on the traditional knowledge of people who have lived around the Phu Phan Forest.

The processing and sale of agricultural products

Here, I describe activities processing and selling agricultural products in Bua Village. They currently make fruit juice, wine, herbal medicine and indigo cloth at the Inpaeng Center.

Maoberry juice

A fruit-processing factory at the Inpaeng Center operates from the time of harvesting the fruit (e.g., July for maoberry) to around October. According to the leader of this project, the factory started producing maoberry juice as its main product with permission from the Food and Drug Administration of Thailand in 1995. It was also certified to meet the organic standards of the Department of Agriculture, Ministry of Agricultural and Cooperatives around 2015. There are three types of maoberry products: 100% pure maoberry juice, 33% maoberry juice containing sugar, and wine. In the case of 100% pure juice in 180cc bottles, the cost is 20 baht wholesale, 25 baht retail, and 35 baht for sale in Bangkok, including shipping costs. The purchase price of maoberry is 40 baht max per kilogram for members of the Inpaeng Network and 35 baht max for other people. Members can determine the prices themselves.

Herbal medicine

A processing factory for herbal medicine is also located on the grounds of the Inpaeng Center. Although two full-time female staff members work there, their salaries are low, and their schedules are not fixed. As they are also farmers, they do not go to the factory during busy farming seasons. When the center requires more labor for processing because of the availability of many herbs, it employs additional local people for the drying process.

The person who manages the factory is Ms. D, mentioned above, who is one of the leaders of the Inpaeng Network in the Bua Village. She took a Thai pharmacy on Thai traditional medicine, passed the exams, and acquired a license for medical practice in Thai traditional medicine (Thai pharmacy) in 1992. The present factory was built using grants from the Agricultural Land Reform Office. More than 800,000 baht, was provided in two installments. The factory was completed in 2014 and started to operate in January 2015.

The stocking of fresh herbs is related to an integrated farming project. Most of the fresh herbs are bought from members of the Inpaeng Network who live near the center, as they cannot afford to pay for gas to buy from distant sellers. The staff members and growers hold meetings to share information on the expected demand for herbs and then decide who will grow and sell herbs during the harvest season. Most of the herbs are harvested during the dry season, but the harvest time depends on the herb. For example, *"fathalaichon"* (*Andrographis paniculate [Burm. f.] Wall. ex Nees*) is harvested during the rainy season. Contract growers have prior training in using non-chemical fertilizers, such as cow and buffalo dung, or granulated fertilizer mixed with chicken manure and cow dung. The staff members collect fresh herbs without washing them. The herbs are washed and dried at the factory. They try to avoid soot and dust adhering to the herbs because they do not have enough space in their houses to wash and dry them. The number of contractors, including small-scale growers, is approximately 20, half of whom are folk healers.

Processing is as follows: First, the bad parts of the fresh herbs are removed. The herbs are then washed with water and cut into small pieces (although "*khamin chan*" [*Curcuma longa L.*] is pounded because a large amount must be prepared for drying before noon). Finally, the samples are dried in the sun. In this factory, the herbs are not dried using gas. Gas is expensive, and the finished products are different from those in the sun. For example, "*kwaokhrueakhao*" (*Pueraria candollei Grah.*) becomes darker and shrinks after a longer drying period in the rain, but it becomes white and flat after a shorter drying period in the sun. After drying, they are sometimes powdered and packed into capsules.

Both individuals and hospitals buy medicinal herbs from the Inpaeng Network. Individual consumers buy them for health, but also to process for resale. The best-selling herb is *khamin chan*, which is beneficial for the stomach. *Fathalaichon* has also become popular. The herbs are mostly consumed in Sakon Nakhon Province. Individual consumers include visitors to the Inpaeng Center or consumers who know about the herbs through word of mouth. The center does not sell prescribed medicines to cure illnesses, but only individual herbs (*ya diao*). Phra Achan Fan Acharo Hospital (*rongphayaban phra achan fan acharo*) in the Phanna Nikhom district buys herbs before they are powdered. The hospital is state-run and staffed by practitioners of both Thai traditional medicine and modern medicine, but not by folk healers. Sakon Nakhon Thai Traditional Medicine Hospital Luang Pu Fab Supatto (*rongphayaban kanphaet phaen thai sakon nakhon luang pu fep suphattho*) in the Waritchaphum district purchases herbs in powdered form. The monthly total sales range from 20,000 to 40,000 baht.

Indigo cloth (pha khram)

Villagers dye cotton threads with indigo and weave the threads into cloth. Most raw materials, such as indigo trees (*ton khram*) and cotton, are purchased from members of the Inpaeng Network. Indigo cloth has received considerable attention in recent years.

Characteristics of integrated agriculture and the relations between the community and outsiders

In this section, I consider the characteristics of Inpaeng Network's integrated agriculture and the relations between the community and the state, capitalism and globalization, while referring to the research on the autonomous village community in the past.

At the beginning of the Inpaeng Network in the late 1980s, members were aware of problems related to debt, increased poverty, and degradation of land and forest that were the result of agriculture focused on selling. They changed their methods of farming from monocultivation of cash crops to integrated farming as agriculture for living. In other words, farmers who had faced problems caused by export-oriented agriculture promoted in the national development plan re-evaluated local practices for self-sufficiency as their parents, grandparents, and ancestors had done and decided to start integrated farming. Behind this movement was the influence of "community culture thought," which was popular among development workers and academics in the 1980s and aimed at development centered around "community culture."

Shifting their agriculture from the then-authorized cash-crop-oriented approach to one based on integrated farming was not just about methods, but rather about changing the approach to life. Mr.

B expressed this as follows: "We are not rich; however, we are not poor either (*bo ruai tae bo chon*). We do not own a lot, but are not in poverty because we can eat properly. This is the point. You first need to change your basic way of thinking (to move into such a new agriculture). This is very difficult to determine." The expression, "We are not rich; however, we are not poor," can been heard from other farmers who followed the method of integrated farming. Their farming based on this approach clearly differs from the preceding modernized and industrialized agriculture in terms of its orientation toward a community movement.

Seri and Hewison address the process of renewal (of farmers' lives) with an invariable role played by religion, which seems to be "a fundamental aspect of the decision by some villagers as they choose to turn their backs on the market-oriented system of production. It is necessary for these people to rid themselves of greed and realize the meaning of sufficiency. They learn to be modest and to recognize their own limitations and to keep a balance between the spiritual and the material" (Seri and Hewison 2001, 136–137). We can thus imagine their determination and will by which the initial 13 members, including Mr. B and Ms. C, turned away from the consumerist way of thinking, as well as the then-authorized market-oriented agriculture, and started on the path toward (more) integrated agriculture.

Nevertheless, a certain portion of cash might be required to lead a modest life. The practice of integrated agriculture, which primarily purports farmers' autonomy from the market economy or globalization, does not necessarily "transcend" transactions in the market. Integrated farming in Inpaeng pursues agricultural products for farmers first, followed by cash income from selling surplus. Rattan and maoberry are typically indigenous to Phu Phan forest. These are products that generate sound income; however, they are not cash products that have no roots in the local soil.

Using "forest produce," or non-timber forest products (NTFP), for local sufficiency could be posed as the latest technique in a long line of local practices that began a century ago. For such an understanding, I refer to Chatthip's argument on "community culture" in his seminal work *The Thai Village Economy in the Past,* wherein he writes that village production under the "*sakdina*" system[6] was subsistence production, meaning production for personal use and not for sale or exchange. Village rice-growing under the *sakdina* system was mainly directed to consumption within the family household (Chatthip 1999 [1984], 16). Farmers had a high level of subsistence: they could produce their own food, make their own clothes, and gather fish, vegetables and timber from nature (ibid., 22). Farmers also gathered forest produce besides animals and vegetables for food. After the rice season was over, villages in Isan and the south often had no surplus rice available to cover tax; thus, the state levied tax in forest produce. The state kept a portion of these forest goods and sold some as exports (ibid., 22–23). Trading in Isan was solely in forest produce, originally for the "*suai*" tax.[7] However, when tax collection changed to cash at the end of the Fifth Reign (at the beginning of the 20th century), villagers sold forest produce to raise the cash to pay the four-baht poll tax (ibid., 67). One such example of forest produce is rattan.

However, I have not yet ensured that the argument on "community culture" would properly cover the possible linkage between collective memory on usage of "forest produce" in Inpaeng areas, which could date back to the era of the *sakdina* system, and agriculture practiced by Inpaeng members. My research needs further investigation of the relationship between Inpaeng and other agricultural practices and methods since the 1980s in rural Thailand. In more practical aspects of farming—for instance, nursing rattan saplings in a more efficient manner—interactive exploration of agricultural methods among members remains a promising issue for further research, because it is an inferred critical factor for understanding assemblage in this community movement.

In the frame of community movement, a demanding argument for the nature of the Inpaeng Network may be deployed in the course of long-lasting self-organization of the village community. In Chatthip's work, the relations within the village and the relations between the village and the state are as follows: "The basic relations of production of the village under the *sakdina* system had two dimensions. First, the village was a community which still had strong internal bonds, similar to the time of the primordial village. Second, the village was exploited from outside—by the state which had by now come into existence" (ibid., 26). For autonomous village communities that are self-sufficient in the region, the external state is an actor of exploitation. In explaining "community culture school of thought," Chatthip states that village communities and peasant culture are recognized as anti-state and non-capitalist (Chatthip 1991, 133).

Conclusion

The initial movement of the Inpaeng Network may be located partly in the context of collective resistance against state-led systems or capitalistic market economies. In contrast, community culture, or indigenous or local knowledge, has been positively incorporated into official discourses and policies since the 1990s, and as has been seen as the sufficiency economy or New Theory farming advocated by the King. The Inpaeng way of integrated farming has come to be regarded as a successful case consistent with the philosophy of the sufficiency economy, which embodies rather mainstream values and methods compared with alternative ones.[8] Various kinds of external institutions provided financial and technical support to the

Inpaeng Network projects, which led to its growth. In the past three decades, the network has accepted various visitors and observers, and has cooperated with various people and institutions both in and outside the country. Recent developments in IT have facilitated this development, along with the input of younger practitioners.

Acknowledging and utilizing globalized surroundings, sufficiency-oriented agriculture in Inpaeng illustrates a new dimension of collective autonomy in villages, which might diverge from an authentic rural community—essentially based on inward-looking autonomy. Tracing the orbit of rise and expansion of the Inpaeng Network, we can recognize that people have been pursuing better lives together with shifting values and ethics, while maintaining each person's autonomy. Both selection of products in their farms/forests and encounters/ collaborations with other farmers have been active in a form of assemblage, keeping and nurturing the sense of communal good.

Endnotes: The Integrated Agriculture and Community Movement in Northeast Thailand

1. During the economic crisis, "The value of the baht fell 40 percent, sharply increasing value of unhedged, dollar-denominated debt," "Unemployment rose; the stock and real estate markets collapsed; most of the country's financial institutions were technically bankrupt," leading to "GDP shrank by more than 10 percent" (UNDP 2012, 23).

2. Considering its wide network covering several provinces, Rado (2013, 194) points out, for example, that members in Bua Village of Kut Bak district did not identify network members in Phuphan district as competitors/rivals when the latter obtained the technique in processing *makmao* (maoberry). Rather, these communities have developed such a relationship as follows: if one community oversupplies *makmao* juice, another community even assists in selling the remaining bottles.

3. The Inpaeng Center offers training to members on producing and processing many household groceries made of raw materials, which can be planted in the area. Suksudaj observed and reported the variety as: juices and wine (local berries: "*kor*", "*ngaew*"), snacks (sticky rice, bananas), body-care products (tamarinds for body lotions, "*anchan*" for hair shampoo); and more than 60 other items including herbal medicine, mosquito repellant, herbal tea and clothing material (Suksudaj 2010, 47).

4. Suksudaj (2010, 52) further reports such an option called "*dek hak tin*" or "kids love homeland" program, in which local adolescents are trained to understand "the interconnectedness between the trainees and their ecosystem." Another program "Inpaeng community ecologists training" aims "to draw the young adult generation back from working as cheap labour in big cities, to sustainable, self-reliance farming in their hometown".

5. Suksudaj (2010, 45) addresses the relationship between the combination of several products and the background idea for the combination as follows: "Theoretically, Inpaeng's members allocated their land into cash crop areas, fishery pond areas, chicken coop or pig pen areas and forest-like plantation areas. Having various kinds of food to consume is the second indicator of food security. Local food is regarded as better food than the 'idiot food' (*ahan panya on*) (market, industrialized, preservative-added foods)".

6. King Trailokanat promulgated the *sakdina* law in 1455. Under the *sakdina* system, the King distributes land to various official positions according to rank. This system remained in force for the 416 years of the Ayutthaya period (Chatthip 1999 [1984], 12). It means the King owns all the land. However, there is disagreement among scholars as to whether the land was actually provided or was merely an indicator of differences in official position and status.

7. "*Suai*" is produce taxes levied on rice and forest goods.

8. The change of the relationship between the network and government is pointed as follows: "In the second phase when the network gathered momentum (1992–1996), villagers became critical of government policies to promote market-oriented farming without effective mechanisms to support small farmers. This created some conflict between the network and government agencies at the local level. However, the situation changed in the mid-1990s when government policy switched towards community empowerment and promotion of the King's ideas. The government began to make funding and technical advice available to projects that demonstrated change from within" (UNDP 2007, 45).

References

Chatthip Nartsupha. (1984) 1999. *The Thai Village Economy in the Past.* Translated by Chris Baker and Pasuk Phongpaichit. Chiang Mai: Silkworm Books.

Chatthip Nartsupha. 1991. "The Community Culture School of Thought." In *Thai Constructions of Knowledge*, edited by Manas Chitakasem and Andrew Turton, 118–141. London: School of Oriental and African Studies, University of London.

Darlington, Susan M. 2019. "Buddhist Integration of Forest and Farm in Northern Thailand." *Religions* 10(9), https://doi.org/10.3390/rel10090521.

Delcore, Henry D. 2004. "Development and the Life Story of a Thai Farmer Leader." *Ethnology* 43(1): 33–50.

Misui, Hisao, Hisataro Horiuchi, Somchai Chakhatrakan, and Shuhei Saito. 2008. "New Theory nouka no shokuryoujikyu to keieiseika: Thai-chaopuraya-gawa-deruta jouryuuiki wo jirei toshite (Food Self-Sufficiency and Farm Income of 'The New Theory' Farm Households: A Case Study of Upper Region in the Chao Phraya River Delta, Thailand.)," *Journal of Agriculture Science, Tokyo University of Agriculture* 53(1): 46–53. (in Japanese).

Mongsawad, Prasopchoke. 2010. "The Philosophy of the Sufficiency Economy: a Contribution to the Theory of Development." *Asia-Pacific Development Journal* 17(1): 123–143.

Office of National Park. 2017. http://portal.dnp.go.th/p/nationalpark. (2017/07/01)

Rado, Istvan. 2013. "Sustainable Community Development in Northeastern Thailand." In *Growing Sustainable Communities: A Development Guide for Southeast Asia*, edited by Linda Brennan, Lukas Parker, Torgeir Aleti Watne, John Fien, Duong Trong Hue and Mai Anh Doan, 179–196. Tilde University Press.

Rado, Istvan. 2019. "Community Economies in the Context of Thailand's Sufficiency Economy Approach: A Positioning Theory Analysis." (https://ssrn.com/abstract=3362711 or http://dx.doi.org/10.2139/ssrn.3362711)

Schliesinger, Joachim. 2001. *Tai Groups of Thailand: Volume 2 Profile of the Existing Groups.* Bangkok: White Lotus.

Seri Phongphit and Kevin Hewison. 2001. *Village Life: Culture and Transition in Thailand's Northeast.* Bangkok: White Lotus.

Seubsman, Sam-ang, Matthew Kelly and Adrian Sleigh. 2013. "The Sufficiency Economy and Community Sustainability in Rural Northeastern Thailand." *Asian Culture and History* 5(2): 57–65.

Suehiro, Akira. 1993. *Thai: Kaihatsu to minshushugi (Thailand: Development and Democracy).* Tokyo: Iwanami Shoten. (in Japanese).

Suehiro, Akira. 2009. *Thai: Chushinkoku no mosaku (Thailand: Exploration in Semideveloped Country).* Tokyo: Iwanami Shoten. (in Japanese).

Suksudaj, Sutee. 2010. "The Thai Social Capital as a Social Determinant of Oral Health." (Doctoral Dissertation) The University of Adelaide, Australia. Available from http://hdl.handle.net/2440/65058

Tanabe, Shigeharu. 2016. "Introduction: Communities of Potential." In *Communities of Potential: Social Assemblages in Thailand and Beyond,* edited by Shigeharu Tanabe. Chiang Mai: Silkworm Books.

United Nations Development Programme. 2007. *Thailand Human Development Report 2007: Sufficiency Economy and Human Development.* United Nations Development Programme.

United Nations Development Programme. 2012. "Thailand's Best Practices and Lessons Learned in Development" Vol. 1 https://www.th.undp.org/content/thailand/en/home/library/democratic_governance/TICA-UNDPV1.html

Chapter 8

CROSSING THE LIMITS
Implications of Rope Bridge-building for
Social Movements in Southern Laos

TOMOKO NAKATA

Introduction

Lao People's Democratic Republic is one of the least developed
countries in Southeast Asia. Its government, based on the goals set
in 1996 at the 6th Party Congress, defined its long-term development
objective as freeing the country from this status by 2020 (Lao PDR
2003, 4). Foreign direct investment has been encouraged, as it is
expected to contribute largely to the country's economic development.
Under such policies, numerous development projects have been
implemented, especially in the hydropower, plantation-agribusiness
and mining sectors (Baird and Barney 2017, 1), with significant
impacts on locals' livelihoods and the culture and environment of
the regions (Baird 2010; McAllister 2015; Obein 2007; Friis et al. 2016).

While its economic system shifted from a socialist to a market-
oriented one in the mid-1980s, Laos has maintained a single-party
regime since its establishment in 1975, as in the cases of such
neighboring countries as China and Vietnam. The present regime
is often characterized as authoritarian, with virtually no freedom
for people to object to the government's policies. Independent
civil society organizations are nonexistent (Kyaw Yin Hlaing
2006, 130), and international NGOs are restricted to extending

and supplementing official government policies, programs and objectives, with few active linkages with local groups (Arnst 2014). Not only is the space for organized opposition to the government limited (Baird 2018, 4), but the typical Laotian also avoids talking about politics in public places, practicing self-censorship for fear of being arrested (Kyaw Yin Hlaing 2006, 130; Singh 2012, 9–10). Although Vietnam and China are also known for their single-party authoritarian regimes, widespread social protests are possible in both countries[1] for urban and rural people who suffer, for example, from water pollution or land-grabbing (Creak and Barney 2018, 6). Moreover, in Cambodia, NGOs support the locals with their land rights claims, as demonstrated by Abe (Chapter 9 in this book), whereas people in Lao PDR cannot count on such help.

A few cases of local resistance have been reported in several parts of Laos: residents resisted or expressed in overt or covert ways their opposition to the acquisition of village land through land concessions granted by the government to Chinese or Vietnamese companies (McAllister 2015; Baird 2017; Kenney-Lazar 2012); villagers, frustrated with the state prohibiting them from exploiting forest resources while sanctioning commercial logging, have illegally felled rosewood in protected areas (Singh 2012, 149). However, these movements have tended to be sporadic, without spreading to other areas, and have engendered no significant consequences. In addition, the government's control of information prevents the movements from becoming publicly known, thereby precluding their spread to wider demographic ranges and geographical areas.[2]

Given the authoritarian single-party regime, which does not tolerate challenges to its policies and authority, do the Laotian people have no choice but to docilely obey the decisions, instructions, laws and rules made and implemented by the government, even when their survival is at risk? If they do have a choice, how can they act?

In this chapter, I attempt to answer these questions by examining how the locals in Southern Laos struggled to sustain themselves after being deprived of a large part of their farmland for large-scale rubber plantations.

For several decades, studies of collective actions have largely focused on new types of social movements, including students, feminists and ecological movements, which are prominent in post-industrial and post-capitalist societies (cf. Melucci 1989), in contrast to labor movements, which have waned. In post-material societies, where people's primary needs are largely fulfilled, freedom of need, rather than freedom from needs, has been increasingly recognized (Melucci 1989, 177). The needs of the participants in such a movement shift toward nonpolitical goals, such as self-realization in daily life and challenging the logic of complex systems for cultural reasons (Melucci 1989). In developing countries in Southeast Asia, including Lao PDR, however, the situation is often different as they are not post-industrial and post-capitalist societies; rather, these nations are in many instances making every effort to become members of the community of industrialized and capitalist countries. People are not free from needs and thus cannot afford to think about self-realization. Therefore, we need to examine social movements in Laos from a different perspective, taking into consideration its specific historical, political and socio-cultural conditions.

The Lao state and its relationship with village communities

Laos, as a state, is often marked by its discontinuities (Stuart-Fox 1993). It has experienced several divisions or breakups in its history, starting with the Kingdom of Lan Xang splitting into three (Luang Prabang,

Vientiane and Champasak) in the 18th century and the annexation of the Kingdom of Vientiane by Siam in 1828, colonialization by the French—who, without regarding Laos as a political entity, "divided [it] at first into Upper and Lower Laos, and subsequently into the protectorate of Luang Prabang plus directly administrated central and southern provinces" (Stuart-Fox 1993, 110). Finally the civil war separated the areas under the Royal Lao government from those controlled by the Pathet Lao, which eventually seized control throughout the territory of the present-day Laos in 1975. Moreover, the population comprises various ethnic groups, speaking languages belonging to the Tai, Mon-Khmer, Tibeto-Burman and other language families, while ethnic Lao "have spread far beyond the geographical boundaries of present-day Laos" (Stuart-Fox 1993, 106). These conditions probably contributed to forming "a weak base on which to build the institutions of a modern nation-state, both economically and politically, and a weak sense of national identity" (Stuart-Fox 2006, 354–5).

According to Taillard, the weakness of the state's hold in Laos reinforced the village institution (1977, 71), and the peasants are deeply attached to their villages, which is conceived in three aspects: unit of housing, community of interest and center of relations (1977, 73). Since 1975, such socialist policies as the introduction of agricultural cooperatives and collectivization and restrictions on the movement of people and goods that were implemented by the Lao People's Revolutionary Party (LPRP) have not been capable of transforming traditional Lao peasants' practices and villages. Rather, villages have become less open and more corporate, and local solidarity has tended "to prevail over outside allegiances" (Evans 1995, 188). In the late 1990s, I still observed similar aspects as described by Taillard and Evans when conducting fieldwork in a village in Southern Laos (herein called K Village), as discussed later.

Meanwhile, the state's hold has been steadily strengthening since the economic reform called *"Chintanakan Mai"* ("New Economic Mechanism," or literally, "New Thinking") was launched in the mid-1980s following the collapse of the socialist economy. Various development projects implemented in the wake of this reform have been affecting people's lives and visions directly and indirectly throughout the country. Not only has that development become "the dominant rhetoric and vision of the Lao state" (Singh 2012, 6), but the people seem to be permeated with them. Poverty eradication has been publicly declared as one of the main targets of the Lao government's development strategy. Development projects have been introduced to improve living conditions, for example by providing roads, water supplies, healthcare and schools. In this context, people's views of the state or government can change. For example, Sarinda Singh argues that local people consider national development to bring them personal prosperity, as under the current government they have experienced improvements in their lives lacking under former socialist policies (2012, 16–7). Holly High demonstrates that the rural Lao people in Southern Laos continue to engage with the state through development programs, despite their disillusionment with and suspicion of the programs, and argues that the state and its programs "were still able to capture desire" (2014, 4) of the people.

Nevertheless, engagement with the state is not unconditional or perpetual. It is necessary that people "believe that the state has the capacity to provide them with benefits" (Singh 2012, 15). Singh studied local perspectives on the Lao state based on fieldwork in Nakai District, Khammouane Province, where a controversial hydropower dam project, Nam Theun 2, was implemented (2012). She repeatedly stresses the pragmatic self-interest of Lao people's engagement with the state. That is, if the state's policies and programs fail to contribute to their prosperity, state authority and legitimacy can be questioned. Although open and collective protest is hardly an option, as mentioned above, they can talk about and act on shortcomings in discreet and limited ways (Singh 2012, 11).

The state is not the only party that has increasingly intervened in living conditions in Laos. Foreign actors, such as international organizations and development agencies, have been involved in various ways. Receiving foreign investment, loans and aid implies that the government should accept outside influences on its law and policymaking.[3] One of the most prominent cases is land-use planning. Various international development agencies took initiatives to make sustainable development a key objective for policymakers, following increasing concerns by the international community, and land-use planning was drawn up and implemented precisely in line with the discourse, which stressed the threats of upland shifting cultivation, population growth, deforestation, etc. (Lestrelin, Castella, and Bourgoin 2012). In this context, a village-scale land zoning system was established "that divided land into five categories of forest: 'protected,' 'conservation' and 'regeneration' forests,[4] where economic activities are prohibited; 'production' forest, where limited logging and collection of forest products are permitted; and 'degraded' forest, which can be allocated for tree plantation, livestock farming or permanent agriculture" (Lestrelin, Castella, and Bourgoin 2012, 587). In addition, a protected area system was established by designating 18 National Biodiversity Conservation Areas. The concept was promoted by the World Bank's Global Environmental Facility and international conservation NGOs (Goldman 2001, 508).[5]

International organizations and development agencies also played an important role in the land law of 1997. The National Land Titling Program, supported by the World Bank and the Australian Agency for International Development (AusAID), aimed to allocate secure land titles in urban areas to provide incentives for land holders to invest in productive and market-oriented land uses (Lestrelin, Castella, and Bourgoin 2012, 588). Meanwhile, people in rural areas found their rights over their farmlands being threatened: "according to the new laws, any land left fallow for more than three years can be claimed by the state, and any land can be expropriated for development projects as long as the users receive compensation" (Goldman 2001, 509). As such, granting land concessions to foreign investors was facilitated by the law.

In summary, since economic reform started in the late 1980s, the rural population in Laos has experienced significant changes in terms of land and forest uses, as the government created domestic laws that had been practically nonexistent. Through such legislature, not only the state but also foreign actors, including the World Bank, Asian Development Bank (ADB), international development agencies and NGOs, have come to intervene in people's lives. That is, people in Laos have been forced to confront the market economy and neoliberalism, as well as environmental protectionism, which has been globally prevalent for several decades.

Possibilities of challenge

What possibilities do the Lao people have, under an authoritarian regime, to challenge the policies and regulations that affect them to the extent that they cannot sustain themselves? The situations described above can be examined by drawing on Michel Foucault's concept of biopower, which, unlike the powers of a sovereign of life and death over his subjects, is meant to produce, increase and command forces, rather than being doomed to block them, force them into submission, or destroy them (Foucault 1976, 179). The Lao state endeavors to improve people's conditions under the slogan, "Fighting

Poverty through Human Resource Development, Rural Development and People's Participation" (Lao PDR 2003, 4). This is consistent with the concept of biopower in that the latter, Foucault maintains, is an indispensable element of the development of capitalism that needs to be ensured at the cost of integration of bodies into the apparatus of production, along with the adjustment of the population to economic processes (1976, 185).

Development studies have increasingly featured the concepts of biopower and biopolitics (Cavanagh 2014, 273), as they can help to reveal "the ways in which development has functioned historically as a technique of liberal governance" (Reid 2013, 107). However, Reid suggests that another type of biopower and biopolitics has emerged over several decades, as environmental protectionism has become a new doctrine of development, contesting traditional models of development as privileging macroeconomic growth while serving to harm environments, and proposing "human development" by freeing the lives of human populations from economic imperatives (ibid.). Therefore, the development policies and programs designed and implemented by the Lao government under the influence of various foreign actors—sometimes in conflict with each other over which objective, economic prosperity or environmental preservation, should take precedence—can also indicate the exercise of such power.

The concept of biopower suggests the possibility of such challenges, as, according to Foucault, where there is power, there is resistance that is by no means exterior to power (1976, 125-6), and life is in no way exhaustively integrated into techniques that dominate and manage it, but constantly escapes them (1976, 188). That is, if we follow Foucault's argument, villagers are neither necessarily nor entirely driven to accept or tolerate such power, but may be able to take flight from it.

Another possibility of challenge arises from the history of the inhabitants treated in this study. A large number have roots in the area named Zomia, where, according to James C. Scott, the inhabitants historically chose to escape the state's reach to evade taxes, corvée, conscription, epidemics and crop failures associated with population concentration and monocropping (2009, 22–3). This statement can be confirmed in colonial administrators' reports from the end of the 19th and the beginning of the 20th centuries, which often refer to villages in areas that were found to be empty, as the inhabitants had seemingly escaped the village as a group to evade the taxes and corvée imposed by the French.[6] However, as Scott recognizes, since the end of the Second World War the relationship between nation-states and people in the area has largely changed with the spread of various technologies, including railroads, telephones and airpower, and as his analysis does not apply to late-20th century Southeast Asia (2009, xii); it is implausible to imagine that the inhabitants today could adopt a similar strategy to deal with the state.

Nevertheless, it would also be fallacious to consider people to have completely broken with the past, abandoning their former practices and knowledge. The fieldwork that I conducted in K Village in the late 1990s convinced me of the political equality within the village, as the roles of such village leaders as chiefs and elders were restricted to administrative or ritual domains, with no privilege of appropriating resources in land and labor. Village affairs were to be discussed and settled not by majority vote, but by consensus at village meetings in which every household participated and in which every household was regarded as equal, endowed with access to farmlands that were cleared by its members and responsibilities to contribute labor and money to collective work and rituals organized by the village. Under such political and economic equalities, discourses stressing mutual aid and solidarity within the village were effective (Nakata 2004).

Although deprived of the possibility of escaping from the state, K Village retained, at least in the late 1990s, certain aspects of self-organization and mutual aid reminiscent of their self-governing ancestors. One typical example that I observed was the construction of a wooden bridge across a river en route to dry rice fields. This was decided at a village meeting, organized by the village and carried out through the participation of all households without intervention by outsiders (Nakata 2000). Housebuilding, various ceremonies and rituals including marriages, funerals, worship of ancestral spirits, and farming, were the occasions where mutual aid among households was prominently observed (Nakata 2004).

Self-organization and mutual aid are, along with voluntary association, the principles that David Graeber refers to as characteristics of an anarchist movement and behavior patterns that are as old as the history of humanity (2004, 3). While stressing the principle of direct action, he maintains that anarchist movements do not try to seize power within any national territory and are thus irrelevant to sudden revolutionary cataclysm; rather, they are concerned with forms of practice, which undermine structures of domination (Graeber 2004). Therefore, without any direct, overt or violent actions of opposition to the state, one can evade the state's domination by following these principles or behavior patterns, as with the villagers in Southern Laos.

Based on ethnographic data collected through the fieldwork that I conducted in K Village in 1998–99 and 2010–2019, I examine the actions of locals in the face of significant changes in livelihoods and living conditions that were largely affected by development projects from two perspectives: bio-power, as it has increasingly intervened in locals' lives, whereas this exercise of power can in turn become a point of resistance and the start of an opposite strategy (Foucault 1976, 133); and local practices, seemingly rooted in historical conditions of the village organization, that have a certain affinity with the anarchist principles referred to by Graeber. This study explores how people in

Laos, deprived of the option of organizing collective actions against the government under the authoritarian socialist regime, can act to fulfill their primary needs and how their actions can be considered as compared to a social movement.

Rubber plantations in Bachiang District and their impacts on local households[7]

As Laos is regarded as underdeveloped while rich in exploitable resources, investors from neighboring countries, including Thailand, Vietnam and China, have invested in many of its economic sectors. Rubber plantations have been an extremely popular investment, especially at the beginning of the 2000s. Following the prominent success of one village in Luang Namtha, Northern Laos, whose inhabitants started planting rubber trees by themselves in the 1990s (Shi 2008), rubber cultivation expanded into many parts of the country. Unlike the northern region, where small-holding production was predominant, mainly due to regional authorities' policies that favored contract farming (ibid.), large-scale rubber plantations were established under concession agreements in many places in the south.

In the case of rubber plantations in Bachiang District, Southern Laos, which were established in 2005 under concession agreements between two Vietnamese companies (the Lao-Viet Joint Company and Dak Lak Rubber Company)[8] and the district authority, locals were deprived of a large part of their farmland with little or no compensation. The district authority claimed that the plantations could offer them employment to earn their living; however, during the seven years in which rubber trees were not productive, labor demand on the plantations was seasonal and unstable. Thus, locals could not rely on wages from plantations to sustain themselves. In K Village, the inhabitants have managed to earn a living by engaging in day labor and selling banana leaves at market, while planting a small amount of rice on their remaining tiny, steep plots of land.

The start of tapping in 2012 largely changed the situation. The Dak Lak Rubber Company was granted land, including that of the households of K Village. Around 1,000 tappers were to be employed on 3,500 hectares of rubber tree plantations in Bachiang District. Although most locals had no experience in permanent employment, many applied for tapping training sessions held by the company and were then employed as tappers. In fact, these workers are employed almost the entire year, except for the month of February when the trees are unproductive. Wages were higher on the whole than previous remuneration by the rubber company, but they varied significantly with a tapper's skill and diligence, as their wages were based on the amount of latex that they collected. Many locals who engaged in tapping had difficulties adjusting to plantation labor, often complaining about the working conditions, regulations and discipline on the plantations, lack of sleep and fatigue because they had to leave for work in the dark, the strictness of their supervisors over attendance and technique, penalties for absenteeism and lack of skill. Some quit and resumed farming or sought alternative employment, while the others continued tapping: they found the job more or less acceptable and could not have found an alternative to their income from tapping.

Within the few years after the start of tapping, the village landscape gradually changed: reinforced concrete houses were built one after another, many households owned several motorcycles, and the majority of households were equipped with a private electric water pump. Meanwhile, some families continued to live the same life as before. The noticeable difference in the households' financial status can be partly attributed to their degree of involvement in tapping. Households with several members engaged in tapping earned much higher income than those with no members or just one member engaged, who may have frequently taken days off or been late for work. For example, one household with four tappers earned in total about 10 million kip[9] per month, while another household with one tapper who was frequently absent or late for work earned less than one million kip a month.

This wage labor also altered the villagers' relationship with money. As plantation labor earned them a somewhat regular income, many began to buy on credit, which had not been possible before. When they purchased something expensive, such as furniture or a motorbike, they could pay in installments. Money lending and borrowing became common among the villagers; young men, for example, often borrowed money from neighbors or relatives for entertainment and, generally would pay only the 30% monthly interest on payday. One villager who worked for the army started lending money in a more regular and systematic way, by drawing up contracts with borrowers who accepted a mortgage on their lands.

Social relations within the village have also been increasingly mediated by money in recent years. As many households have shifted to tapping, abandoning or largely reducing their involvement in farming, labor exchange has been eliminated in cultivation, especially in sowing. When a household needs help to clear a piece of land, they now often have to pay for the work, as it is impossible to call on their neighbors to help based on reciprocity; their neighbors, in fact, may not necessarily have any plans to clear land. In addition, labor has been progressively recognized as a commodity in the village, since tapping as permanent rather than temporary wage labor has permeated the area.

Labor is not the only commodity newly recognized in K Village. Farmland has also become a commodity that can be bought and sold between the villagers. This had previously been unthinkable; it was the norm that one had to ask for permission to cultivate a piece of land owned by a neighbor who had left it uncultivated due to lack of labor, for example, and such use was generally permitted free of charge. However, after the establishment of rubber plantations, cultivable land had scarcity value so villagers came to recognize it as a commodity. In particular, the production of rubber trees has recently been declining for such reasons as aging of trees and heavy, continual rains that have prevented tappers from working. Thus, wages have largely decreased, with some households seeking farmland in the vicinity to resume cultivation. Households with money would buy land owned by a neighbor but left fallow long term due to lack of labor or deemed uncultivable due to the gradient, who then chose to sell it out of necessity. The purchasers tended to plant cash crops, including cashew nuts and cassava, instead of dry rice, as the yield on a tiny plot, they assumed, would be insufficient.

Economic disparity has become increasingly obvious within the village. While some households have accrued savings to invest in a truck, to launch a business or to purchase a plot of land to plant cash crops, others, excluded from plantation labor due to age, health or lack of adaptability, had practically no land to cultivate, no jobs, and thus no other choice than to rely on family members or relatives. Under these conditions, homogeneity within K Village has totally disappeared, and solidarity is now a thing of the past, when it was a core element of village rituals and festivals and also daily life.

Amid the dramatic changes in livelihood that transformed social relations and value systems in K Village, some households chose to continue farming by unprecedented means, namely deciding to clear conservation forest (*pa sanguan*) to convert it to farmland.

Clearing conservation forest

According to my interviews with the villagers, many households started clearing conservation forests situated more than 10 kilometers from K Village[10] after the rubber companies began to plant trees based on land concession agreements. They found their farmland so reduced that they could not produce enough rice to sustain their families. They had previously never done this because they understood that it was prohibited and would put them in danger of arrest or penalties. In addition, the river lying between the residential area and the conservation forest made access difficult. In the dry season, when the river level falls, it is relatively easy to ford; whereas in the rainy season it rises, meaning that villagers must swim across, sometimes at risk of drowning. Those who dared to go to clear conservation forest did not mind taking such legal and physical risks. They told me that they had no choice but to go to "the other side [of the river]" to earn their livings, since there was no land left to cultivate on "this side: the Vietnamese had seized almost all of our lands." In fact, those who were not young had little possibility of employment, as the rubber company employed, in principle, those who were in good health and aged between 18 and 35 years. Even if they could find employment, the wages were often insufficient, at least until tapping started in 2012. Some were probably reluctant to become plantation workers, as they had been working on their own lands for many years without any experience of being employees and having to obey the regulations and orders of the company and supervisors. However, when tapping started, many households abandoned farming fields in conservation forest to engage in tapping, probably expecting an increase in and stabilization of wages.

The few households that continued cultivation gradually shifted to cash crops, because forest that could be cleared was in increasingly short supply due to successive arrivals from surrounding villages seeking farmland. The common practice was to plant dry rice in the same field for two consecutive years; in the third year, however, they shifted rice cultivation to a new plot. It was apparent that sooner or later it would be impossible to find forest to convert into farmland, so they began to plant cash crops to cover the expense of rice as yield was insufficient. These cash crops included a plant called *khem* (*Saccharum arundinaceum*), a material for brooms, and cashew nuts. However, the commoditization of *khem* was extremely labor-intensive, so many households abandoned it. Cashews were introduced by the Dak Lak Company in the early stage of rubber plantation. Along with rubber trees, the company planted cashew trees by employing locals who would learn to plant the crop through this experience. Observing that cashew nuts fetched high prices, the locals began to plant them by themselves on the tiny plots that remained or on land that they bought from others. The number of villagers planting cashews increased rapidly. However, in recent years the price of cashew nuts has been decreasing, so villagers have been shifting to cassava, the price of which has been increasing. In any case, clearing conservation forest instead of engaging in plantation labor does not imply that the locals could continue to live their traditional lives.

Meanwhile, the district authorities did not entirely overlook the clearing of conservation forests by locals. According to the villagers, those who cultivated crops in former conservation forest, were sometimes summoned to the district office and required to pay a penalty. However, they were adamant in refusing to pay, claiming that they had no choice but to clear conservation forest to sustain themselves, since no land remained to cultivate on "this side" due to the rubber plantations. They maintained that the district authorities ended up condoning their cultivation by not taking any measures to stop them. Locals interpreted this as implicit consent of the authorities and thus continued cultivating "the other side."

Rope bridge-building

The households who were farming by covertly clearing conservation forests began to build rope bridges, also covertly, to improve access between "this side" and "the other side" of the river. Four or five rope bridges seem to exist across the river, although I only visited one of them and did not meet any locals who knew exactly how many there are. Here, I examine the case of the one that the households of K village have mostly been using after having participated in its construction.

The rope bridge in question was built around 2010. A resident of T Village, which had merged with two neighboring villages, including K Village, to form one village in 2006, met someone in a former conservation forest turned into farmland and decided to build a rope bridge to ease traffic flow and simplify the transportation of products. He explained that many people, especially women, elderly persons and children, could not swim, yet they had to go weed their fields during the rainy season. The two approached others, who also cultivated the lands close to theirs. Finally, eight households from two villages participated in building the rope bridge, each contributing 150,000 kip (about 20 US dollars) toward the cost of materials, in addition to labor. However, the rope bridge had to be remade every year, as it was carried away by the torrent of the river at the end of the rainy season. The number of participants increased from the second year, with each household contributing 50,000 kip per year. Several years ago, they began using metal ropes instead of vegetable-fiber ropes and widened the bridge so that motorbikes could cross. Observing that the rope bridge helped not only foot traffic between the two sides of the river, but also the motorbikes, the locals crossed the river to turn conservation forest into farmland in increasing numbers.

While no households in K Village participated in building the first rope bridge, some joined soon thereafter. An inhabitant of K Village, who was the first in the village to clear conservation forest and has been farming ever since, was charged with the task of collecting expenses from the households in K Village. According to an interview with him conducted in 2019, six households paid 50,000 kip each, and two or three households that paid 20,000 kip. The former group had farmland on the other side and used the bridge frequently, while the latter did not cultivate any crops there, but occasionally used the bridge to forage in the forest. Some households that had cleared land but had stopped cultivation to engage in tapping, for example, did not pay for the bridge, as they did not use it. The villager mentioned above stated that the total amount of money to be collected from all the households of several villages that participated in building the rope bridge would be around 7 to 8 million kip, which would be spent on materials, especially metal ropes. However, he did not know exactly how many households from how many villages would contribute to construction, and seemingly had no interest in knowing. No leaders appeared to have been in charge of planning, management or operations related to bridge- building because no one could answer my questions as to who had the best overall knowledge about the rope bridge.

Not all households in K village that had farmland in the former conservation forest used the same rope bridge. One household used another bridge together with people from other villages, paying 50,000 kip a year for the other bridge because it was more convenient. As each household chose independently which part of the conservation forest to clear, without consulting their neighbors in the village, it was quite common for the fields of different households from different villages to be adjacent. Besides, the choice of clearing conservation forest itself was made independently—something that only some village households dared to do, at least in the beginning; others hesitated, probably for fear of sanctions by the district authorities.

All four or five rope bridges seemed to have been built by the locals who had cleared conservation forest so needed to frequently cross the river. It is highly probable that each of them was built in the same way as the above case, that is, a few persons farming close to each other talked and decided to build it jointly, asking others who also had farmland in their vicinity to join them. Each bridge was built where it was most convenient for its users. There were obviously no leaders or schemes in building these rope bridges; rather, they were made independently and quite spontaneously.

The villagers maintain that the district authorities were well aware of the rope bridges, but did not take any actions against them, in much the same way as they turned a blind eye to those clearing conservation forests.

Conclusion

The processes of change in livelihoods and social relations experienced by the villagers following the establishment of rubber plantations through large-scale land concessions in Bachiang District demonstrates the infiltration into K village of a market economy and capitalist relations of production, marked by the commodification of land and labor. This development project was launched under the state's policies that stress the efficient use of human and natural resources to eradicate poverty. The official papers published by the government are full of rhetoric related to poverty eradication, such as "fighting poverty," "improvement of the poverty situation in the poorest districts," and "improving the well-being of the people through greater food security" (Lao PDR 2004). These discourses are spread through district officials and village chiefs and drive people to expect the state and its programs to bring them prosperity. However, once people discover that the program fails to provide them with any profit, while depriving them of access to various resources, the same discourses serve as a frame of reference for them to justify their illegal actions, such as clearing conservation forests to ensure food security. The determined refusal of villagers to pay penalties for having cleared conservation forest on the grounds that they had no choice as they had no land to cultivate nor any way of sustaining themselves, reveals the relational character of biopower (Foucault 1976).

The process of building rope bridges indicates both new and old aspects of the organization in the area. As mentioned above, it was organized and implemented not on a village basis but on an individual basis. Formerly, such projects were initiated and undertaken on a village basis. However, as the livelihoods of village households diversified, especially since tapping was introduced in the area, the economic disparity among households has become salient and social relations within the village are increasingly mediated by money. It has therefore become impossible to mobilize all the households for such projects as bridge-building. Those who chose to clear conservation forest came across people from other villages who had taken the same risk, probably for the same reasons, such as the impossibility of employment by the rubber company or reluctance to become plantation workers. They found it possible to cooperate with them in place of their fellow villagers. Crossing the river to clear conservation forest brought them to cross village boundaries.

However, their building methods were quite similar to those used when K Village had built a wooden bridge, in that decisions were made by consensus and work and expenses were equally borne by all households. Rope bridge-building was spontaneous and voluntary, without no rulers or even leaders to plan, conduct or administer the entire work. All participants, recognizing the utility of the rope bridge, autonomously decided to be involved in its construction and to contribute equally with their labor and money to execute the project together. This can be regarded as self-organization, mutual aid and voluntary association, as the participants' commitment was voluntary, detached from village affiliation and for a specific purpose.

In contrast with open manifestations or revolutionary movements, which are practically impossible for the Lao people, building rope bridges was implemented quietly and without attracting public attention. This, however, attracted other locals, finding it easier to cross the river. Others joined successively to clear conservation forest, to the extent that, according to the villagers, there is no more forest left. The district authorities could do nothing to prevent their actions. This implies that the locals rendered the law virtually ineffective and achieved their goal of finding plots of land to cultivate.

One may wonder why the authorities did not take sterner measures to stop their clearing of the forests, as in the case of Sulawesi's Lore Lindu National Park, in which landless farmers had their crops completely destroyed by a party of forest guards (Li 2008, 126). Asking officials such a question directly is impossible, so we can only make assumptions. It is often suggested that there is a "persistent gap between policy and practice" in Laos (High and Petit 2013, 427), that is, "policy as it appears on paper bears little resemblance to implementation on the ground: . . . fines are levied but not enforced." Accordingly, rural residents have "a degree of manoeuvre in their engagements with the state" (ibid.). District officials' sympathy for the locals might be a reason for their reluctance to take coercive measures like those taken by forest guards in Sulawesi. Local officials may be sympathetic to the concerns of the villagers because they are partly responsible for their well-being (Kenney-Lazar 2018, 27). In addition, their relationships with local inhabitants are not restricted to professional interactions, but extend to certain kinds of familiarity represented by "friendly conversations, sharing food and alcohol in homes or drinking venues, small gifts or 'fees,' and possibly a wrist-tying ceremony" (High and Petit 2013, 426). Local officials in the area supplement their income, which is quite insufficient, by engaging in farming on the side. As their lifestyles do not largely differ from those of villagers, they understand the difficulties locals face due to the rubber plantations and thus might hesitate to take proactive action toward them. Moreover, the laws and regulations concerning conservation forests are permeated with global concepts and values as they were initiated and drawn up by foreign actors, including the World Bank and the ADB. It is uncertain whether local officials are fully aware of protection of the environment and forest to the extent that these actors might expect. It is unlikely that they consider environmental conservation to have a higher priority than the local population's subsistence. For them, "development melds the interests of the Lao state and all Lao people in their quests for prosperity, whereas conservation reflects the interests of the foreign other" (Singh 2012, 56).

Admittedly, the locals' actions reflecting somewhat anarchistic characteristics might fall under the tolerance and leniency of the local authorities within a presumably authoritarian state. In other words, they are overlooked precisely because the officials know that the villagers' goals are far from political, without any intention of changing the existing social structure, much less of overthrowing the government. Without "trying to seize power within any national territory" and instead of taking "the form of some sudden revolutionary cataclysm" (Graeber 2004, 40), their movements, which have gradually eroded the conservation forest, eventually rendered the laws and regulations related to it ineffective by resorting to their former practices and knowledge in terms of organization and by associating with their fellows across village boundaries with a view to creating less alienated ways of organizing their lives (ibid.) out of the reach of various powers. Their course of actions may not be considered a social movement as such, as they had no intention of organizing one, but rather a movement of the people who, in an unfamiliar situation, met and then found that they could cooperate for a common objective, eventually proving they were capable of achieving their goals without recourse to open protests.

Endnotes: Crossing the Limits

1. In Vietnam, there are also some cases of organized protest conducted by factory workers (Tran, 2008).

2. For more details on the control of information in Lao PDR, see Baird, 2018.

3. According to Stuart-Fox, the majority of some 50 laws that have been adopted since the inception of the New Economic Mechanism in 1986 were prepared with the assistance of foreign experts, who paid particular attention to developing a corpus of commercial laws to serve as a basis to encourage foreign investment (Stuart-Fox, 2005, 24).

4. The law defines protected forest *(pa pongkan)* as forest to conserve watersheds, guard against soil erosion, and protect dense forests; conservation forest *(pa sanguan)* as forest preserved to conserve wild animals and plants; and regeneration forest *(pa hun hu)* or young fallow forest as forest area to be regenerated immediately (Inoue et al. 1998, 403).

5. The number of National Biodiversity Conservation Areas expanded to 20 areas in the late 1990s, and the name was changed to National Protected Areas in the early 2000s (Lestrelin, Castella, and Bourgoin, 2012, 587).

6. One such example can be found in "Rapport sur l'exode de Phon Thong, 1 Novembre, 1907," Fond: Résidence Supérieure au Laos, E//6, Archives Nationales d'Outre-Mer, Aix-en-Provence.

7. The changes in livelihoods and social relations that have been observed in K village since the establishment of the rubber plantation are described more in detail in Nakata (2021).

8. In 2006, another Vietnamese company, Dao Thieng, was granted a land concession to plant rubber trees.

9. One US dollar is worth around 8,000 kip (Laotian Kip).

10. This conservation forest is, in fact, officially categorized as one of the National Protected Areas, but the locals never refer to it as such, calling it just *pa sanguan*. It is uncertain whether this category is well-known among the rural population. Therefore, I just call it "conservation forest."

References

Arnst, Randal. 2014. *The Decline of Lao Civil Society*. New Mandala. June 15. http://www.newmandala.org//the-decline-of-lao-civil-society/.

Baird, Ian. 2010. "Land, Rubber and People: Rapid Agrarian Changes and Responses in Southern Laos." *The Journal of Lao Studies* 1(1): 1–47.

———. 2017. "Resistance and Contingent Contestations to Large-Scale Land Concessions in Southern Laos and Northeastern Cambodia." *Land* 6(16): 1–19.

———. 2018. "Party, State and the Control of Information in the Lao People's Democratic Republic: Secrecy, Falsification and Denial." *Journal of Contemporary Asia* 48(5): 10.1080/00472336. 2018. 1451552.

Baird, Ian and Keith Barney. 2017. "The political ecology of cross-sectoral cumulative impacts: modern landscapes, large hydropower dams and industrial tree plantations in Laos and Cambodia." *The Journal of Peasant Studies* DOI: 10.1080/0306150.2017.1289921.

Cavanagh, Connor J. 2014. "Biopolitics, Environmental Change, and Development Studies." *Forum for Development Studies* 41(2): 273–294, DOI: 10.1080/08039410.2014.901243

Creak, Simon and Keith Barney. 2018. "Conceptualising Party-State Governance and Rule in Laos." *Journal of Contemporary Asia*. DOI: 10.1080/00472336.2018.1494849.

Evans, Grant. 1995. *Lao Peasants under Socialism and Post-Socialism*. Chiang Mai: Silkworm Books.

Foucault, Michel. 1976. *La volonté de savoir, Histoire de la sexualité 1*, Paris: Éditions Gallimard.

Friis, Cecilie et al. 2016. "Changing local land systems: Implications of a Chinese rubber plantation in Nambak District, Lao PDR." *Singapore Journal of Tropical Geography*, 37: 25–42.

Goldman, Michael. 2001. "Constructing an Environmental State: Eco-Governmentality and other Transnational Practices of a 'Green' World Bank." *Social Problems* 48(4): 499–523.

Graeber, David. 2004. *Fragments of an Anarchist Anthropology*. Chicago: Prickly Paradigm Press.

High, Holly. 2014. *Fields of Desire: Poverty and Policy in Laos*. Singapore: NUS Press.

High, Holly and Pierre Petit. 2013. "Introduction: The Study of the State in Laos." *Asian Studies Review* 37(4): 417–432.

Inoue, Makoto et al. 1998. "Toward Institutionalization of various participatory forest management systems in Lao P.D.R." Proceedings of IUFRO Inter-Divisional Seoul Conference, October 12–17, Seoul, Korea.

Kenney-Lazar, Miles. 2012. "Plantation rubber, land grabbing and social-property transformation in southern Laos." *Journal of Peasant Studies* 39: 3–4.

———. 2018. "Excavating the Hidden Politics of Land Governance in Laos." *CSEAS Newsletter* 76: 26–29.

Kyaw Yin Hlaing. 2006. "Laos: The State of the State." *Southeast Asian Affairs* 2006: 129–147.

Lao PDR. 2003. National Growth and Poverty Eradication Strategy (NGPES).

Lestrelin, Guillaume, Jean-Christophe Castella, and Jeremy Bourgoin. 2012. "Territorialising sustainable development: The politics of land-use planning in the Lao People's Democratic Republic." *Journal of Contemporary Asia* 42(4): 581–601.

Li, Tania Murray. 2008. "Contested Commodifications: Struggles over Nature in a National Park." In *Taking Southeast Asia to Market: Commodities, Nature, and People in the Neoliberal Age*, edited by Joseph Nevins and Nancy Lee Peluso, 124–139. Ithaca & London: Cornell University Press.

McAllister, Karen. 2015. "Rubber, rights and resistance: the evolution of local struggles against a Chinese rubber concession in Northern Laos." *The Journal of Peasant studies* 42(3–4): 817–37.

Melucci, Alberto. 1989. *Nomads of the Present: Social Movements and Individual Needs in Contemporary Society*, edited by John Keane and Paul Mier. London: Hutchinson Radius.

Nakata, Tomoko. 2000. "Minamilaosu, Ngezokunomuranohashizukuri (Building a bridge in a Ngae village, Southern Laos)." *Shanti 2000, Travels in Southern Laos*. Tokyo: Shanti International Volunteer Association 58–63. (in Japanese).

———. 2004. *Minamilaosu-sonrakushakai-no-minzokushi: Minzoku-konjyujyokyoka-no-rentai-to-toso* (Ethnography of a Village Society in Southern Laos: Solidarity and Struggles in a Multi-Ethnic Environment). Tokyo: Akashi-shoten. (in Japanese).

———. 2021. "After dispossession: Shifting livelihoods and lives since advent of a rubber plantation in southern Laos." *Journal of Southeast Asian Studies* 52(3): 492–514.

Obein, François. 2007. *Assessment of the Environmental and Social Impacts created by the VLRC Industrial Rubber Plantation and Proposed Environmental and Social Plans*. Final Report, Agence Française de Développement.

Reid, Julian. 2013. "Interrogating the Neoliberal Biopolitics of the Sustainable Development-Resilience Nexus." In *The Biopolitics of Development: Reading Michel Foucault in the Postcolonial Present*, edited by Mezzadra, Sandro, Julien Reid, and Ranabir Samaddar, 107–122. New Delhi, Heidelberg, New York, Dordrecht, London: Springer.

Résidence Supérieure au Laos, Rapport sur l'exode de Phon Thong, 1 Novembre, 1907, E//6, Archives Nationales d'Outre-Mer, Aix-en-Provence.

Scott James C. 2009. *The Art of not Being Governed: An Anarchist History of Upland Southeast Asia*. New Haven & London: Yale University Press.

Shi, Weiyi. 2008. *Rubber Boom in Luang Namtha: A Transnational Perspective*. Vientiane: GTZ RDMA.

Singh, Sarinda. 2012. *Natural Potency and Political Power: Forests and State Authority in Contemporary Laos*. Honolulu: University of Hawaii Press.

Stuart-Fox, Martin. 1993. "On the Writing of Lao History: Continuities and Discontinuities." *Journal of Southeast Asian Studies* 24(1): 106–121.

———. 2005. *Politics and Reform in the Lao People's Democratic Republic*. Working Paper No.126, Asia Research Centre, Murdoch University.

———. 2006. "The challenge for Lao historiography." *South East Asia Research* 14(3): 339–359.

Taillard, Christian. 1977. "Le Village Lao de la Région de Vientiane : Un pouvoir local face au pouvoir étatique." *L'Homme* XVII (2–3): 71–100.

Tran, Angie Ngoc. 2008. "Contesting 'Flexibility': Networks of Place, Gender, and Class in Vietnamese Workers' Resistance." In *Taking Southeast Asia to Market: Commodities, Nature, and People in the Neoliberal Age*, edited by Joseph Nevins and Nancy Lee Peluso, 56–72. Ithaca & London: Cornell University Press.

Chapter 9

GLOCAL ASSEMBLAGE IN COMMUNITY MOVEMENTS

Transforming Collective Actions in Cambodian
Land Rights Movements

TOSHIHIRO ABE

International tide and context of large-scale land acquisition in Cambodia since 2000

People in countries on the global periphery cannot ignore their direct involvement at the edge of the radical tide of globalization. Impacts may appear as rises in the prices of everyday commodities and gasoline, but more vital and crucial effects on their lives can take the form of deprivation of farmland. The phenomenon of land loss by local farmers in the global south has been called "land grabbing" or "land rush," particularly by international investors and regional entities operating for foreign enterprises.

Numerous large-scale enclosures of farmland were recorded worldwide between 2007 and 2012 (Hennings 2018: 521), in a phenomenon thought to have resulted from the world food and financial crises of 2007–2008 (Sherchan 2015: 7). Another scholar has indicated more precisely when discourses on large-scale land acquisition began to circulate internationally: "The global land grabbing meta-narrative . . . first emerged in October 2008 when the non-governmental organisation (NGO) Genetic Resources Action International (or GRAIN), based in Barcelona, released a report entitled "Seized: The 2008 Land Grab for Food and Financial Security"

(Baird 2017: 17). This report analyzed phenomena relating mainly to "governments of countries unable to meet their own food needs trying to gain control of land for food production" and "corporations and private and institutional investors looking for opportunities in the midst of a deepening financial crisis" (ibid.). However, Baird asserts that this earliest report "presented [an] overly simplistic picture" of the reality of each affected place."

Accordingly, in 2012 the Land Matrix project, which has conducted comparative worldwide research on this issue, identified various types of investors: "investment originates from three groups of countries: emerging countries (Brazil, South Africa, China, India, Malaysia, Korea); Gulf states; and countries in the 'Global North' (USA, European countries). There is a strong trend of intra-regional transactions with, for example, firms from Brazil, Argentina and South Africa seeking to replicate domestic success through investments in their regional neighborhoods" (Anseeuw et al. 2012: viii): "the new regionalism" is one of the keys to this global trend, while not necessarily blaming wealthy countries in the north and on the gulf coast as the primary drivers of the recent trend. Ian Baird admits that this behavior can also be found in Southeast Asia among such actors as Vietnam, China and Thailand (Baird 2017: 17–8).

The Land Matrix project also identified a common negative concern in such cases relating to various stakeholders having different motives: "In addition to the complexity of the topic, there is a huge lack of transparency on land governance matters, in particular regarding planning and decision-making processes, contractual agreements, and issues of community involvement and compensation. Little is known about the short- and expected long-term effects of these investments. Even with the data collated by the Land Matrix project, the picture of large-scale land acquisitions remains hard to decipher" (Anseeuw et al. 2012: vi).

Cambodian law on economic land concession says, for instance, that these large-scale land acquisitions are formally intended to "develop intensive agricultural and industrial-agricultural activities; and to increase employment in rural areas within a framework of intensification and diversification of livelihood opportunities and within a framework of natural resource management based on appropriate ecological system" (Sub-Decree No 146 on Economic Land Concessions, Article 3, 16 December 2005).[1] The policy is thus expected to help solve problems of land ownership in a post-conflict society, to activate the land market economy and to enhance the modernization of agriculture. However, such factors as "lack of transparency" in the decision-making process might create a gap between its formal objective and its actual managerial process.[2]

In order to present a basic picture of policy implementation for large-scale land acquisition in Cambodia, this article partially follows the approach of these preceding works, bearing in mind the gap between official objectives and managerial process and the "new regionalism" when focusing on stakeholders in the ongoing phenomenon. The argument then diverges at the point where unique factors in the local context are observed, followed by consideration of how society has coped with this global tide over the past decade. During the period addressed in this article, strategic shifts in the local movement for land rights have been identified, specifically in the framing of collective action and the targeting of actors involved as responsible stakeholders.

The final section considers the unique autonomy of their movements and unintended factors affecting the current movement within the frame of community movement. This article adopts Shigeharu Tanabe's theoretical connotation of the term "community movement," whereby "the people participate in a community to transform their life circumstances and join its movement articulating with multiple and heterogeneous forces, groups and institutions," creating "new values and ethics through their experiences within such a movement" (Tanabe 2011). Referring to Delanty (2003), Tanabe defines the term "community" to be "a process of and product of imagining and reflexive practices of the people who intend to expand and revitalize their lives and their spaces" (Tanabe 2016: 14), diverging from the classic image of community with unified collective identity and shared values/norms. Rather, a community movement, in theory, generates "the social" within itself "from people's intention to create new values and ethics through reflexively problematizing their community itself" (Tanabe 2011).

Can a community movement work in specific contexts under political pressure if it involves political motives? Does any condition, such as arguments about the political opportunity structure in social movement theory, affect the continuity and cohesiveness of a community movement? To examine these questions in the Cambodian landscape, this article incorporates the term *"glocalization"* and Manuel DeLanda's notion of "assemblage" into the inquiry, exploring a possible type of community movement in a politically restricted context by comparing the local land rights movements over two periods (the first and the second halves of the 2010s).

Rise of large-scale land acquisition in post-conflict Cambodia

Social and historical context

While studying common features of international trends relating to this issue, we must also identify unique aspects of this issue in the Cambodian context. Scholars have identified two specific points relating to local cases: land titling in a post-conflict society and implementation of economic land concessions (ELC) since the enactment of the 2001 Land Law.

The concessions economy of the 1990s

During the Khmer Rouge regime (1975–1979), which forbade private land ownership, official documents on land ownership were lost (Hak 2018: 1–2). The period between the end of the civil war and the early 1990s was marked by unregulated movement of people, possession of land by occupation and state-sanctioned allocation of large-scale forest concessions under the 1992 Land Law (Oldenburg & Neef 2014).

In this situation, "the concession system was reintroduced with strong support from international organizations, particularly the World Bank" (Hibou 2004) and it was expected to function as the main tenure system for natural resource management in Cambodia.

The ruling party at the time, the CPP, used this opportunity in 1994 to offer "alternative livelihood solutions for demobilized soldiers," so that for instance, "an area equivalent to 5% of the total Cambodian territory was allocated to the military" (Diepart 2015: 13–4).

Large-scale land acquisition in the form of ELC since 2001

However, revenues from forest and fishery concessions in the 1990s were largely "captured by provincial and district authorities, members of the military and policemen, political party representatives and high-level civil servants" (McKenney and Prom 2002)' (Diepart 2015: 13–4). International actors, such as the World Bank, no doubt saw this result as a negative one, prompting their request for a more comprehensive policy with a legal basis (Hak 2018: 1–2; Neef et al. 2013: 1087; Diepart and Sem 2018: 30–1).

The main pillars of the 2001 Land Law are the adoption of economic land concessions (ELCs) and social land concessions (SLCs). The latter essentially refers to the allocation of land, according to the ELC implementation, to domestic migrants, veteran soldiers and people in serious economic difficulties, partly supplementing use of ELCs to promote construction of processing factories for agricultural products (Office of the United Nations High Commissioner for Human Rights 2018).

State public land includes spaces characterized by their use in the public interest, including forests, rivers, lakes, harbors, railways and roads. Notably, the classification of state public land can be changed, "if the property has lost its public interest," to state private land (Oldenburg and Neef 2014: 57).

In the relevant subdecree of the 2001 Land Law published in 2005, "rental fees for concessionaires are low and lie between 0 and 10 USD/ha," much cheaper than "rental fees among locals [, which] range from 100 to 250 USD/ha" (Oldenburg and Neef 2014: 57).

According to data accumulated by the local NGO Cambodia League for the Promotion and Defense of Human Rights (LICADHO), as of 2012 more than 2 million ha of land, almost 53% of arable land in Cambodia, had been provided to 227 ELCs (Vrieze and Naren 2012, cited in Neef et al. 2013: 1087). Amid the local context of institutional large-scale land acquisition/allocation, this article focuses on ELCs.

A subdecree of the 2001 Land Law of 2005 stipulates that ELCs are granted for land less than 10,000 ha for a maximum of 99 years. No restrictions are set on applicants, so foreigners can apply to obtain concession contracts. The subdecree requires that safeguards for local residents be put in place, including through prior consultation and design of resettlement solutions and by conducting environmental and social impact assessments (Diepart and Sem 2018: 49; Sperfeldt et al. 2012).

Diepart and Sem (2018: 51–2) identified four stages of ELC policy implementation, which reflect foreign actors' involvement as well as governmental responses and societal reactions to the policy. (1) Prior to promulgation of the Land Law in 2001, mainly forestry concessions were granted. (2) In the second stage, between the enactment of the 2001 Land Law and the 2005 subdecree of the Land Law, a few ELCs were granted, but the legal framework was not sufficiently established. (3) Since 2005, when the subdecree was released, elaborating further on governmental institutions, "the number of ELC contracts has increased and the nature of ELCs has changed" (Diepart and Sem 2018: 52). The remarkable result of ELCs in this period was the rush to create rubber plantations, even in "Protected Areas (under the management of the Ministry of Environment) and in Protection Forests (under the management of the Forestry Administration)" (Diepart and Sem 2018: 52). The boom continued until 2012, when a moratorium on ELCs (Order 01) was ordered by the prime minister. (4) Since 2012, although Order 01 banned new registrations, ELC contracts approved before the order's publication have been signed.

Most ELC areas allocated since 2007 are occupied by rubber plantations, but the variety of agriproducts and the nationalities of concessionaires have broadened, formally corresponding to such official goals as those espoused in Cambodia's National Strategic Development Plan for 2009–2013, which "identified the agriculture sector as an important engine towards poverty alleviation and economic growth . . . by improving productivity and diversification, and commercialisation of agriculture with environmentally sound protection and food security".[3]

Local problems under the positive slogan of globalism and/or regionalism

In addition to several scholars' general concerns about the implementation of large-scale land acquisition, the Cambodian case has been the subject of specific critical inquiries. Although ELCs started with a positive future vision of combining commercialization, industrialization and diversification of agriproducts and increasing employment in rural areas based on appropriate ecological systems, Diepart and Sem (2018: 53) says that "[t]here is a broad consensus in Cambodia among NGOs and researchers that the process of authorising and implementing Economic Land Concessions shows clear deviations from the established legal and policy framework (Sperfeldt et al. 2012). We have discussed above the lack of transparency surrounding the granting and monitoring of these concessions. . . . Public consultations and social and environmental impact assessments that should be carefully undertaken before any agreement is signed are rarely conducted properly, if at all (Sperfeldt et al. 2012)" (Diepart and Sem 2018: 53).

Put differently, contrary to the vision of empowering various locals, actual beneficiaries were "Cambodian business tycoons, political elites and foreign investors since the mid-2000s, mostly for agro-industrial plantations" (Neef et al. 2013: 1086). Criticizing local implementation of ELC, Shercan directly points to the negative effects on residents and farmers: "Contrary to the stated goals, ELCs have been documented by the civil society, in particular human rights groups and academics, as leading to the dispossession of private and common land; displacement of small-holder farmers and indigenous communities; loss of housing, land and property; deterioration of livelihood and loss of income; increased food insecurity and impoverishment, among others. Over 700,000 people have been reported to have been dispossessed through ELCs nationwide since 2000. . . . The UN Special Rapporteur on the Situation of Human Rights in Cambodia, Surya Subedi, in his 2012 report to the Human Rights Council, has stated that '. . . There are well documented serious and widespread human rights violations associated with land concessions that need to be addressed and remedied' (Sherchan 2015: 1–2)."

Hak et al. (2018) describes local residents' and farmers' experiences of ELCs as involving "land conflicts, dispossession, and forced displacement" (Hak et al. 2018: 1).

Local residents and farmers have been placed in a situation in which such expressions as dispossession, deprivation and conflict are generally suitable. With their social condition defined by recent domestic politics, affected local populations do not seem to have deployed active movements against governmental land policy. However, in several remarkable cases of collective action local affected populations creatively searched for a new framework and repertoire to increase their supporters and to remedy their situation. The following section traces some of these movements during the past decade and examines their unique characteristics.

Repertoires of local protest and appeal against eviction by ELC

After rapid increases in ELC implementation nationwide resistance was increasingly evident from around 2010 until the social disturbances that followed the results of the 2013 national election, to the point that the government halted new approvals of ELCs. Everyday resistance and protests, involving residents and farmers "blocking off . . . provincial roads to create disturbance, delivery of thumb-printed letters to local government officials, formation of village networks to share information and defend land" (Milne 2014) were common. Furthermore, some newly emerged forms of protest appeared during this period, gathering widespread attention, particularly from local youth, media and foreign observers, for their "unusual" elements in the local context.

However, the ruling party's reaction to these civil movements was oppressive in the run-up to the 2018 election. The diversity of movements diminished, as did expectations that mobilizing local partners would cause the ruling party to shift its track on land issue policy. Disqualifications of politicians of the opposition party and the banning of some local (English) news media since September 2017 continued after the 2018 national election, leaving residents and farmers pessimistic about the likelihood of positive changes on the issue in the local political arena.

Amid such circumstances, local protesters have changed the framework of their movements from domestic pursuit of political justice to global negotiation for institutional compliance. As a result, they have developed an alternative strategy for land recovery involving new actors rather than focusing on local government.

Collective actions for local mobilization and support: Binding contemporary trend and customary/traditional images

Avatar performance by ethnic minorities in mountain areas

An *Avatar* performance by indigenous people in mountain areas suggests the atmosphere of the earliest resistance movement against land concessions. Famed for having used images from the popular Hollywood movie, the performance appealed not only to local people, particularly the younger generation, but also to foreign media, which connected images of exotic residents in the tropical forest with the global entertainment phenomenon. Since May 2011, residents of mountain forest areas in northwest Cambodia, wearing green clothing, leaf hats and with faces painted in primitive designs in an intentional mimic of characters from the Hollywood film, have repeatedly gathered in Phnom Penh and their hometown to appeal for an end to "illegal logging and mineral mining and taking a toll on the ancient forest".[4] Many ethnic minorities in mountainous areas have participated in the movement, centered in the greater Prey Lang area, where an estimated 350,000 people reside.[5]

The film *Avatar* describes a war between humans and the indigenous population of the planet Pandra, the Na'vi. Humans came to Pandra to acquire specific natural resources needed to cope with a severe energy crisis on Earth. The Na'vi were a forest people who worshiped a sacred tree and lived in harmony with nature. The *Avatar* performance represented local mountain people as protectors of the forest, living in an ecologically responsible manner, making investors participating in the ELC project destroyers and thieves of natural resources. These roles create a direct allegory between the movie and local culture and lifestyles.

Some might wonder whether the Khmer majority living in the plains, the audience for this *Avatar* performance, felt more empathy with rice fields than mountain forests. However, local activists have explained that many audiences—even the performers themselves—were not entirely clear on the plot and character of the film, with the *Avatar* costumes being conflated with local images of scarecrows. In this way, incomplete understanding of images and symbols from the global phenomenon could be smoothly bridged with the customary stock of meanings.

One such demonstration on 18 August 2011 saw residents of Prey Lang join other groups such as "fishers, farmers, forest communities, moto-taxi and tuk-tuk drivers, and urban community activists representing a range of faiths—Buddhist, animist and Muslim" to pray at Preah Ang Dangkor in Phnom Penh in front of Royal Palace for "the wisdom of their leaders, more rational development, the conservation of natural resources, and inclusion and respect for the poor who most depend on those resources".[6] At 146 sites outside Phnom Penh, various protest networks conducted related events on the same day.

This movement achieved partial victory in 2012 when four ELCs in Sandan district, Kampong Thom of Prey Lang, totaling 40,618 ha, were canceled—although other firms have continued their logging (Boyle 2012).

Political appeal by "multimedia monks"

The same period (2009–2014) saw, in addition to these *Avatar* performances, protests by activists called "multimedia monks," who visited sites of conflict around the country and recorded clashes between local residents and security personnel through film and photographs. These digital data were quickly shared online and provided concrete evidence of abuses of authority. Monks are usually thought to remove themselves from secular life, so their political actions using IT devices, particularly SNS such as Facebook and Twitter, caught the interest of young people and media alike. Additionally, as their activities became more aggressive after the results of the 2013 national election some locals perceived their activities as akin to the Arab Spring.[7] Anti-governmental movements by "multimedia monks" thus combined another global trend, that of the Arab Spring, with possible input by local youth in an unusual phenomenon whereby traditional figures made full use of IT devices, much as in the *Avatar* performances.

One of the leaders of this movement, Luon Sovath, began these activities in 2009 when police violently evicted villagers in Chi Kraeng district of Siem Reap. Four farmers, two of whom were his relatives, were shot and beaten by police in the incident. His video became counterevidence against police claims of having fired into the crowd in self-defense.

He and other monks organized the Independent Monk Network for Social Justice (IMNSJ) in 2013 and have continued uploading videos daily ever since. As of 2014, IMNSJ had 5,000 members. But Bunenh, leader of IMNSJ, explains that "I want everything to stay informal and I do not want to register as an NGO under this government because it would mean I would accept Hun Sen's law" (Le Coz and Besant 2014).

Opposing the movement, in 2013 Phnom Penh's governor warned people to "see whether each monk is genuine or not because there have been fake monks on the street" (Le Coz and Besant 2014). In 2014, Luon Sovath was barred from all pagodas registered in the country (ibid.). What's more, elderly monks began criticizing use of IT devices, such as laptops, tablets, and smartphones.

Luon Sovath and other activists faced charges of incitement in November 2014, when they were accused of plotting to commit an attack and disrupt the 2013 election by "the distribution of t-shirts urging people not to vote and handing out flowers to soldiers in Phnom Penh accompanied by stickers calling for them to 'turn your guns against the despot'" (Crothers 2014). Finally the court dismissed the case because the charges were made on an improper basis. Many supporters gathered in front of the court began parading through the city after his release from custody. Even so, crackdowns on the activities of these "multimedia monks" worsened, leading to arrests in May 2017 at a rally of the opposition party. The monks were released only after agreeing "to delete their videos and promise not to use social media to cover the event".[8]

Female leadership in protest: "the women-at-the-front concept"

Women protestors have been prominent among the opposition to land acquisition. Female activists, like the multimedia monks, have rarely been portrayed visibly in local social contexts because of "the traditional role assigned to Cambodian women of caring for the home and the family" (Wight 2015; Lamb et al. 2017: 10) as well as "their generally lower level of education, poorer access to powerful networks and ignorance of their rights" (Kent 2016: 19). However, a local observer indicated that one such activist figure was accepted by locals in the course of the rise of the female politician, akin to Aung San Suu Kyi in Myanmar.[9]

Scholars have recognized female rights activists' role on the front lines of the land protest (Henning 2018; Kent 2016; Lamb et al. 2017). Lamb et al. reported in 2015 that "[i]n the protest, the reason women are at the front line is because they think that if men are at the front line, it might be easy to provoke the situation or cause violence. The protestors believed that men can't protest strongly as women did; if they did, men could be caught or arrested. If men challenged authorities, it could more easily result in violence" (Lamb et al. 2017: 10).

Female protesters are highly conscious of their role in the movement. Lamb et al. (2017: 10) describes two episodes that they experienced in 2014–2015, both illustrating protesters' intention behind performances: ". . . one woman who participated in the Phnom Penh protests explained that 'I have to cry and yell in the protest things like . . . 'Kratie Provincial Governor please help me because now, no house, no pot, no plate, nothing! Please help now!' "; Srey Mom [a local organizer] further explained that 'the authorities pay less attention in terms of taking action or responding to the women,' and thus this is seen to reduce the likelihood of violence. This positioning of 'women at the front' was strategic."

Anne Hennings (2019) attributes the design of this strategy to NGOs: "Notably, peace and land rights activists apply feminine images and are in many cases advised by NGOs to use (or manipulate) gender as a strategic weapon for the benefit of the group's legitimacy . . . NGOs in Cambodia skillfully use these features of gender" (Hennings 2019: 105). She also observed that these NGOs "have urged female activists to engage in emotional resistance" to elicit the sympathy of observers/supporters (Hennings 2019: 109). Accordingly, emotional performances of appeal by female activists have appeared on numerous local news media during active periods of local civil movements.

However, this strategy depends on the policy and attitude of authority. Although it was broadly valid in the early stages of the demonstrations, the escalation of protests finally brought counterattacks by the authorities. As early as 2015, the national assembly began examining drafts of media laws that would restrict freedom of speech, agricultural laws that would restrict farmers' crop choices, and NGO laws that would require greater government oversight of NGOs (Beban 2015).

When Hennings conducted field research in 2017, negative comments on the strategy were also heard: "I don't know if you have come across the saying that if women are at the front, there will be no or less violence. I find it absurd and crazy! We see that those women are beaten, harassed and jailed. It's false and unfair to say with women in the front, no violence will happen to them" (Action Aid staff member, Phnom Penh, January 12, 2107) (Hennings 2019: 111).

A typical female activist, Tep Vanny, was arrested in August 2016 and detained until August 2018, just after the national election. She was finally released with the King's pardon after signing an agreement not to participate in the movement.

Collective action ongoing: International actors to be involved

The preceding collective actions all incorporated new social elements in different ways. Such juxtapositions as monks and IT tools, political movements and female leadership, and Hollywood symbols and indigenous peoples in "traditional" mountain areas were eye-catching, particularly for members of younger generations not previously involved in political activity.

However, as noted, since around 2015 the government has gradually adopted hardline reactions to these movements. In 2017, the Ministry of Interior required "all CSOs to notify local or national authorities before carrying out any activities, and empowering authorities to ban activities on broad and vague grounds"[10] and stipulated that prior permission did not imply future approval.

Faced with such reactions, stakeholders' expectations that the government would change course on this issue and compromise to achieve desirable solutions also needed to change. Following these recent political changes in local circumstances, movement actors have shifted their strategy from mobilizing locals for governmental policy change to negotiating with foreign stakeholders on ELC land issues, incorporating the movement framework of pursuing global justice.

Sugar plantations in Oddar Meanchey Province

One such case dealt involved residents who lost their farms and houses amid ELC developments for a sugar plantation. The "accused" were Bonsucro (UK) and Mitr Phol (Thai); the "plaintiffs" were residents of Oddar Meanchey, a local NGO and a U.S. NGO; the "judge" was UK National Contact Point. The actions involved were clearly different from the collective actions described in the previous sections, which aimed at negotiating with the Cambodian government. The local government took no position in these processes. The case involved land acquisition directly by "regional actors," brought to the international context.

The timeline of this case was as follows:

2008–2009: Soon after Angkor Sugar company took the land by ELC, Mitr Phol was given the rights to the land and began evicting more than 700 families to construct a plantation. The evictions were violent, including arson of residences and jailing of protesters, and the resulting images were widely publicized in various media.

2011: Residents filed a complaint with a third party, Bonsucro, through its grievance mechanism. This supervisory entity, based in London, cited its responsibility to require ethical certification of its member company, Mitr Phol. Bonsucro manages a certifying system by which sugar producers prove their compliance with EU ethical standards for environmental conditions, resident support and laborers' rights. Thanks to Bonsucro's certification, "Mitr Phol's biggest customers, past and present—including The Coca-Cola Company, PepsiCo, Mars Wrigley, Nestlé and Corbion— could advertise their sugar as responsibly sourced".[11]

2012: Mitr Phol suddenly withdrew from the Bonsucro network without addressing the complaint.

2013: Residents and NGOs asked for an independent investigation by the Thai National Human Rights Commission.

2014: In August, the Thai National Human Rights Commission conducted field research. Thai commissioner Niran Phitakwatchara backed claims against Mitr Phol, stating that "[t]he concession has resulted in the illegal [taking] of land from local people, destruction of their homes, killing of livestock and shooting, beating, threat[ening] and intimidation and harass[ment] of the villagers. . . . In conclusion, our finding is the collapse of the community".[12]

2015: Bonsucro readmitted Mitr Phol to its network, although the latter had never answered complaints by residents of the concession area.

2016: Residents and Cambodian NGOs filed a new complaint with Bonsucro against Mitr Phol.

2018: In April, Thai lawyers representing approximately 3,000 victims brought a suit before the Thai court. The court ordered the parties to enter mediation in September, but Mitr Phol refused.[13] Bonsucro dismissed the 2016 case on the grounds that "it did not receive cogent evidence of a breach".[14]

2019: In March, the NGOs filed a complaint on behalf of over 700 locals with UK National Contact Point (UKNCP), claiming that "the sugar association violated the OECD Guidelines for Multinational Enterprises by failing to hold its member company, Mitr Phol, accountable after the Thai sugar giant grabbed the families' land and left them homeless and destitute".[15] UKNCP accepted the complaint, suggesting mediation, and promised an independent investigation if mediation failed.

The land rights activities in this section focused on an international body which affected a local company with regard of ethical compliance with the EU standards. The company that was allocated the land under the ELC policy had a relationship with a supervising entity in the EU framework and was thus indirectly to be controlled by EU regulations. Here, a Cambodian local problem was repositioned in a global context. No longer were Cambodian domestic politics involved. Rather, a Thai company was accused, involving an actor in an economically superior country in the region (Southeast Asia). This is not directly framed in a simple argument that a developed country in the north was exploiting a developing country in the south. Yet actors from developed countries in the north engaged in the case indirectly, at least in the following two regards: (1) Cambodian zeal for sugar production has been heightened by the EU's preferential trade scheme "Everything But Arms," which "provides duty-free access to the European market and a guaranteed minimum price for sugar that has been on average three times the world price" (Sherchan 2015: 2), so that "Thai and/or Taiwanese sugar companies in partnership with well-connected Cambodian businessmen have developed seven industrial sugarcane plantations through ELC leases to produce raw sugar for export to Europe" (Sherchan 2015: 2). (2) a multinational company in the region—Mitr Phol, in this case—has fixed its position in the global market by obtaining ethical certification from an EU entity. Against such a background and context, the local actors' reframing strategy involved entering the arena for problem-solving where the seed of the problem generated.

The case of rubber plantations in Ratanakiri Province

A similar picture of collective action is found in Ratanakiri province, where ELC land for rubber plantations given to a Vietnamese company was a matter of contention for a decade before being reclaimed by locals. The accused here was Hoang Anh Gia Lai (HAGL) of Vietnam; the plaintiffs were the residential Highlanders Association; and the mediators or facilitators were the International Finance Corporation (IFC) of the World Bank Group and the Compliance Advisor Ombudsman (CAO), an independent accountability mechanism for the IFC, and the Multilateral Investment Guarantee Agency (MIGA), which reports directly to the president of the World Bank Group. Cambodian governmental entities were not named.

The timeline of the negotiation process was as follows:

2012: The IFC invested in HAGL through a Vietnamese private equity fund, and HAGL began developing a rubber plantation in Ratanakiri province, where ethnic minorities (Jarai, Kachok, Kreung, Tampoun) have historically had non-timber livelihoods, spirit mountains, traditional hunting areas and burial grounds.[16]

2014: Residents and NGOs filed complaints concerning local land and destruction of resources with the CAO. The complaints addressed the failed investment by the IFC, which indirectly invested in HAGL through a Vietnamese private equity fund.

2015: HAGL agreed to return the land already developed. In subsequent negotiations, HAGL offered to return 20 spirit mountains and two burial grounds to the villagers, whereas local residents demanded return of all 64 areas that the company had already planted with rubber and fruit trees.[17]

However, the "IFC bought equity stakes totaling $125 million in two other Vietnamese financial institutions, TP Bank and VP Bank," which provided "financing of more than USD200 million to HAGL, specifically to fund its rubber plantations in Cambodia, despite the pending complaint with the CAO".[18]

2009: Just before the final mediation meetings, HAGL withdrew, citing "an overall restructuring of the company after the Vietnamese car manufacturer THACO bought a majority ownership stake in HAGL's agricultural subsidiary".[19] The governor of Ratanakiri announced in the return ceremony that all 64 areas that local communities had demanded would be excluded from the HAGL concession areas "for the indigenous people to practice their beliefs, cultural traditions and to support their livelihoods".[20]

The strategic approach used in this case, as in Oddar Meanchey, was one of negotiating with a foreign ombudsman that supervised the activities of the member organization. Even negotiations over returning the land were not held directly with the company developing plantations in the conflict area. In short, residents addressed their local problem with an institution far removed from their everyday lives, drawing in the direct "perpetrator" of their victimhood. The Ratanakiri case used protection of the cultural rights of ethnic minority/indigenous people, an issue which has recently been circulating in the global context of rights-related discussions and leaves no space for local political discourse.

Changing the movement framework

The framing of the land rights movement in the first half of the 2010s is a plea for political justice in a domestic context, using elements found among global cultural and societal trends. The strategy involved an unusual mixture of cultural/customary aspects and global/contemporary aspects in the leading figures of the movement, such as indigenous minority groups in mountain areas and Hollywood films, monks and IT devices/SNS, and ordinary female residents and political activism. Yet the styles of these movements have changed in response to political pressure since the 2013 national election. In the past few years, certain land rights movements have increasingly adopted different framings for their actions, namely pursuit of global justice in a local context. Local actors in these movements no longer negotiate with the government, but go over the heads of the companies that evicted them, approaching international institutions acting remotely far from their everyday lives. Negotiations for land recovery with such entities begin indirectly, speaking of compliance with specific business ethics regulations or the responsibility of supervising member organizations.

No doubt this shift of movement framework—and subsequent movement repertoire—has been affected by political restrictions in the local context. However, the goal of reclaiming land has not changed. What has changed during the past decade is the framing of collective action, as well as the actors involved in the collective action, with the exception of residents and farmers.

A glance at cases focusing on appeals to international organizations could suggest that local initiative has diminished in politically restrictive local situations thanks to instruction by foreign NGOs, with locals able to follow the NGOs' direction. Such a view might be reasonable, because residents and local NGOs have little negotiating experience with such international entities. Certainly, support by a European or U.S. NGO is needed to process formal negotiations through bureaucratic procedures.

However, the practical views of local NGO staff members reveal an aspect of local input in this shift in movement character.[21] According to the members' view, one point of reference is the rise and fall of ADB projects, with lessons learned from the preceding negative experiences of local activities relating to the project serving a crucial role in analysis of recent shifts in such movements' direction.

The ADB project was conducted in 2010–2015, led by the Asian Development Bank (ADB) with the Australian Agency for International Development (AusAID), mainly for rehabilitation and reconstruction of national railways to support residents who were resettled by the railway project. The project was financed by the ADB through a USD84 million concessional loan and by aid from AusAID of USD23 million. The Cambodian government was to comply with the ADB's policy on involuntary resettlement of more than 4,000 households by offering compensation and assistance. "As financiers of the project, the ADB and the Australian Government have a duty to monitor, supervise and support the resettlement process to ensure compliance with the policy and human rights obligations. The reality, however, is that the Cambodian Government, the ADB and AusAID routinely ignored the policy and legal obligations, as well as the warnings and evidence provided by affected communities and NGOs".[22] The supporting project thus finally collapsed without obtaining substantial compensation from the government. The affected people and communities were not provided with continuous safeguards, and the movement faded out with no concrete results. However, at least one positive reaction to the ADB was that the Compliance Review Panel (CRP), the ADB's internal accountability mechanism, admitted that "the ADB failed to comply with its policies and procedures, leaving a substantial number of affected households worse off and impoverished".[23]

Remembering this experience, local NGO staff members, in their words, gained insights into future social action, as expressed in the slogan "connecting the dots," or more directly, "following the money".[24] The foreign entities that provide legitimacy to a business entity—or local authority—in Cambodia are inevitably required to comply with a code of conduct, usually as assessed by a superior supervising entity or a larger alliance system. Even though Cambodian authorities are formally required to be such a supervising figure, compliance has not been properly implemented, causing local problems. The essential motivation of residents in each region is to reclaim their land, not to persuade the local government to be politically correct. Bypassing the local government is thus a strategic as well as practical choice for local actors. This strategy, in the words of local NGO staff members, was developed by reflecting on the failure of movements to gain local compensation related to the ADB railway project.

An interesting observation by local actors is that the recent shift to the international justice field in the movement for land recovery was rooted in the failure of an international initiative and by local civil entities' perception of and learning from that initiative. At the time of the project, local actors in related movements were not aware of the possibilities that would unfold in other movements in the near future. The failure of one collective action has led local actors to form an assemblage through other collective actions by involving various international actors to achieve the objectives of residents.

Glocal Assemblage in community movements in a context of harsh globalization and intra-state political restriction

Glocalization with inward/outward orientation

The series of negative experiences of residents/farmers should be attributed to the implementation of the ELC policy. Yet ELC was not introduced and initiated by the Cambodian government alone, nor was large-scale land acquisition in general. Rather, as a starting point, such international entities as the World Bank, IMF, FAO, ADB and EU played prominent roles in pushing the idea that Cambodian agriculture and agribusiness would be modernized through foreign investment. For instance, until the early 2000s there was a scant sugarcane market for export from Cambodia, but the scale of the market has ballooned since the EU put its policy in place in 2001. Cambodian ELCs to develop sugarcane plantations piggybacked this trend, joined with other "political" objectives, such as institutional acquisition of land by political elites.

In this situation, residents first deployed their strategy for gaining nationwide recognition and mobilizing local partners to garner their support. The various "new" movements had a common characteristic that can be described as the juxtaposition of images or by unusual combinations of local elements and global trends. "Traditional" indigenous people from mountain areas appeared in the capital of Phnom Penh, performing as characters from the popular Hollywood film *Avatar*. Monks in religious garb made full use of IT devices and SNSs to support land activism, reminiscent of the Arab Spring. Females took an active role in opposing land grabbing, gaining wide attraction and support inside and outside mainstream society. Efforts to enact political change through female leadership paralleled global trends at the period embodied in Aung San Suu Kyi in Myanmar and Hillary Clinton in the United States.

When focusing on these local appearances of global elements and signs through interactive forms or interconnectedness, the word *"glocalization"* has been coined, particularly referring to an inward orientation. This term has been used with varying interpretations, Robertson (1995) suggesting a basic understanding of the term as a global product or service's tendency to indigenize its guise when planted in a local context, with the local culture simultaneously vitalizing itself in facing global culture. Other works (Canclini 2001; Roudometof 2005) have tended to emphasize the aspects of interconnectedness and the fluid reconstruction of local, national and international dimensions. Giulianotti and Robertson (2006: 173–174) stressed the simultaneous occurrence of opposite vectors of homogenization and heterogenization in a socially constructed reality, such as in the spread of football's popularity. This article shares the viewpoint on the simultaneous occurrence of homogenization-heterogenization vectors with Giulianotti and Robertson, emphasizing inward/outward orientation.

However, domestic political restrictions rendered these *glocal* movement repertoires less than fully influential in society. Local authorities did not enter the negotiation arena. Civil society movements' efforts to mobilize local partners have been gradually eliminated from the public space by the government, including through surveillance and limitations on their relationships with foreign NGOs.

In such a constrained environment, residents and farmers, with the support of local NGOs, have shifted their strategy. Instead of seeking to change domestic authorities, they have recontextualized the problem through global discourse, discovering which foreign stakeholders are responsible for the problem and entering into negotiations with them. For this to happen requires a reframing of the social problem—not with domestic concepts and discourses, but with global concepts and discourses. Now stakeholders need not cooperate with political opposition in a context of an upcoming general election and the possibility of regime change. Rather, they have developed discourses around lack of compliance of foreign entities obliged to be ethically legitimate in their activities in a developing country, or they have emphasized their claim to support traditional life and the environment (see the movements in Ratanakiri), which resonates with international values on environmental issues. This orientation of local movements could be called a case of *glocalization* with outward orientation.

This argument has common points with two other chapters on "community and development" in this volume (cases from Laos and Thailand) in terms of local farmers' collective action/movement adopted to cope with the negative influences of globalization, which appeared to force locals to abandon the established pattern of agriculture. These arguments thus report similar, but different, patterns of resilience and survival embodied by local farmers.

The Lao case of building rope bridges across a river to clear protected forest emphasizes spontaneity, which functioned retrospectively to elicit unpredicted cooperation with locals of other villages. The chapter on the Inpaeng Network in Thailand focuses on loose complementary interactions among neighboring communities in the network, where each community pursues its own sufficiency in an independent manner. These two cases address the appearances of cooperative interactions through spontaneous engagement in autonomous actions/movements, whereas the Cambodian cases in this chapter shows the changes of collaborators reflecting political circumstances.

Community movement as *glocal* assemblage under political pressure

Another feature of the current action in Cambodian land movements is the conscious reliance on the previous failure of a social movement. Put differently, although the referred case did not achieve its aim, its failure has affected practical insights and strategies taken in subsequent movements.

This process of deploying collective action neither comes from an internal logic that is divorced from circumstances nor accepts foreign activists' instruction, which might be construed as an enlightenment package. Certainly the current orientation toward negotiation with international entities through effective discourse in a global context requires input by foreign experts in the field of justice, but as a basic and final actor in decision-making for the movement, local actors are conscious of the lessons learned from the "failures" of past movements. This is not a feature directly attributable to the inner factors autonomous to the movement body, because two "outer" factors were crucial drivers of the new avenue of action:

international initiatives by such bodies as the World Bank and EU in local contexts; and the unexpected outcomes—negative results— of local actors' engagement. Indirect autonomy, having appeared as assemblage of various actors, could be identified in the digestion of these two "outer" factors by locals/local movements in the course of their continuous actions. DeLanda (2006: 256) explains his use of the term as "a multiplicity which is made up of heterogeneous terms and which establishes liaisons, relations between them, across ages, sexes and reigns—different natures," being characterized only by its "co-functioning." Applied to such realities as those involving daily conversations and territorial states (DeLanda 2006: 259, 265), the term "assemblage" points to an ontological law of perpetually changing condition of any substance. It thus works as a tool to describe and observe heterogeneous relations in function among components of a social group, network or movement.[25]

Yet arguments might proceed differently when "assemblage" is used to illustrate a social group, movement or network, depending on whether a discussant presupposes that core members of the group, network or movement under examination intend to organize and manage their actions with a view to preserving the active body's heterogeneous character. Put differently, when using the term in social reality, arguments might proceed in two directions: one admitting an intentional action to acquire assemblage in organizing a collective entity, and the other adopting an understanding that assemblage appears outside/beyond actors' intentions, observed only retrospectively. The former direction rejects organization of a rigidly structured collectivity with fixed rules and norms. Otherwise, as DeLanda notes, the "collective unintended consequences of intentional action" (2006: 257) applied to the term assemblage on a larger social scale implies that even intentional actions may bring about unintended consequences, which are also included as elements of assemblage. Using this logic, this article's interpretation is inclined toward the latter position, though considers both as interconnected behind the scenes. When addressing assemblage as the autonomous character of Cambodian local movements, this article deals with the term assemblage in the preceding sense of unintended appearances in reaction to such factors as foreign business interventions involving land, deterioration of the local political landscape and ensuing loss of context in which other locals could be in solidarity with actors, failure of preceding land rights movements in separate contexts, and involvement of outside actors, such as Cambodian NGOs from the capital and INGOs from foreign countries.

This article explored "a possible type of community movement with political motive in a politically restricted context, comparing Cambodian land rights movements in two periods." The *"glocal assemblage with outward orientation"* illustrates a theoretical answer from the local context, appearing as a heterogeneous strategy essentially composed of unintended responses to social situations, while including negative experiences of former movements. However, while exploring the possible appearance of assemblage as a community movement in politically restricted conditions, I was not able to obtain sufficient data concerning the actual process of generating and maintaining such assemblages in local micro-aspects. Inquiring about the validity of such an assemblage for community movements in other social situations under similar political difficulties would require further empirical data.

Endnotes: Glocal Assemblage in Community Movements

1. https://www.ajne.org/sites/default/files/resource/laws/7208/sub-decree-146-economic-land-concession.pdf (accessed on 25 April 2021).

2. The gap between an official objective and a real managerial power in local politics is indicated as follows: "Delineation of national parks, reserved forest areas, and military-based protected areas are a way of legitimizing the exercise of exclusive managerial power of national governments over natural resources. Claiming and classifying forestland and forest resources as 'state property' has been a common strategy of ordering and appropriating nature in most Southeast Asian countries (e.g., Peluso 1992; Forsyth and Walker 2008)" (Neef et al. 2013: 1090).

3. Kingdom of Cambodia, National Strategic Development Plan, Update 2009–2013 (30 June 2010), para. 97 (cited in Sherchan (2015: 7)) https://extranet.who.int/nutrition/gina/sites/default/files/KHM%202010%20NSDP%20Update%202009-2013.pdf

4. https://www.pri.org/stories/2011-05-25/indigenous-protest-cambodia

5. "The majority of these residents are from the Kuy ethnic minority who live traditionally and rely on non-timber products from Prey Lang, which straddles Thom, Stung Treng, Kratie and Preah Vihear provinces" (Boyle 2012).

6. https://ourpreylang.wordpress.com/2011/08/19/pray-long-for-prey-lang/

7. Arab Spring is the term which designates a series of large-scale anti-governmental movements/actions in countries in Middle East and North Africa mostly in the years 2010-2012. The political protest spread from Tunisia, where democratization has been realized after the collapse of former regime in this uprising.

8. "Buddhist monks detained over social media posts in Cambodia" https://www.ucanews.com/news/buddhist-monks-detained-over-social-media-posts-in-cambodia-/79348

9. Author interviews with local NGO staff members, August 2012 and March 2013, Phnom Penh.

10. "Cambodia Fundamental Freedoms Monitor: April 2017–March 2018," p. iii (The Fundamental Freedoms Monitoring Project) https://cchrcambodia.org/admin/media/report/report/english/FFMP_Second%20Annual%20Report_EN.pdf

11. https://www.inclusivedevelopment.net/uk-government-body-accepts-oecd-complaint-against-sugar-sustainability-body/

12. "Thai human rights body says plantations stole land" (Zsombor Peter 14 August 2014) https://www.cambodiadaily.com/news/thai-human-rights-body-says-plantations-stole-land-66456/

13. "Thai court accepts Cambodian land grabbing case, orders mediation" (5 September 2018, Bangkok) https://www.inclusivedevelopment.net/thai-court-accepts-cambodian-land-grabbing-case-orders-mediation/w

14. https://www.inclusivedevelopment.net/uk-government-body-accepts-oecd-complaint-against-sugar-sustainability-body/

15. Ibid.

16. "Cambodian indigenous communities win back their sacred land from Vietnamese rubber developer" (26 March 2019) https://www.inclusivedevelopment.net/cambodian-indigenous-communities-win-back-their-sacred-land-from-vietnamese-rubber-developer/

17. Ibid.

18. Ibid.

19. Ibid.

20. "Cambodia: Hoang Anh Gia Lai Rubber Plantations" https://www.inclusivedevelopment.net/campaign/cambodia-rubber-land-grabs/

21. Author interview: March 2019, Phnom Penh.

22. https://www.inclusivedevelopment.net/campaign/cambodia-adb-and-australia-financed-railway-project/

23. Ibid.

24. Author interview with local NGO staff: March 2019, Phnom Penh.

25. Given his usage of the term in explaining a process of conversation and communication in general, local actors' performative combination of opposite images and unusual mixtures of local elements and global trends are a credible embodiment of assemblage.

References

Anseeuw, Ward, Mathieu Boche, Thomas Breu, Markus Giger, Jann Lay, Peter Messerli and Kerstin Nolte. 2012. "Transnational Land Deals for Agriculture in the Global South: Analytical Report based on the Land Matrix Database." https://landportal.org/library/resources/mokor05925/transnational-land-deals-agriculture-global-south-analytical-report

Baird, Ian. 2017. "Land Grabbing in Laos and Cambodia: Understanding why it happens." *Geography Review* 31(3): 16–19.

Beban, Alice. 2015. "Time to sow the seeds of land reform in Cambodia." http://www.eastasiaforum.org/2015/03/26/time-to-sow-the-seeds-of-land-reform-in-cambodia/

Boyle, David. 2012. "Economic land concessions in Prey Lang rejected." *Phnom Penh Post* (6 August 2012). https://www.phnompenhpost.com/national/economic-land-concessions-prey-lang-rejected

Canclini, García. 2001. *Consumers and Citizens: Globalization and Multicultural Conflicts*. Minneapolis, MN: University of Minnesota Press.

Crothers, Lauren. 2014. "Activist monk to 'put Cambodia's legal system on trial': 'Multimedia monk' Luon Sovath faces incitement charge with dissident leader." https://www.aa.com.tr/en/world/activist-monk-to-put-cambodias-legal-system-on-trial/103787

DeLanda, Manuel. 2006. "Deleuzian Social Ontology and Assemblage Theory." In *Deleuze and the Social*, edited by Martin Fuglsang and Bent Meier Sørensen. Edinburgh: Edinburgh University Press.

Delanty, Gerard. 2003. *Community*. London: Routledge.

Diepart, Jean-Christophe and Sem Tho. 2018. "Cambodian peasantry and formalisation of land right: Historical perspectives and current issues." French Technical Committee on Land Tenure and Development (AFD-MEAE).

Giulianotti, Richard and Roland Robertson. 2006. "Glocalization, Globalization and Migration: The Case of Scottish Football Supporters in North America." *International Sociology* 21(2): 171-198.

Hak, Sochanny, John McAndrew and Andreas Neef. 2018. "Impact of Government Policies and Corporate Land Grabs on Indigenous People's Access to Common Lands and Livelihood Resilience in Northeast Cambodia." *Land* 7(4): 1–20.

Hennings, Anne. 2018. "Plantation assemblages and spaces of contested development in Sierra Leone and Cambodia." *Conflict, Security & Development* 18(6): 521–546.

Hennings, Anne. 2019. "The dark underbelly of land struggles: the instrumentalization of female activism and emotional resistance in Cambodia." *Critical Asian Studies* 51(1): 103–119.

Hibou, Béatrice. 2004. "Cambodge: quel modèle concessionaire?" In *Le Royaume Concessionaire: libéralisation économique et violence politique au Cambodge*, edited by Jean-François Bayart, 77. Paris: Fonds d'Analyse des Sociétés Politiques (FASOPO).

Kent, Alexandra. 2016. "Conflict continues: Transitioning into a battle for property in Cambodia today." *Journal of Southeast Asian Studies* 47(1): 3–23.

Lamb, Vanessa, Laura Schoenberger, Carl Middleton and Borin Un. 2017. "Gendered eviction, protest and recovery: A feminist political ecology engagement with land grabbing in rural Cambodia." *The Journal of Peasant Studies* 44(6): 1215–1234.

Le Coz, Clothilde and Daniel Besant. 2014. "Holy activism: Media-savvy monks." https://southeastasiaglobe.com/holy-activism-cambodia-loun-sovath-but-buntenh-independent-monks-network-for-social-justice-southeast-asia-globe/

Milne, Sarah. 2014. "Can Cambodia's sites of struggle become sources of hope?" http://www.eastasiaforum.org/2014/04/01/can-cambodias-sites-of-struggle-become-sources-of-hope/

Neef, Andreas, Siphat Touch and Jamaree Chiengthong. 2013. "The Politics and Ethics of Land Concessions in Rural Cambodia." *Journal of Agricultural and Environmental Ethics* 26: 1085–1103.

Neef, Andreas. 2016. "Cambodia's devastating economic land concessions." http://www.eastasiaforum.org/2016/06/29/cambodias-devastating-economic-land-concessions/#more-51099

Office of the United Nations High Commissioner for Human Rights. 2018. "Assessing the Impact of Social Land Concessions on Rural Livelihood in Cambodia," 1–77. https://cambodia.ohchr.org/sites/default/files/Clean-English%20SLC%20report%20-%20FINAL%20version%2013%20Mar%20 2018.pdf

Oldenburg, Christoph and Andreas Neef. 2014. "Reversing Land Grabs or Aggravating Tenure Insecurity?: Competing Perspectives on Economic Land Concessions and Land Titling in Cambodia." *The Law and Development Review* 7(1): 49–77.

Robertson, Roland. 1995. "Glocalization: Time-Space and Homogeneity-Heterogeneity." In *Global Modernities*, edited by Mike Featherstone, Scott Lash and Roland Robertson. London: Sage Publications.

Roudometof, Victor. 2005. "Transnationalism, Cosmopolitanism and Glocalization." *Cuurent Sociology* 53(1): 113–135.

Sherchan, Depika. 2015. "Cambodia: The Bitter Taste of Sugar Displacement and Dispossession in Oddar Meanchey Province." https://cambodia.actionaid.org/publications/cambodia-bitter-taste-sugar-displacement-and-dispossession-oddar-meanchey-province

Sperfeldt, Christoph, Farrah Tek, and Billy Chia-Lung Tai. 2012. "An Examination of Policies Promoting Large-Scale Investments in Farmland in Cambodia." Cambodian Human Rights Action Committee (CHRAC).

Tanabe, Shigeharu. 2011. "Outline of Research Project 2011–2013: Community Movements in Mainland South East Asia." Unpublished paper.

———. 2016. "Introduction: Community of Potential." In *Communities of Potential: Social Assemblages in Thailand and Beyond*, edited by Shigeharu Tanabe. Chiang Mai: Silkworm Books.

CONTRIBUTORS

Chapter 1

SHIGEHARU TANABE is professor emeritus at the National Museum of Ethnology in Japan and currently teaches anthropology and Japanese studies in Chiang Mai University, Thailand. Recent works include *Anthropology of Spirits: Politics of Communities in Northern Thailand* (Iwanami Shoten, 2013, in Japanese), "An Animic Regime Subjugated: The *Pu Sae Ña Sae* Spirit Cult in Chiang Mai" (*Bulletin of the National Museum of Ethnology* 43(3), 2019) and an edited volume, *Communities of Potential: Social Assemblages in Thailand and Beyond* (Silkworm Books, 2016).

Chapter 2

RYO TAKAGI is professor at the Faculty of Business Administration, Kanagawa University (Japan). He has conducted anthropological field research in Nakhon Sawan province, and published his book, *Micrology of Oder: An Ethnography of Interaction in a Thai Village* (Kanagawa University Press, 2014, in Japanese). His recent works include "Community Radio Movement in Rural Area of Northern Thailand," in *Modern Nations and Coloniality* edited by Hidekazu Sensui (Ochanomizu-shobo, 2022, in Japanese).

Chapter 3 and Introduction

RYOKO NISHII is professor at Research Institute for Languages and Cultures of Asia and Africa, Tokyo University of Foreign Studies. Her recent works include *Ethnography of Affect* (Kyoto University Press,

2013, in Japanese), "A Corpse Neccessitates Disentangled relationships: Boundary Transgression and Boundary-Making in a Buddhist-Muslim Village in Southern Thailand," in *Buddhist-Muslim Relations in a Theravada World*, edited by Iselin Frydenlund and Michael Jerryson. (Palgrave Macmillan, 2020), and co-edited book "Affectus: Touching the Outside of Life (Kyoto University Press, 2020, in Japanese).

Chapter 4

KEIKO TOSA is professor at the Graduate School of Global Studies, Tokyo University of Foreign Studies. Recent works include *Study on Weikza Belief in Myanmar* (Keiso syobo, 2000, in Japanese), an co-edited volume, *Living in Myanmar at a Transition: Anthropology of "control" and public sphere* (Fukyosha, 2020, in Japanese) and "The Cult of Thamanya Sayadaw: The Social Dynamism of a formulating Pilgrimage Site" (*Asian Ethnology* 68(2):240–64, 2009).

Chapter 5

AYAKO SAITO is part-time lecturer at Tokyo University of Foreign Studies in Japan. She is interested in the Muslim community in Myanmar and has been conducting her research there. Her recent works include "The New Challenges of Democratization and the Muslim Community" in *Living in Myanmar at a Transition: Anthropology of "control" and public sphere* edited by Keiko Tosa and Katsumi Tamura (Fukyosha, 2020, in Japanese)

Chapter 6

TADAYUKI KUBO is associate professor at Faculty of Comparative Culture, Otsuma Women's University in Japan. He has been carrying out anthropological research on the displacement and settlement processes of Karenni refugees from Myanmar. He published *Anthropology of Refugees: Displacement and Resettlement of Karenni*

Refugees on the Thai Burma Border (Shimizu Kobundo, 2014, in Japanese). His recent works include "Ethnocentrism or National Reconciliation: Rethinking Ethnic Relations and the History of Karenni" (*Journal of Burma Studies* 25(2), 2021).

Chapter 7

NOBUKO KOYA is lecturer at the Faculty of Sociology, Otani University (Japan). She has conducted anthropological research on folk healers' role in Thai society for many years. Her recent works include "The Folk Medicine Revival Movement in Northern Thailand: The Exercise of Healers' Capacities and Legitimization of Healing Practices," in *Communities of Potential: Social Assemblages in Thailand and Beyond*, edited by Shigeharu Tanabe (Silkworm Books, 2016).

Chapter 8

TOMOKO NAKATA is professor at the Department of International Relations, Kobe City University of Foreign Studies (Japan). She has been conducting research in Southern Laos for many years, focusing on social and cultural changes in village communities. Her recent works include "After dispossession: Shifting livelihoods and lives since advent of a rubber plantation in southern Laos" (*Journal of Southeast Asian Studies*, 52(3), 2021).

Chapter 9

TOSHIHIRO ABE is professor of sociology at Otani University in Japan. His research interests principally relate to transitional justice, migration, social movements, and global governance in the South African and Cambodian contexts. His publications include *Unintended Consequences in Transitional Justice: Social Recovery at the Local Level* (Lynne Rienner Publishers, 2018) and the edited volume *The Khmer Rouge Trials in Context* (Silkworm Books, 2019).

INDEX

f=figure; n=endnote; **bold**=extended discussion or key reference

A

A Thousand Plateaus (Deleuze and Guattari, 1980) 52n3, 60
Abe, Toshihiro 12, **14**
acoustic body (Yamada) 87n18, 91
active utopianism **43–44**, 54n18, 54n20
actor-network theory (ANT) **86n6**, 87n8
actualization of potential 25, 28, 29, 46, 53n8, 60
affective contacts 41, 44, 47
agencement 130; *see also* assemblages
agribusiness **212–213**, 239, 290
Agricultural Land Reform Office (Thailand) 222, 228
agroforestry 214, 216, 217, 222
alternative agriculture 214, 217
Althusser, Louis 127
Amnesty Ordinance 66/23 (1980) 93, 98, 108
anaphora relations 183, 197
anarchism 2; anarchist 3, 45, 248; anarchistic 4, 60
Anderson, Benedict 5, 188
anti-government movements (Myanmar) 7, 183,184; anti-government agitations 185; anti-government activities 186
anti-Muslim movement (Myanmar) 6, 129, 135, 136, 140, 145, 161, **162–166**, 171, 175, 176
Appadurai, Arjun 45
Arab Spring 1, 278, 291, 296n7
Arabic schools **166**
arahant ideal 52n6
Arendt, Hannah 5; "cause" versus "origin" **95**
Ashin Wirathu 136
Asian currency crisis (1997) 12; economic crisis **215**, 216, 235n1
Asian Development Bank (ADB) 13, 245, 260, **288–290**

assemblage of resistance (Tanabe) 4, **22–26**; conclusions **48–51**; counter-hegemony function 22; use of term **23**
assemblages 9, 75, 76, 82, 88n24, 95, 297n25; Bennett's description 95; configuration **52n2**; constituent parts 11; DeLanda's notion 270; Deleuze's concept 52n3; Deleuze and Guattari **211–212**; glocal **293–295**; human and non-human elements 9–10; man-horse-stirrup 9, 86n7
Association for Protection of Race and Religion (MaBaTha [*q.v.*]) **6**
Aung Min, U 187
Aung San 182
Aung San Suu Kyi, Daw 5, 135, **145–146**, 156n13, 280, 291; by-election (2011) 128
Avatar performance by ethnic minorities 14, **276–278**, 291

B

baisri ornaments (cooked rice offerings with folded leaves and flowers) 29, 35, 36
Bamar Muslims **6–7**, 161, 163, **177n3**; charitable activities 7, **165–166**; discrimination experienced 163–164, 166; educating children outside of religious schools (significance) **166–170**; minority within Muslim community 6, 170
Bangkok 62, 68, 71, 79, 99, 227; demonstrations (2010) **74–75**
becoming (*devenir*) 26, 27, 28, 29, 40–41, 44, 46, 48, 49–50, 52n6, 53n10
becoming a Buddha 26, 41, 53n7
Benjamin, Walter 94
Bennett, Jane 9–10; *Vibrant Matter* (2010) **95**
Bergson, Henri 16n4, 24

www.ingramcontent.com/pod-product-compliance
Lightning Source LLC
Chambersburg PA
CBHW031356270326
41929CB00010BA/1208